The seven essays in this volume break new ground in the theory of the business firm and its applications in economics. A leading analyst of industrial organization, Professor Demsetz first critically examines current debates on existence, definition, and organization of the firm, discussing conceptual treatments of the relation between business ownership, wealth, and economic development. Subsequent essays offer new perspectives on competition, profit maximization, and rational behavior, shedding light on managers' compensation, antitrust policy, and the accuracy of firms' accounting data. The latter themes in particular make the collection of interest to business audiences, as well as to professionals and students in economics.

These previously unpublished essays derive from lectures originally presented at Uppsala and Lund Universities in Sweden, the Mont Pelerin Society meeting in Prague, and the Center for the Study of Economy and State at the University of Chicago.

The economics of
the business firm

The economics of the business firm
Seven critical commentaries

HAROLD DEMSETZ
University of California, Los Angeles

CAMBRIDGE
UNIVERSITY PRESS

Published by the Press Syndicate of the University of Cambridge
The Pitt Building, Trumpington Street, Cambridge CB2 1RP
40 West 20th Street, New York, NY 10011-4211, USA
10 Stamford Road, Oakleigh, Melbourne 3166, Australia

First published 1995

Printed in the United States of America

Library of Congress Cataloging-in-Publication Data
Demsetz, Harold, 1930–
   The economics of the business firm : seven critical commentaries /
   Harold Demsetz.
   p. cm.
   Includes bibliographical references (p.   ) and index
   ISBN 0-521-48119-8
   1. Managerial economics.   2. Industrial organization.
   3. Corporate profits.   I. Title.
   HD30.22.D45   1995
   3338.5–dc20   94-42703
                                               CIP

A catalog record for this book is available from the British Library.

ISBN 0-521-48119-8 Hardback

To Armen Alchian, Ben Klein, and Ronald Coase,
friends and colleagues whose works on the firm
have influenced several parts of this volume

Contents

vii

Preface

The commentaries contained in this volume are being published for the first time. Most began as lectures I have been privileged to give during the last five years at Uppsala and Lund Universities in Sweden, at the Mont Pelerin Society meeting in Prague, and at the University of Chicago during a brief stay as guest of that university's Center for the Study of Economy and State. Although the present commentaries differ from the lectures that gave them birth, many key points remain.

The main objective in publishing this set of essays and studies is to set several ideas about the economics of the firm before readers. While I long ago learned that seldom is an idea completely new, I believe that plausible claims of originality can be made for several of the ideas set forth in this volume. The commentaries make no pretense at extensively surveying the topics discussed, but, to set these ideas before readers in proper context, it often is useful to discuss critically selected works that already form part of the growing literature of the firm. The works to which I refer appeared over a long time span, beginning with F. H. Knight's *Risk, Uncertainty, and Profit,* published more than seven decades ago, and ending with contemporary work on profit measurement and tournament theories of management compensation. I hope that readers find both the critical and the constructive parts of this volume useful to their own thinking and work, and that it can serve as supplementary reading material for courses that focus on the firm. The audiences for the original lectures were heavily weighted with graduate students and with faculty from economics departments and business schools. The present volume is aimed at the same somewhat heterogeneous audience. However, the nontechnical style of the writing makes the material accessible to upper-level undergraduate students in economics.

Each commentary, reflecting its origin in a separate lecture, is meant to stand on its own, but several are interconnected in obvious manner through the core themes of the economics of the firm. The first two commentaries, on the existence and organization of firms, discuss conceptual and theoretical issues in the presently emerging theory of the firm. The third seeks to alter our notions of what belongs in the firm's production function, and it presents an important illustration of implications of the altered function for matters as broad as wealth distribution and economic development. Maximizing behavior is the topic of the fourth commentary. Commentaries five and six are more appropriately titled studies, since they feature not only debate and discussion, but also statistical analyses of the measurement of profit and the compensation of executives. The final commentary broadens the inquiry into a discussion of competition.

Harold Demsetz

The firm of theory:
its definition and existence

The central theory of economics remains the neoclassical theory. It is essentially a theory that imparts much understanding about the price system as an allocator of resources, but it also contains a simple model of the business firm. Why is there a firm in the theory of price? What defines the firm in this theory? This, the first commentary of the present volume, is the proper place to settle these two epistemological issues. How I do settle them is at considerable variance from the manner that has become popular in the newly emerging theory of the firm. The answers to these questions lead quite naturally to the second commentary, which deals with theories of the internal organization of firms. Modern treatments of the firm do not cleanly separate the organization of the firm from the question of its existence. In the writing of this volume, I have become convinced that mixing these two issues is a source of confusion. Just as a theory of the existence of the atom need have no close relationship to a theory of the inner workings of its electron system, so an explanation for the existence of the firm may have little to do with an explanation of the firm's inner organization.

The most important example of comingling these two issues is found in R. H. Coase's 1937 classic article, "The Nature of the Firm." Coase sets his task explicitly at the beginning of part II of his article. "Our task is to attempt to discover why a firm emerges at all in a specialized exchange economy." His reply, which has become extremely influential, is that the market, or price guidance, is not free. Transaction cost, if high enough, justifies the substitution of managed coordination for price-guided coordination. But then Coase goes on to apply transaction cost analysis to the inner organization of the firm, inquiring about the degree to which the firm is vertically integrated and the reliance it places on long-term employment contracts.

The interest that economists have shown in the existence of firms, by and large, has not expressed itself in an examination of facts pertaining to firms. Instead, there has been a search for a logical theory by which to justify the existence of firms in a price system. This purely theoretical slant is a result of the fact, alluded to by Coase, that the firm as a theoretical construct fits uncomfortably into the important body of price theory we call neoclassical economics. I now believe that the fit is not a poor one if the role of the firm in the theory is correctly perceived. The uncomfortable fit results from the

1

improper way in which we have viewed the firm in this theory. I shall come back to this important issue later in this commentary; there I will give an alternative perception of the firm.

Contemporary literature perceives the identifying element in the firm to be its reliance on managed coordination. So does the older literature, and I begin by contrasting the two most influential early views about managed coordination and the existence of firms, those of F. H. Knight and R. H. Coase. The existence of the firm seemed not to be recognized as a problem in need of addressing by the literature surrounding neoclassical theory. That literature concerned itself with a related existence problem, the existence of profit in a supposedly highly competitive economy. In such an economy, the value of the marginal productivity of a factor determines the price it receives in the market. The competitive market tolerates no factor payment in the absence of a productive contribution. Profit is a payment to the owners of the firm, but the productive contribution made by owners, unlike the sweat of laborers, is unclear, and its rationalization is complicated by the fact that profit is in the nature of a residual, not a specified or easily calculated sum. The older literature found a productive function for ownership in the risk borne by a firm's owners, and the existence of profit was attributed to the necessity for rewarding risk taking if there was to be risk taking. This rationalization of profit, which we may associate with the factual divergence of the real economy from the full information assumption of the perfect competition model, is a major target of the critical attack made by F. H. Knight in his influential book *Risk, Uncertainty, and Profit* (1921). It is as a consequence of this attack that the need to explain the existence of the firm is first recognized.

Knight's explanation

The primary task assumed by Knight in his book is not to explain the existence of the firm or even its organization, but to explain the existence of profit. Knight shows that, even if the full information assumption of perfect competition is dropped so that risk can exist, risk offers no good explanation of profit because it is associated with known probability distributions of event outcomes. An insurance company can calculate an actuarially fair premium for the risk of fire and, upon charging this premium to business firms for insurance against the event of fire, it converts this risk to just another cost of doing business. Entry, exit, and competition generally must then treat risk as any other cost of production. As such, risk cannot give rise to profit. Business prospects that exceed all costs, including this risk cost, cannot exist in competitive equilibrium. Sufficient entry is attracted to eliminate the possibility of profit.

Knight then goes on to argue that imperfect information must reflect something more than risk before it can give rise to profit (or loss). Events must be unpredictable, so that no conversion of uncertainty into a known cost of production is possible. Knight creates a new classification of imperfect knowledge to fit this need, and he labels it *uncertainty*. This is distinguished from risk by associating it with possible outcomes about which so little is known that no calculation of an actuarial type is possible. Uncertain events can give rise to profit or loss because entry into or exit from markets cannot rationally construct an anticipation of these events.

In acknowledging the presence of uncertainty, Knight fails to face the problem of how to redefine competitive equilibrium or of how to demonstrate the existence of equilibrium when competition and uncertainty are commingled. Uncertainty is a strange source of profit if Knight's objective is to resuscitate the role of profit in guiding resources in a price-directed economy. Being unpredictable, it cannot rationally influence resource allocation decisions. Yet what makes profit an important variable in neoclassical theory, and in Smith's earlier work on the *The Wealth of Nations,* is the guidance it gives to resource flows. Moreover – and now at last we come to the point regarding the existence of the firm – uncertainty as the sole source of profit undermines an explanation of the existence of firms if firms are thought to exist in order to seek profit. Knight, rejecting risk as a source of profit and substituting an unpredictable source of profit for it, needs a new theory of why firms exist. This, at least, is my interpretation of why Knight strays from the central topic of profit to deal with the question of the firm's existence. He does not himself acknowledge this, but he does deviate from the chain of reasoning that moves his analysis from risk to uncertainty to profit in order to offer a rationale for the firm's existence. The rationale, significantly, depends not on profit but on risk, or, more accurately, on risk redistribution.[1]

Knight sees in the firm advantages of redistributing risk between owner-manager and employees. The profit and loss consequences of fluctuations in business outcomes are absorbed by the owner-manager, who contracts to pay relatively stable wages to employees. Employees are thus insulated at least partly from fluctuations in the business outcomes. This reallocation of risk is efficient in Knight's view, for he sees it as putting a greater proportion of risk on the party that he believes is less averse to bearing it, the owner-manager. Presumably, risk is not handled as well without firms.

In return for offering stable wages to employees, the owner-manager requires them to allow their activities within the firm to be supervised. To accept this supervision, employees in turn require a contractually fixed wage that attenuates risk. Hence, Knight explains the existence of the firm, the wage system,

---

1. Knight never really reconciles the uncertainty source of profit and the sensibility of having resources guided by profit considerations. On this and other aspects of Knight's uncertainty theory, see Demsetz (1988b).

and recourse to managed direction of employees, all as concomitant to the desire to allocate risk efficiently. This improvement in the distribution of risk among the cooperating parties may be identified here as Knight's *productivity explanation* of the firm's existence. An economic explanation for the existence of firms must insist on a convincing description of conditions, hopefully frequently encountered, that make the firm a productive arrangement, and I shall couch my discussions of other theories of the firm's existence in terms of their productivity explanations.[2]

Knight's search for an explanation of the existence of firms is, in some ways, echoed by the different explanation put forward later by R. H. Coase. Just as Knight's explanation of superior risk allocation can be interpreted as an explanation based on cost reduction, so can Coase's. However, where Knight relies on reductions in risk cost through risk reallocation, Coase relies on reductions in coordination cost through the substitution of managed coordination for price-directed coordination.

Coase's explanation

In putting forward his now famous explanation of the existence of the firm, Coase looks to transaction cost (although risk may be one factor among many that influences transaction cost). Managed allocation of resources within the firm becomes viable if the cost of coordinating resources through market arrangements (i.e., transaction cost) exceeds the cost of managing them within the firm. The reduction in *coordination* cost achieved through managed coordination is Coase's productivity explanation of the existence of the firm.

To argue against Knight's view, Coase observes that risk is often accepted without the counterbalancing shift in control that Knight claims to be necessary. He points to the fact that when firms buy goods from other firms, they usually pay a relatively riskless contracted amount to suppliers, much as the Knightian firm pays contracted wages to employees. Yet the firms doing the purchasing do not ordinarily insist on, or acquire, supervisory control over suppliers.[3]

Coase's counterexample is not so telling a criticism as it first appears. Knight can be interpreted to say that a *difference* in risk-bearing ability between

2. The reader must remember that our topic is the existence of the firm, not its organization. As to existence and the use of the management/wage system, Knight relies mainly on risk redistribution. As to other aspects of the firm's organization, Knight offers insightful considerations of moral hazard.

3. Coase might have added, but did not, that stabilizing employee wages would bring about an increase in the variability of employment. The wage system, if this increase in variability were great enough, would increase the risk of income fluctuation borne by wage earners rather than by owner-managers. Knight's theory requires that this not be so.

cooperating parties is required to justify the formation of a firm. This difference is taken by Knight as obvious when it comes to owner-managers and employees, but, he might argue, not when it comes to two firms. No improvement in risk allocation is achieved by adopting contractual arrangements between firms like those that exist between a firm and its employees if the owners of these firms do not have systematically different risk preferences. Hence, Knight might argue, two firms cannot on grounds of superior risk allocation justify a merger into a single firm.

There is, however, a more serious problem with Knight's theory. The owner-manager can be compensated through market transactions for bearing a greater proportion of the risk inherent in the firm's operations. The smaller the share of risk borne by employees, the lower is the wage that satisfactorily compensates them for their work. There is no clear need for the owner-manager to receive his reward for risk-bearing through the supervision of employees. Similarly, the price that governs exchange between firms and their suppliers, in Coase's counterexample, should reflect how risk is shared, and Coase, in discussing this counterexample, makes passing reference to the market's ability to set prices that compensate for risk bearing. Since wage or price adapts to accommodate to the actual distribution of risk, risk *redistribution* cannot, in and of itself, provide an acceptable rationale for the firm or for the supervision of employees. The price system, unaided by institutions such as the firm, can cope with the risk distribution problem. It is somewhat surprising that Knight should have overlooked this, for his discussion of the problem of basing profit on risk clearly recognizes the existence of a market-determined price for risk bearing.

But Knight might have a reply even to this point. Although he writes about risk redistribution as already described, he might claim that he has been misinterpreted. The fluctuations in outcomes that the firm experiences are really due to uncertainty, not to risk. The predictability that is required to gauge the wage concessions appropriate to compensate owner-entrepreneurs for their agreement to pay relatively fixed wages is lacking if the fluctuations in the outcome of business activity reflect uncertainty. This cannot be, however. The value of these concessions *is* measured by the value of the control over employee actions that has shifted to the owner-entrepreneur in return for the payment of fixed wages.

Knight's rationalization of the existence and organization of the firm makes more sense if one simply views the management of employees as a method for *reducing* risk, not merely redistributing it. Reduction of risk is obviously in the interest of owner-managers, given that they have taken on a large share of the risk inherent in business operations. Reduction of risk may be what Knight really had in mind, but, if so, he did not make this claim with any clarity, and a literal interpretation of his theory justifies the existence of firms in terms of risk redistribution.

The profession is indebted to Coase for pressing it to pay attention to transaction cost and for showing how this cost affects institutional arrangements such as the firm. Coase's theory of the firm's existence does not suffer from some of the same weaknesses as Knight's. But coordination cost, like risk cost, offers only a possible avenue by which the existence of a firm might be justified for reasons of productivity enhancement. Potentially there are many paths to cost reductions, and each may have a bearing on whether the firm or the market is the chosen instrument of economic organization. Coase's reliance on reduction in coordination cost may be sufficient to explain the existence of firms within an otherwise price-directed economy, but it may not be necessary. More important is the question of empirical significance. The empirical significance of Coase's explanation and of other explanations is a more unsettled issue than is supposed by the emerging modern theory of the firm.

One important alternative source of the firm's productivity is implicit in neoclassical theory, but to understand it fully we must understand more clearly just what we mean by a firm. It is a peculiarity of Coase's and Knight's discussions, and of much of the new literature on the firm, that precise definitions of the firm are lacking. "Managed coordination" is used to represent the firm. These discussants treat the firm as if the managed coordination of resources is unique to the firm, but managed coordination is not so clean a cutting edge as their discussions suppose. Management takes place in households, which, I presume, are not firms. Furthermore, market transactions, which certainly are not regarded as firms in this literature, almost always require at least a modicum of management. A customer instructs a clerk to select one item from the shelf and not another; at purchase, he instructs the clerk to use a particular credit card and to put the item in a bag. The clerk responds as if he is being managed by his department head rather than by the customer. An investor instructs her stockbroker to check on the correctness of information that has come to her attention, to enter orders in certain amounts at certain times, and to call back with verifications of transactions. Do we have managed coordination within a firm or managed coordination across a market? Moreover, if market transactions involve conscious management, so conscious management involves market transactions. The firm is itself a nexus of contracts. So, if transaction cost rises, there is a substitution in favor of managed coordination only if contracts used to form the firm do not rise in cost as much as do other transactions.

A reexamination of the firm in neoclassical theory

The firm as conceptualized by neoclassical theory is not a mere appendage to the theory; it is an important aid to the theory's search for understanding of the price system. To understand why this is so, one must recognize the nature of the coordination problem that neoclassical theory tackles. The problem is to see how the price system works, and the task of the price system is to cope with the interdependencies that exist in a modern economy. The theory confronts this problem by constructing a hypothetical economy in which people depend on others. The construction depends on two characteristics of economic activity: extreme decentralization and extreme interdependency. Extreme decentralization deprives all firms and households of influence over price. So they do not set price; the system does. This aspect of neoclassical theory is well understood. The need for interdependency is not.

Self-sufficiency, the opposite of interdependency, is production for one's own consumption. An economy populated by self-sufficient persons poses no social coordination problem with respect to resource use (although it does with respect to the distribution of wealth). The social dimension of the production problem contemplated by neoclassical theory comes from reliance on others, especially on strangers. It therefore serves this theory to populate its hypothetical economy only with persons who are not self-sufficient, especially with persons who are dependent on strangers. The importance of interdependency to an understanding of the price system becomes obvious in a comparison of the following two scenarios:

1. Robinson Crusoe, stranded alone on his island, must decide how much water to consume from his inventory of fresh water and how much time and effort to allocate to securing new supplies of water.
2. Hundreds of thousands of individuals in a populous society secure water from thousands of different persons who own and operate wells.

The first scenario involves decisions but poses no social coordination problem. Plans are conceived and executed by a single person. If Crusoe makes no calculating errors, his plans lead to appropriate actions and predictable outcomes. The chain from decision to action to outcome is direct, open, and conscious, and, I may add, it is managed coordination. The fact that Crusoe manages his own time and effort, rather than someone else's, does not deprive his decisions, plans, and activities of the "managed" label, especially if there exist potential intertemporal inconsistency problems in Crusoe's behavior. Management does not depend on the existence of complex organization. But self-sufficient management lacks the interesting social dimension that motivates neoclassical theory. The potential for conflict and inconsistency between Crusoe's use of resources and the use of resources by others does not exist.

The second scenario poses a significant social coordination problem. Water is produced from many sites by persons whose activities are not coordinated in any obvious way, and this water is made available to many other persons who do not consciously plan or control water production. Is there any reason to believe that sensible quantities of water are produced and consumed? This type of question is a central concern to neoclassical theory. To face this question squarely, a hypothetical economy is modeled so as to be so interdependent that no one is self-sufficient in the sense that Crusoe is.[4]

This is accomplished with the aid of two "black boxes": the household and the firm. The household sells its services to others and buys goods from others. It does not self-employ resources to produce goods for its own members; it offers its resources to firms. Firms buy or rent these resources, and they produce goods that are not for consumption by their owners and employees as such, but are for exclusive sale to households. The role of prices in accommodating this high degree of interdependency is of interest, not the manner in which households and firms manage their internal affairs. The contribution made by the household and the firm in this theory is to make the price system deal with extreme interdependency and decentralization. "In-the-household" production and "on-the-job" consumption are ruled out. This is implicit in the circular flow diagrams that once were a popular expository device of basic economics texts, but the theoretical significance of the circular flow was poorly understood. The texts mistakenly emphasized the circularity of the flow rather than the interdependency and decentralization exhibited in the transactions it pictures.

The firm as a specialized production unit

For lack of a better word, I use *specialized* to describe a production unit that produces for outsiders; this usage is different from specialized in the sense of doing only one thing, although the narrowing of tasks ordinarily accompanies specialization in the sense of doing for others. The firm in this theory is not just a black box, it is a specialized black box. It may do more than one thing within its boundaries, but whatever it does is directed toward use by outsiders, not insiders. No attention is paid to the complexities of managing production (or, as a counterpart, to the problems of dispute resolution within households). The role of this concept of the firm is *to separate production from consumption,* so that Crusoe-type self-sufficiency is absent. The coordination system for linking production and consumption that remains when self-sufficiency is absent is comprised of but two components: impersonally determined market prices and personally defined tastes. The two react to each other as described in neoclassical theory. The perfectly competitive firm is thus an important building block for a scenario that puts the price system to a test in which it is the only coordination mechanism for joining production to consumption. The firm in

---

4. Persons remain self-sufficient to the extent that they make their own decisions relative to the prices they face.

this theory need not be an organization at all. A single owner-manager-employee is all that is needed, and indeed neoclassical theory pays no attention to the organization problems that abound within real firms. *Organization* unnecessarily complicates things, when all that is needed from the firm is that it separate production from consumption; production must be exclusively for consumption by outsiders. What is needed is a concept of the firm in which production is exclusively for sale to those who are formally outside the firm. This requirement defines the firm (for neoclassical theory), but it has little to do with the management of some by others. The firm in neoclassical theory is no more or less than a *specialized unit of production*, but it can be a one-person unit.

The transaction and specialization theories compared

This concept of the firm differs from that widely used in contemporary literature on the firm and in the older works of Knight and Coase. In that literature, firms and markets are viewed as substitutes because the emphasis is on alternative ways of coordinating the use of resources. Here the emphasis is on specialized production, not on the internal organization of the firm. From this perspective markets and firms are *not* substitutes; if there is a relationship between the two, it is a complementary relationship. Markets do not produce goods for others, because they do not produce. Hence, in the specialization theory of the firm, markets cannot substitute for firms, and neither can the price system. Markets are conceptualized arrangements for matching bids and asks, for exchanging entitlements, and for revelation of the prices that accomplish these exchanges, but the activities that accomplish these things are housed in firms. These firms may be brokers, members of organized exchanges, contract lawyers, financial news gatherers and promulgators, etc. All are specialized producers of exchange services who may or may not rely heavily on managed coordination in the production of these services.

In a world in which everyone possesses perfect information about prices and technologies, price coordination is a pseudonym for self-management, so that what might be considered as substitutes are self-management and management by others. Prices do not coordinate; they supply information. Each owner of resources, knowing all there is to know in a perfect information world, can self-manage his or her resources, placing them in their highest value uses. As information becomes costly and less perfect, self-management gives way to management by others because this is an efficient way to take advantage of specialized knowledge. The relevance of specialized knowledge to the internal organization of the firm is a topic to which we return in the next commentary.

The specialization theory gives an entirely different perspective on the existence of firms from that given by the transaction cost theory. In transaction cost theory, if transaction cost becomes lower (relative to management costs), activities previously undertaken within firms are now accomplished in markets. In the limit, if transaction cost goes to zero, firms cease to exist and all activities are accomplished by markets; this is interpreted as the substitution of markets for firms. And if transaction costs are prohibitively high, the market is abandoned in favor of within-the-firm allocation of resources. In the specialization theory, a reduction in transaction cost causes firms to subdivide, with each firm tending to focus production on a smaller part of the goods spectrum. This subdivision is what the transaction cost theory calls the substitution of the market for the firm, but the specialization theory calls it only an increase in the number of firms. While it is true that the interface between these new firms is not managed (if these firms are price takers), whereas before the subdivision the interface was managed, and this make it appear as a reduction in reliance on managed coordination, it is also true that the larger number of firms require more central management units. Hence, one cannot claim that there is less reliance on managed coordination if transaction cost is reduced. And if transaction cost goes to zero, firms do not disappear from the face of the earth. They cannot, in the specialization theory, because goods are still produced for sale to others. Firms simply achieve a maximum feasible division of activities or a maximum feasible number of separate management units.[5]

The specialization theory, analyzing a reduction in transaction cost, views the interposition of a market between activities previously carried on within one firm, not as the substitution of market for firm, but as the substitution of two firms for one. Assuming that specialization is productive, this substitution can increase both the total output of the economy and the fraction of this total that is produced in firms (as compared to the fraction produced in self-sufficient fashion). The degree to which persons rely on others (strangers) is increased as a result of a reduction in transaction cost. Reliance on markets also increases, but not by eliminating firms. The number of firms and the degree to which they sell to outsiders increase, as does reliance on markets. The importance of firms and of markets in the economy correlates positively.

From the perspective of the specialization theory, an increase in transaction cost reverses this process; the number of firms decreases. This change is also called for by transaction cost theory, but the interpretation is again very different. Transaction theory interprets this as a substitution of firms for markets and therefore as an increase in the importance of managed coordination. Specialization theory treats it simply as a reduction in the number of firms and in the number of independent management units, but not as a substitution of

5. Just how many firms might exist if transaction cost were zero depends on considerations of economies of scale and scope, but each firm would tend to specialize more than if transaction cost were positive; "specialization" here means that production is focused on a smaller number of goods.

managed coordination for price-guided coordination. There is an increased role for management in allocating resources internally that would otherwise have been bought and sold across markets, but there is a reduced role for management in that two independent management teams are replaced by a single team. The number of firms and the use of markets are both reduced. Firms do not become more important in the economy; the loss in specialization might result in a smaller fraction of an economy's output being produced in firms and a larger fraction in self-sufficient operations. If an increase in transaction cost is thought of as raising not only the cost of exchanging goods but also the cost of devising the nexus of contracts that links multiple members of a team together in a firm, the result clearly is a move toward self-sufficiency and a move away from markets and from production for others. Coase's view of the change is of the substitution of firm for market, for which the measure of change turns on how many more activities take place within a firm (especially vertically related activities). The view of the change offered by the specialization theory, however, is of the substitution of firm for self-sufficiency, and its value turns on the fraction of output produced for sale to others. This fraction can increase even while vertical integration decreases, and it can decrease while vertical integration increases. More can be produced within the business sector, relative to self-sufficient production, if firms are highly specialized than if they are highly vertically integrated, so that lower transaction cost increases the degree to which the economy relies on firms for its total product. The bottom line of specialization theory is that *firms exist because producing for others, as compared to self-sufficiency, is efficient; this efficiency is due to economies of scale, to specialized activity, and to the prevalence of low, not high, transaction costs.* And if Smith's proposition is true (that specialization is limited by the extent of the market), then it should follow that (1) the transaction cost per dollar of goods exchanged is lower the larger is the market and (2) the importance of firms to an economy's output is greater the larger is the market.[6]

Recognition of specialized production as the distinguishing characteristic of the firm reveals quite easily why neoclassical theory requires profit-maximizing behavior from the firm's owner. Since the firm produces only for sale to others and not for internal on-the-job consumption, its owner maximizes utility by using the firm to maximize profit and then by saving or consuming this profit from within his or her household. Since the transaction cost theory of the firm does not emphasize the interdependence-specialization consideration, it does not logically require profit maximization of the firm; managed coordination can be directed toward any end because the firm need not be limited to

---

6. There is evidence that at least for highly organized markets there are inverse relationships between transaction cost and size of market (Demsetz, 1968a) and between vertical integration and size of market (Demsetz, 1989).

producing only for outsiders. On-the-job consumption may go on in a real firm, but not in its neoclassical caricature.

Critics of the neoclassical profit-maximizing assumption err in supposing it presumes that only profit matters to owners of real firms. No doubt profit is an important consideration of these owners, but the profit-maximizing assumption is a necessary consequence of broadly conceived *utility* maximization in a regime in which production is completely specialized for sale to others. The assumption does not preclude the firm's owner from acts of consumption and charity, it simply places these in that other black box, the household. Strangely enough, neoclassical theory's characterization of the firm as a unit that produces for outsiders is not explicitly acknowledged by the theory. The theory does not define what it means by a firm. And it fails to perceive that the profit-maximizing behavior of firms' owners is not a result of their psychology but of its unstated presumption that the firms they own produce only for consumption by outsiders.

One final difference between the transaction cost and specialization theories of the firm should be noted. Management, as this term is used in the transaction cost explanation, is not an essential ingredient of the specialization theory's firm. It is difficult to imagine the complete absence of management because the firm produces, and production requires the manipulation of resources in one way or another. This manipulation cannot be distinguished from management even in a one-person firm. However, the firm in neoclassical theory is simply a conceptualization that formalizes and represents the actions of input owners in placing their inputs in highest value uses. With an assumption of full knowledge of prices, no owner of the firm is required to accomplish this. Inputs are put into the right places to work with an appropriate batch of other inputs solely by the independent actions of input owners (households) responding to prices. The prices for joining an inappropriate mix are lower than for joining an appropriate mix, and all households use these inputs correctly because there is full knowledge of technologies; an inappropriate technology yields a lower set of prices for inputs.

We tend to think of the owner-manager *of the firm* as necessary to this process. In the firm of the real world the owner-manager is necessary, but not in the firm of perfect competition. This firm is merely a verbal convenience in neoclassical theory, standing in for a description of specialized production for others. All one needs for this firm are fully informed owners *of inputs* who respond to relevant prices. Owners of inputs behave toward the placement of their inputs as they behave toward their consumption expenditures, simply matching tastes against the opportunities offered by market prices. Although this "coming together" of inputs follows a profit maximization prescription, competition assures the absence of profits and losses in equilibrium, so that there is no need for a recipient of the *firm's* residual. Economic rent, should it exist, accrues to owners of inputs in scarce supply. No supervision within the firm is needed. Because production is for sale to others, this coming together of inputs qualifies as a firm in the specialization theory of the firm, even though the owner of the firm has been replaced by the owners of inputs who simply respond to known market prices and technologies. This does not qualify as a firm in the transaction cost theory, because this theory insists on the substitution of managed coordination for price-guided coordination. The puzzle of explaining the existence of firms in the perfect competition model of neoclassical theory, in which prices seem to do everything, is now solved. No firm in the managed coordination sense is needed. Only specialization in the sense of production for others is needed. Although this firm is not difficult to conjure from the neoclassical theory's price system, it is a highly unrealistic firm, just as perfect competition is highly unrealistic.

Specialized production for sale to others is a mainstay of real firms also. One does not go into business to produce for oneself; so specialization for sale to others is not irrelevant to an explanation for the existence of real firms. The importance of the firm has increased measurably over the last century. One hundred years ago, rural life was dominant even in developed economies, and it was marked by a high degree of self-sufficiency. Farm families burned wood from their own wood lots, they obtained a large fraction of the food they consumed from their own crops, and they produced much of their own clothing during the winter season. Cash crops were also grown, and to this extent farms were firms, but then, much more than now, efforts of these families went into activities that helped them be self-sufficient. Sales to others *and* purchases from others now dominate rural and urban life alike, so that the modern farm is much more a firm. At the same time as this transition took place, the fraction of employment in rural activities dropped considerably, substituting the much greater specialization of urban life for that of rural life. These two dramatic transformations have made the firm much more important in the activity of all economies, but especially in developed economies. To recognize this, one needs only to see the firm is as an institution defined by its specialized production for others.

The sources of these important changes are found in economies of large-scale production, the result of which is to make efficient output rates much greater than are needed for self-sufficiency. Economies of scale also were a result as well as a cause of the transformation. Reductions in transport cost and increases in population enlarged markets and thereby made specialization more productive. This improved productivity may be, but is not necessarily, linked to reductions in transaction cost. To the extent that larger markets have lower transaction cost, this increased, rather than decreased, the relative importance of firms in the economy, just the reverse of the implication of the transaction cost theory of the firm. The reduction in the cost of transporting goods is not to be confused with a reduction in the cost of transacting. Transaction cost is reflected in the cost of becoming informed about buyers and sellers and in executing contracts that change who owns entitlements to goods. Transporting goods is different. The cost of shipping goods is an ordinary production cost, one that is incurred by a firm between the separated parts of its activities or in the shipment of goods to buyers. The specialization theory of the firm easily incorporates the role of improved transportation into a picture of increased interdependence and, therefore, of increased importance of firms in the economy. Transaction cost theory does not.

Agency and nonagency explanations
of the firm's organization

In the first commentary, I treated the internal organization of the firm as a different topic from that of the firm's existence. This creates a communication problem that we had best face here. The concept of the firm that is familiar to readers who have followed recent writings about the firm identifies the firm with a type of organization that relies heavily on the managed coordination of a work force. In this literature, for example, a reduction in the cost of transacting is viewed not only as a source of vertical integration, which clearly is an aspect of the firm's organization, but also as a substitution of the firm for the market, which comes close to identifying managed coordination as the essence of the firm. Consistent with this impression is the notion, deriving from Coase's work, that positive transaction cost is the reason the firm exists. In the first commentary, the firm is defined as an institution that specializes in the production of goods for others; on this view, a firm may exist if the efforts of some are managed by the direction of others, but this interpersonal direction is not necessary and is not the essence of the firm. A single person can constitute a firm, producing goods for the use of others.

Clearly organizational questions must be faced by the single-person firm. How big should the firm be? How vertically integrated should its activities be? What controls should the owner-worker in this firm use when dealing with suppliers? How should the owner-worker plan and execute tasks? Management of one sort or another is always involved when production takes place. Even when the firm is comprised of one person only, and no interpersonal management of workers is involved, the activities of this person and the use he or she makes of resources must be self-managed.

The literature of the firm in economics is much more concerned with the multiperson firm than with the single-person firm. The multiperson firm introduces a rich menu of agency problems. The material that follows is directed at understanding some organizational issues that face the multiperson firm, but much of what is said can be extended to the relationships between the owner of the single-person firm and those with whom it contracts for supplies and other services. No doubt, however, organizational problems arise for the multiperson firm that do not arise for the single-person firms, and vice versa. Essentially, the organizational problem is the problem of achieving efficient production for the use of others. In some instances, efficiency obtains with multiperson teamwork, but in other instances the single-person firm is more efficient.

Rather than create a new vocabulary to exposit these organizational issues in a way that makes clear that I am writing about a multiperson firm and not necessarily about all types of firms, I use old terminology and rely on the reader to keep this issue in mind. I write about *team* production, which can be properly identified in context as a multiperson cooperating group of persons working within a single institutional entity that can be called a firm, but team production is not necessarily a characteristic of all firms. The single-person firm is comprised of no team *unless* the cooperative arrangement is thought of as extending beyond the formal limits of the firm to include working relationships with suppliers. As the reader will discover, I do not think this thought is wrongheaded at all. As economists, our interest is in understanding how production by some for others (specialization) is organized; if the contractual arrangements between a firm and its suppliers share characteristics with the contractual arrangements between a firm and its workers, and if these characteristics respond to the same types of forces, why should we distinguish between them?

Shirking, opportunism, and agency

As discussed in the preceding commentary, the perfectly competitive firm of neoclassical price theory presents no internal organizational problem and certainly no agency problem. Full knowledge of prices and technology, along with errorless use of this knowledge to maximize profit, guarantees this. Even though transaction cost is implicitly zero for perfectly competitive firms, they are firms nonetheless. They are specialized production units. If perfect information obviates internal organization problems, then the existence of interesting organization problems rests at least partially on costly, imperfect knowledge. A look back at some of the major developments on the organizational front reveals the importance of imperfect knowledge.

Team production, synergy, and shirking

Alchian and Demsetz (1972) turn away from explanations of the firm's wage/management system based on risk or transaction cost, and emphasize instead the need for a firm to tailor its organization to cope with problems created by conflicts of interest between members of the team we call a firm.[7]

---

7. Marxians also centered their concern on the wage/management system, seeing it as a reflection of class exploitation. Knight does not openly attack Marxian thought in *Risk, Uncertainty, and Profit*, although his explanation of the wage/management system certainly diverges from that of the Marxians. Since he held no fear of debate, and did not hesitate to make it known when he was on the attack, it is likely that his thoughts were not on the Marxians when he set forth his explanation of the wage/management system.

Two assumptions underpin the analysis: (1) Cooperation often is more productive when achieved through team organization than through the linking of individual efforts across impersonal markets, and (2) team organization exacerbates the problem of measuring and parceling out responsibility to members of the team for the team's success or failure. The second assumption obviously brings imperfect knowledge to the issue of organization, but the impact of imperfect information on the theory of the firm extends beyond this to involve the first assumption also. A few words about this are in order because Alchian and Demsetz give so little attention to the sources of productivity enhancement found in team production.

In neoclassical theory the value of the marginal product of an input is a function of only one controllable variable, the quantity of the input. Product price, technology, and quality of work performed by an input also affect productivity, but these are given to the firm when we assume full knowledge. The value of the marginal product of an input is then solely a function of the quantity employed; quantity is the only parameter regarding input use that is decided, and decided correctly, from within the firm. Full knowledge of prices and technologies denies the management any claim to superiority or to specialized knowledge. Wages of management are quite difficult to rationalize in this model of the firm because there is no productive function for the owner-manager to perform.[8] Indeed, older Marxian views of the firm treat the value of the firm's output as created entirely by the efforts of labor. The consequence of introducing imperfect information is to create a productive role for owners and management, both of whom lay claim to different types of knowledge than is possessed by regular employees.

In a world of imperfect information, product price, technology, and quality of work performed are not known for certain. Errors can be made, including, importantly, errors made by management. The value of the marginal product of an input, such as of labor input, no longer is a function of just the quantity of labor. It is also a function of the quality of management in its determination of which goods to produce, which technologies to employ, and how to monitor the performance of inputs. Specialization of knowledge removes from the employees' shoulders the responsibility for determining these matters. Yet decisions about these matters influence the value of the marginal product of any and all inputs used by the firm, this marginal product being determined solely by multiplying price (or marginal revenue) and the increment to physical output

8. These management tasks can be restored if the full information assumption is given a different interpretation. Present prices and technologies may be assumed to be known, but the future may remain obscure. This preserves a productive role for management but raises difficult problems of dividing present from future. What does it mean to say that present price is known? For how long can present price be acted upon? If there is no duration to present price, are we not really referring to knowledge of past price? Past price may give no clue to tomorrow's price and no rationale for management decisions.

or service occasioned by marginal alterations in quantity of input. If such decisions are wrongly made, the quantities of inputs and the uses made of them will not maximize profit. A team aspect to production arises as a result of these interdependencies. This synergistic interaction makes it difficult, even impossible, to isolate the contributions to the value of output purely attributable to a single input. In addition to creating this measurement problem, synergism may also enhance the productivity of team organization as compared to persons acting on their own as production units. This is one explanation for the viability of multiperson firmlike organization. This source of team productivity owes little to Knightian risk redistribution or to Coasian transaction cost.

The increased difficulty caused by synergy in isolating the marginal product of a specific input used in team production makes the shirking problem more important than it would be otherwise. Exacerbation of the shirking problem has its sources in costly information and in the tendency for each member of a team to maximize his or her own utility even at the expense of the team's efforts. Costly information undermines attempts to discover shirking (i.e., to measure the productivity contributions, plus and minus, across team members) and to impose its cost on the shirkers (i.e., to mete out rewards to individuals that are in proportion to productivity contributions). Since the gains from shirking tend to be focused on the shirker and the costs of shirking tend to be diffused throughout the team, utility maximization causes team members to behave in ways that compromise the team's effectiveness.

Under describable, but not under all, circumstances, the shirking problem is reduced in severity by a management/profit/wage system. For Alchian and Demsetz, the key determinant of the efficient compensation system is taken to be how well it works to resolve the "shirking" problem that inevitably arises in the presence of costly information and that is more severe in the presence of synergistic interaction.

Because standard textbook treatment of the firm prior to 1970 neglected both the agency relationship and the diffuse ownership structure of the modern corporation, the firm that seems to be described in these texts is one that is owned and managed by a single person who employs others to perform factory-like manual labor. If the shirking problem is imported into this picture, and if manual labor is assumed to be susceptible to observationally based monitoring, an effective incentive organizational system for such a firm might well involve the following components: contracted wages for employees, the monitoring of their efforts by the owner-manager who possesses the right to dismiss and promote employees, and, finally, owner-manager compensation derived exclusively from the residual left to the firm after paying its contracted costs. These elements are suggested by the need to control the amount of shirking that takes place in the work place, with supervision accomplishing this at the level of manual labor and with profit retention accomplishing it at the level of owner-manager. Smaller firms and firms relying on the mental efforts of their employees may find that profit-sharing arrangements yield better overall results because of their enhancement of worker incentives, even though these arrangements also encourage higher levels of shirking by owners.

Note once more that the difficult problem of productivity apportionment among synergistically interacting team members makes team organization especially susceptible to shirking problems. The opposite view is adopted in the literature on opportunism; vertical integration is seen as the substitution of the firm for the market *and* as a way of reducing or eliminating the problem of opportunism. This is of interest because shirking and opportunism are both the result of inconsistent interests and of the desire to take advantage of others. One would think that activities with so much in common would also share a common solution, but the contrast between these approaches seems to reject this expectation.

Opportunism and asset specificity

Before ideas of opportunism became popular, explanations of vertical integration were not based on the inherent nature of the firm but on the imperatives of price discrimination, successive monopoly, and the desire to heighten barriers to entry. The main exception to this, of course, is Coase's article on the nature of the firm. Coase framed the issue of firm versus market in terms of vertical integration. Should the firm make or buy an input? Work by Williamson (1975) and by Klein, Crawford, and Alchian (1978) produced an explanation of vertical integration based on asset specificity and avoidance of opportunism. Control of assets by a single ownership interest is viewed as an effective method for reducing the scope and impact of opportunistic behavior in the performance of these activities.[9] The propensity toward opportunism is heightened when the value of assets important to achieving low production cost is heavily influenced by the specific identities, or economic situations, of those who have entered into a cooperative agreement. The productivity of vertical integration in this context is in its ability to reduce the resources needed for the protection of cooperating parties from opportunistic behavior. Vertical integration thereby increases the amount of economically viable cooperation that can take place. To Knight's risk redistribution, Coase's reduction in coordination cost, and Alchian and Demsetz's synergy of team production, we now add a fourth possible source of the productivity of complex firm organization – reduction in the severity of opportunism problems.[10]

9. Vertical integration is never complete. Thus, it only *tends* to bring assets under a single ownership interest. Physical assets are more easily owned by a single interest, but human capital continues to belong to the employees in whom it is housed.

10. The reader is reminded of the distinction between the problems of the firm's existence and its organizational complexity. It is the second of these that this commentary deals with even though terminology, at times, suggests the first problem. The firm exists simply because specialization is productive.

Perspective about this last source of productivity gain is gained by discussing its relationship to Coase's contribution. The paradigm problem discussed by Coase asks whether a firm should produce an input in-house or purchase it from an independent supply source across a market – a question of whether or not to vertically integrate. For Coase, the answer is given by comparing transaction cost and management cost. Reduction in transaction cost is also a source of the firm's productivity in the opportunism explanation, for vertical control by a single ownership interest substitutes for contractual arrangements made across markets. Yet, since the authors of the opportunism explanation attach great weight to its ability to explain vertical integration, they believe that opportunism problems are (the most?) serious sources of difficulties in coordinating vertically related activities through markets. Presumably, vertical integration reduces transaction cost without an offsetting increase in management cost when significant asset specificity is involved. Williamson, for example, believes that if opportunism is absent, efficiency in cooperative efforts demands reliance on "high powered incentives" intrinsic to market exchange; that is, exchange across markets is a more productive form of cooperation if opportunism is absent.

Opportunistic behavior is not a problem that is mentioned by Coase in his famous paper, but it is clear from his later writings (1988) that he does not believe opportunism offers a *special* justification for vertical integration. Therein lies a difference between Coase and those who see opportunism as an important source of vertical integration. Coase believes that there is a wide variety of coordination problems, of which opportunism is only one, and that all of these are candidates for resolution through managed coordination *or* through contractual arrangements made across markets. Which institutional arrangement seems best requires a judgment about the tradeoff between transaction and management costs, even in the case of opportunism. Those who believe opportunism is an important part of the explanation of the extent of vertical integration would not disagree in principle, but they would make, and have made, the claim that opportunism is quite generally better solved through vertical integration than through contractual arrangements. Their judgment is based mainly on the appeal of their theorizing and their ability to describe noteworthy examples of the link between opportunism and vertical integration. I harbor few doubts that opportunism affects economic organization, or that it is a stimulus to vertical integration in many instances, but enthusiasm for this explanation seems to me to have outrun the logical case and/or the evidence available to support the explanation. If the main explanation of vertical integration lies in its capacity to mitigate opportunism, vertical integration should be considerably less important in an economy in which opportunism in dealings between cooperating owners of resources is absent. Consider now a thought experiment based on this claim. Suppose everyone behaves honorably and has the same understanding of agreements as everyone else. Suppose further that nothing unexpected happens. There is then no basis for opportunism; it must be completely absent. Yet, vertical integration still must be plentiful. That this is so follows simply from the fact that any productive activity can be subdivided, and subdivided again and again, so that all activities actually undertaken are, and must always be, vertically integrated to a very considerable extent. There is no unit of product, no unit of production process, and no unit of human activity that is the analog of an indivisible subatomic particle. Opportunism, therefore, cannot explain all or even most vertical integration. Additional explanations are needed.

We know of several other explanations. Price controls, successive monopoly, and transaction cost (even absent opportunism) are three, but even after taking account of these there would still remain considerable amounts of unexplained vertical integration. Two other explanations appeal to me as sources of much of this unexplained vertical integration. Simply put, these are *economies in continuity of operations* and *informational advantages accruing to managed direction of activities.* The first is discussed here, the second later.

A coat of paint can be brushed on a house or sprayed on a car by several different persons, each picking up the task where his predecessor finished. Applying paint in this manner requires repeated motions of starting and stopping and raises the problem of beginning, either in place or time, where or when a predecessor ended his contribution to the total task. Cost is raised and/or quality impaired when one person is not allowed to apply the paint. That is why several painters attacking the job of painting a house undertake parts of the task that are less likely to require continuity of task performance. One painter does the siding, another does the trim; one does the front and one side, the other does the rear and the other side. It is efficient in many instances of teamwork to avoid switching personnel, not (only) because of transaction cost or opportunistic behavior but because task performance would be compromised.

This applies to the duration of a person on a "job," where a job is a series of connected operations, which are not only physical but mental also. Similar reasons explain much vertical integration. Assembly lines are not divided into two separate segments, with the output of the first part delivered to the second part over a disrupted path. Transaction cost and opportunism have little to do with the demand for continuity throughout the entire assembly operation. It simply is costly in time and effort to link the output of one part of the assembly line into the second part, breaking continuity of operations. Such breaks can be justified at times by savings of one sort or another (such as might be obtained by dividing the assembly line to accommodate midstream quality checks or space configuration problems), but the cost of such breaks can run high, and, when it does, vertical integration is the better form of organization. When theories of vertical integration are more fully worked out, I believe that an important source will be found in vertical integration's ability to reduce costs in ways having little or nothing to do with opportunism or transactions but much to do with the preservation of continuity of operations. It is difficult to imagine a world in which all economies of continuity of operations are absent. This difficulty tallies well with the corresponding difficulty of imagining the complete absence of vertical integration.

Opportunism may be the proper and the important explanation of vertical integration in many instances, but, of course, this is more likely for situations in which contractual arrangements have not successfully resolved potential conflicts. Court cases, therefore, are not a random sample of vertical relationships. Disagreement, which is the source of court cases, usually implies an element of alleged opportunism. So a sample of evidence secured from court cases, such as the much discussed GM-Fisher case (Klein, Crawford, and Alchian, 1978), exaggerates the importance of opportunism to vertical integration. A random sample of vertical integration situations is more likely to support other explanations. Coase's (1988) position, which is that opportunism problems are frequently dealt with by contractual agreements different from institutionalized vertical integration, is more likely to find support in a random selection of organizational arrangements. A contract well designed to cope with potential opportunism is not likely to appear in court.

A fair gathering of evidence would include statistical studies of large numbers of organizational arrangements. Although the inventory of such studies is growing, it does not yet offer compelling evidence one way or the other. In an early empirical study, Paul Joskow (1987) carefully examined the effect that location specificity has on vertical relationships in a subsector of Eastern coal mines and power plants. He finds that more permanent relationships exist between suppliers of coal and users of coal when their sites are location-specific toward each other. But, *apropos* of Coase's view, these relationships are not exclusively expressed in vertical integration. They are also expressed in long-term contracts. There also has been a showing that complex specialized components are more likely to be produced in-house (Masten, 1984). This has been interpreted as supportive of a linkage between asset specificity/opportunism and vertical integration. Securing such parts across a market exposes buyer and seller to opportunism because neither is easily replaced once assets are committed to the production of such specialized components. This may explain the in-house production of components like these, but the phenomenon also may be explained by a proposition like Adam Smith's observation that specialization is limited by the size of the market. It may be too costly (other than for opportunism reasons) to commit overhead and start-up cost to a new enterprise if the market for specialized components is small.[11]

11. A more general attack on the evidence regarding vertical integration can be found in Demsetz (1988). Using the relative importance of durable assets in a firm's asset structure as an index

Imperfect information is taken to imply difficulty in devising contracts that mitigate opportunism problems, and this, in turn, is judged to motivate solutions involving vertical integration. But the vertically integrated firm also holds dangers for cooperating parties when the future is uncertain. The more difficult the future is to forecast, the more important it becomes to work flexibility into the design of a cooperative arrangement. This argues against relying on firm-like organization, because reliance on markets generally offers greater flexibility in dealing with unforeseen contingencies. The organizing implications of imperfect foresight are not so clearly in the direction of substituting managed for contractual coordination. The partial directional effect of imperfect information that runs through the catalyst of transactor-specific assets and opportunism calls for vertical integration, but the total effect, which also reflects the usefulness of flexibility, may not. The consequence of imperfect foresight for business organization is not yet clearly discernible, but the firm's inflexibility of response to unexpected changes in conditions makes imperfect information a possible source of vertical "disintegration." The assertion of the firm's inflexibility in response requires logical defense, however obvious its truth may be empirically. Elements of such a defense will be suggested later in this commentary, but, before turning away from agency-type problems, let us consider a framework for analyzing the cost of the agency problems we have been discussing.

The cost of agency

Jensen and Meckling (1976) describe the cost of agency as the sum of monitoring expenditures incurred by the principal, bonding expenditures incurred by the agent, and the value of the lost residual borne by the principal and attributable to the agency problem (by which they mean the dollar equivalent of the reduction in welfare experienced by the principal). These are classifications by name of some of the categories in which the cost of agency may be found, that is, monitoring cost, bonding cost, and so on, but they are not analyses that offer guidance about the behavior that will affect the magnitude of agency cost. An analytical framework is needed that allows one to incorporate rational adjustments to the phenomenon of behavioral problems. Neoclassical thinking tools are of help in providing this framework.

One important adjustment that should be taken into account is the compensation or price that is asked by persons before they join in a cooperative activity subject to agency problems. A party to a prospective agreement, which, once entered into, requires highly specific investments and exposes the party to

of the specificity of its assets, I find no correlation between this index and the degree of vertical integration. One or two other studies have shown a relationship between vertical integration and indexes of asset specificity.

being "victimized" by future dealings with a monopolist, is well advised to insist on a price that is high enough to outweigh this danger. The importance of this anticipation factor extends to all sorts of relational behavior problems, including those that are not associated with asset specificity. A simple – perhaps too simple – way of looking at the anticipation factor will be given shortly. Before discussing this, we should distinguish two types of on-the-job consumption: that which is arranged through explicit negotiations and that which is not.

Explicitly negotiated on-the-job consumption may be understood by supposing first that the monitoring of behavior is perfect. Two cases of perfect monitoring may be distinguished. The first involves self-monitoring. This is relevant to the theory of the firm if the behavior of the sole owner of a firm is at issue. An owner may vacation frequently, she may devote only a small portion of the day to her firm, and she may use the firm to gratify her demand for prestige and authority rather than for profit. In these instances, and many others that could be listed, the owner is engaging in on-the-job consumption, but not in shirking. She is simply substituting utility maximization for profit maximization, and the benefits and the cost of this substitution are borne entirely and solely by her. So we may treat them as explicitly negotiated through her mental calculations. The rational owner is not inclined to take advantage of herself.

However, it is not completely silly to think that an agency problem can be wrapped up within a single individual. Time inconsistency problems create the possibility of self-contained agency problems. An owner may have difficulty staying the course of some rationally calculated plan, such difficulty arising because of a shift in the discount factor he applies to his behavior in the future. This introduces an element of what is, at least, a pseudo agency problem. The owner at time zero can be viewed as different from the owner at a future time; so the "same" person can be both principal and agent. If a person can impose constraints on his future behavior at no cost to himself, he will do so, and this will solve his agency problem. Consistent with this possibility, we may define monitoring cost to include both the cost of knowing or deciphering behavior and the cost of censoring or disciplining behavior. Given this definition, if monitoring cost is zero, there should be no behavior that constitutes shirking or opportunism.

The second case of zero monitoring cost involves dealings between an owner of a firm and those whom he employs, especially professional managers. In a regime of perfect monitoring, managers do not shirk, but they may engage in on-the-job consumption. All that is required is for this consumption to be more efficient when it takes place on the job than when it takes place elsewhere (in employee households). Professional managers who derive utility from heading larger firms or from possessing more corporate jets than seem to serve their firms well, but who find great difficulties consuming such goods outside the institutional framework of the firm, will negotiate with the owner of the firm to be allowed to consume them on the job. The firm's owner, of course, insists that revenues used to purchase this on-the-job consumption for managers is at least made up by revenues gained by reducing other compensations that managers receive such as salary. On-the-job consumption of this sort is not shirking; it is only an efficient form of compensation. Indeed, if the owner of the firm disallows such on-the-job consumption, he must pay higher total compensation to obtain the same quality of effort from management. By assumption, because such consumption on the job confers more utility to managers than consumption of them in the household, the maintenance of a given level of consumption utility for managers requires that wages be increased by more than the cost of this on-the-job consumption should it be barred by the employer. This type of on-the-job consumption, should it be allowed, actually lowers the firm's cost of production.

The empirical consequence of this is that on-the-job consumption is not a reliable measure of the severity of relational behavior problems. A firm may be used by its owner as a plaything. It may be used by professional management as a source of desired perks. It may be treated by both owner and management as if it were a cornucopia of goodies. None of this necessarily signifies the existence of a relational behavior problem.

We are now in a position to assess more carefully the cost of agency. In Figure 2.1, let D and S be the demand for and supply of management services, on the assumption that monitoring is free and perfect. Equilibrium compensation is b, and equilibrium quantity of management services is L. Compensation is measured as the cost to an owner of the firm of securing another unit of management services. The exchange of management services yields a combined management-owner gain from exchange equal to triangle abc. The price per unit of management labor services might be paid in cash, in explicitly negotiated on-the-job consumption, or in some combination of these. We now alter this case by supposing monitoring is imperfect. The firm's owner now incurs a cost to monitor management, but this expenditure does not eliminate all non-negotiated on-the-job consumption. Assume a constant monitoring cost per unit of management services and also a constant dollar cost to the owner of the non-negotiated on-the-job consumption that persists. The sum of these two costs per unit of management services is the amount by which the owner's demand for management services shifts downward from D to D'.

However, one dollar spent by the owner on this on-the-job consumption yields less than the utility of a dollar to management, since it is less fungible than cash. Consequently, the supply of management services to the firm must be shifted to the left, as from S to S', when part of the compensation received

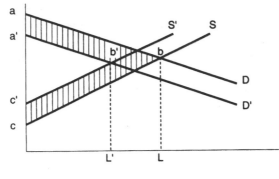

Figure 2.1

by management is non-negotiated on-the-job consumption. The new equilibrium compensation (dollars of cash plus dollars of goods in-kind) is b', and the new equilibrium quantity of management services is L'.[12]

The cost of agency is the difference between triangles abc and $a'b'c'$, the lined area in the text figure. This measures the difference between the gains from exchange in the absence of any agency problem and the gains from exchange in the presence of agency problems. The agency problem reduces the quantity of management services employed from L to L'. The sources of this reduction, but not its measure, are in the cost of monitoring, in the cost of producing non-negotiated on-the-job amenities, and in the cost of reductions in the fungibility of compensation. The measure of agency cost is the reduction in gains from exchange, as illustrated in Figure 2.1. In principle, these costs can be large enough to reduce the equilibrium quantity of management (or of other employee) service to zero, in which case the firm could not exist if agency relationships are necessary.

Clearly, it is in the collective interest of owner and professional management (and/or other employees of the firm), taken as a group, to attempt to reduce the amount of non-negotiated on-the-job consumption.[13] Individual employees have no interest in reducing the scale of this consumption if others do not

12. I am assuming that only negotiated on-the-job consumption is efficient. No deduction for loss of fungibility is required for this because management gets more utility consuming this on the job than at home. I am further assuming that management would rather have the dollars spent on non-negotiated on-the-job consumption, to be spent or saved in their households, than have in-kind on-the-job consumption – if only this could be arranged. This on-the-job consumption is worth less to management than its dollar cost to the firm's owners.

13. The "taken as a group" qualification is needed because particular employees may have a comparative advantage in the "art" of shirking.

participate in the reduction. Effective monitoring of management offers a method for assuring individual managers that reductions in this on-the-job consumption are absorbed by the entire management team. For a given technology of monitoring, the employer will increase monitoring expenditures if these yield a reduction in the cost of non-negotiated on-the-job consumption that is at least as large. The net result, then, is to reduce the downward shift from D to D'; in the limit, with monitoring being perfectly effective for minuscule monitoring expenditure, D does not shift at all. The consequent increase in fungibility of the compensation package decreases the difference between S and S'. The net effect is to bring equilibrium b' closer to b. The efficient amount of monitoring will be that which, as a result of the combined shifts in these curves, makes $a'b'c'$ as large as possible.

It may also be the case that efficiency wages can be used to increase the gains from exchange. If paid a premium, management has a greater desire to avoid being forced to leave the firm's employment. Individual managers reduce the probability of involuntary separation by reducing the amount of non-negotiated on-the-job consumption. The use of a wage premium has the virtue of substituting a monetary transfer payment for the expenditure of real resources on monitoring. But efficiency wages cannot achieve their goal without at least some monitoring. The compensation premium has no force in altering management behavior if there is no fear of involuntary separation from the firm, and there is no fear if there is no monitoring. Management behavior, therefore, must be monitored to some extent, but it may be that the amount spent on monitoring can be reduced by introducing an efficiency wage premium. If this substitution is effective, it is in management's interest to bring it about, for management prefers cash compensation to monies spent on monitoring and on in-kind amenities (setting aside tax considerations). Management brings this about by asking for, or by being offered, a wage premium that is not so large as to leave the firm's owner indifferent between additional monitoring and paying the wage premium.

We have already noted that in the hypothetical case of perfect, zero-cost monitoring, neither this premium wage nor the use of resources for monitoring is required. Non-negotiated on-the-job consumption simply does not take place. The negotiated on-the-job consumption that remains enhances efficiency because the job is the superior place for some consumption to take place, and this consumption cannot be thought of as shirking or as a cost of agency. The negotiation involves a reduction in pecuniary wage in return for an increase in non-pecuniary wage. But such a negotiation is implicit in the case of "non-negotiated" on-the-job consumption also, as is apparent in Figure 2.1. That is, wages and employment are affected by "non-negotiated" on-the-job consumption much as they would be if negotiations have taken place. How does negotiated on-the-job consumption differ from non-negotiated on-the-job consumption? In both cases, management (and other employees) pay for what is consumed through compensation adjustments. The only reason for distinguishing these two situations is that with imperfect information the compensation package is not ideally tailored to an *individual* employee's consumption. The owner of the firm cannot easily determine who accounts for how much of the total on-the-job consumption. As a result, the parties with whom he contracts will tend to receive a compensation package that incorporates adjustments for amenities but where these adjustments tend toward equality for all employees of a definably relevant group. The average amount of amenities consumed on-the-job by a class of employees, such as management, tends to be the adjustment factor. The lack of fineness in this adjustment leaves room for, and provides an incentive to, individuals to attempt to consume more than this average, and this raises the total of on-the-job consumption above what it would be if monitoring cost were zero. With zero monitoring cost, no one acts on the premise that he or she can take advantage of others. With positive monitoring cost, there is the possibility of taking advantage. On average, management (and other employees) and the firm's owner benefit from any technology or organization that reduces monitoring cost and thereby reduces the non-negotiated portion of on-the-job consumption.

Actions motivated by the possibility of taking advantage of others seem to merit the shirking, agency cost, or opportunism labels. These actions would be absent not only if monitoring cost were zero but even if this cost were positive, as long as persons attach no value to gains secured in this way. Ethical beliefs matter here. But we must be careful in economics when ethical beliefs are brought into the analysis. Economic analysis neither makes nor needs an ethical presumption regarding motivation. Analysis depends only on the assumption of rational maximization.

The measure of agency cost in Figure 2.1 takes the situation that would prevail if monitoring were costless and/or perfect as a norm, and this suggests that, in some sense, agency cost is to be avoided whenever possible. This hardly differs at all from a belief that raw material cost, capital cost, and labor cost are to be avoided whenever possible! What makes all these costs worth bearing is the impossibility of simultaneously avoiding them while still accomplishing other desirable goals. Raw material cost is worth bearing because it is desirable to convert raw material into goods under conditions in which these raw materials have alternative valuable uses. The same approach should be applied to an interpretation of agency cost. Agents offer valuable services that are worth buying even if part of the purchase price is non-negotiated on-the-job consumption. More to the point, organizations of the firm that accomplish desirable objectives may make the cost of monitoring agents higher. We may examine this with respect to the firm's ownership structure.

The cost of monitoring is higher for firms in which the ownership structure is very diffuse. If agency cost were the only desideratum in choosing the firm's organization, all firms would be owned and managed by a single person. This person would also be the only employee of the firm. In this way, agency cost would be held to a minimum. Save for the time inconsistency problem previously referred to, agency cost would be zero! No doubt, many single proprietorships function in just this manner or approximately so. But this cannot be the optimal organization for most firms. Specialization and scale can be productive, but they usually require the use of agents. Potential providers of equity to a firm that is about to be organized need to decide on the ownership structure they will agree to (or on some hierarchal structure of control that will be allowed to influence ownership structure). A positive amount of management entrenchment is desirable simply because the expertise and full-time attendance of professional management is productive. For management to be productive, it needs the rights to make a variety of business decisions. The exercise of these rights necessarily brings a dose of management entrenchment to the firm. This applies to small and large firms alike.

For the large firm, the rational amount of management entrenchment is likely to be still greater because owners will be more desirous of a diffuse ownership structure. Investors in equity find firm-specific risk a cost. This cost is related to the share of their wealth that they put into a single firm. The larger the firm, the greater is the share of an investor's wealth that is needed to maintain a given degree of control of professional management. Rational investors, to reduce the firm-specific risk they bear, prefer to own a smaller share of a large firm than of a small firm, giving rise to greater diffuseness of ownership. By choosing a more diffuse ownership structure, owners are choosing to increase the agency cost they bear. However, this reduces the risk-weighted cost of capital to the firm, so that the total cost of operating the firm is not necessarily raised by greater agency cost. Rational investors will choose to increase the agency cost they bear only if this yields a larger decrease in the risk-weighted cost of capital to them. Choosing the more diffuse ownership structure, therefore, does not imply the choosing of a less effective form of organization or a more costly method of producing.

By the same line of reasoning, we would conclude that a team of prospective management-entrepreneurs, seeking to create a firm from capital raised from others, should elect to subject itself to a positive amount of effective monitoring. Capital markets provide the motivation, for prospective investors do not relish the thought of being fleeced by a strongly entrenched management.

Whichever perspective one adopts – that of prospective shareholders or that of a hypothetically completely entrenched potential management group – we are led to the conclusion that the degree of management entrenchment that is sought is greater than zero but less than complete entrenchment. One cannot conclude from this that the severity of the agency problem chosen is unaffected by which group is doing the choosing. Transaction and information costs are positive; these, along with the comparative severity of free rider problems, may lead to different choices, but the differences between the chosen degrees of severity are likely to be much less than one might suppose if the supply of and demand for capital were ignored. Should developments occur that make ownership structure too diffuse or that, for other reasons, transfer too much control to professional management, the cost of capital to the firm must increase. It is also true, however, that too little diffuseness of ownership structure and too little reliance on professional management raise the risk-adjusted cost of capital. The correct degree of diffuseness of ownership structure and, by implication, the correct severity of the agency problem are functions of maximizing behavior of the sort presumed by neoclassical theory, and applying this theory's tool kit can help us make sense of this problem even though its origin is in imperfections in knowledge.

Nonagency explanations of the firm's organization

Although transaction cost is involved in the agency explanations of the firm's organization, it is not necessarily the key element in these explanations. Shirking, for example, can take place even though the cost of searching for, negotiating with, and formalizing contractual arrangements is zero. It is the positive cost of monitoring these arrangements, combined with a lack of congruence between the interests of the parties, that gives rise to shirking. The cost of monitoring, however, is as much a cost of management as it is of market transacting. In addition to ascertaining the effort a worker puts into a job, the monitoring of the performance of suppliers is important also. This is a general problem of empirical implementation of the Coasian transaction cost/management cost tradeoff. An increase in the cost of an input used to measure or discipline the efforts of others may impact management and transaction costs, and in the same direction. But if we suppose that we do know when the relative magnitude of these two costs has changed, as we would, for example, if the government placed a tax on transactions between firms, we could inquire into the significance of this for the firm's organization. This inquiry is independent of whether an agency problem is also present.

Transaction cost theory thus offers a nonagency explanation of the firm's organization. A reduction in transaction cost leads to an increase in the number of firms and in the number of different management teams. The typical firm becomes smaller and more specialized. Both changes ought to influence the firm's organization, at least by making the management hierarchy smaller and by reducing its reliance on formal organizational rules. Additional changes in organization are likely to flow from a reduction in transaction cost, but the literature has not gone much beyond the vertical (dis)integration aspect of organization. The impact and rate of response to changes in market prices might be very different in small, more specialized firms than in large, less specialized firms. Small size and specialized activity make it easier to judge the consequences of price changes, probably of technological changes also, and this greater ease should lead to quicker and more decisive response. The incentive systems used within a firm are also likely to reflect its size and degree of specialization, particularly the relative emphasis given to fixed wages and to profit sharing or performance compensation. The broader implications of changes in the transaction cost/management cost tradeoff need more attention in the literature. Too much attention has been given to the vertical integration issue, even though vertical integration is an important dimension of the firm's organization.

Turning away from these speculations about the consequences of transaction cost, let us now consider three other dimensions of organization. They are the degrees to which the association between input owners is (1) long-lasting, (2) based on supervision, and (3) devised and monitored by a central contractor. The greater the degrees to which the association is durable, directable, and centrally arranged, the more it seems to characterize a complex organization of the sort the literature seems to have in mind by "the firm."

Durability and directability of the association

What advantages are conveyed to the specialist producer by greater reliance on the durability and directability of the association? To answer this, we must first acknowledge the generally true proposition, to which there undoubtedly exist some exceptions, that the specialist producer makes the same goods over long stretches of time. To obtain the bulk of its revenues, the General Motors Corporation does not produce automobiles, trucks, and locomotives on one day or during one year and then turn to producing food products the next day or year. Approximate stability in required tasks is the result of this constancy of goods output, and this allows the durability and directability of the association between team members to achieve economies that otherwise would not be possible. The main sources of these economies are investments in durable equipment that is at least somewhat specialized to the tasks it is designed to perform and investments in specialized knowledge. Because durable, specialized equipment is discussed extensively in the literature, my emphasis here is on the role of specialized knowledge.

The technique of having some persons direct the activities of others uses knowledge more efficiently by reducing the cost of its acquisition and the cost of extending its use through the organization. With the ability to direct the actions of others, only a few persons need become possessors of the specialized knowledge on which the organization's future rests. This reduces knowledge acquisition cost because the cost of acquiring incremental knowledge is lower the more knowledge one already possesses about a particular body of facts and theories; there are economies of scale to specialized knowledge acquisition. Reliance on the direction of some by others allows this knowledge to be put to use guiding these activities without requiring those who actually execute them to master the knowledge themselves. Stability in the team's tasks and continuity of the association of the team members further facilitate the use of specialized knowledge. Persons learn the capabilities and limitations of team members in tasks that are undertaken frequently.

These knowledge-based enhancements in team productivity have implications for the scope of activities that can be carried on within a single organization if it is to be competitively viable. Increasing the number of different lines of activities or the degree of vertical integration forces the organization to settle for less than the full advantages of specializing in the knowledge base on which it operates and requires the central control center of the firm to digest knowledge of different types. The broader the scope of activities, the more burdensome the lack of specialization becomes. A cut-off point is reached beyond which the burdens of acquiring and dealing with so many different types of knowledge are so great that the firm ceases to remain competitively viable. Hence, there is productivity enhancement in specialization that extends beyond task manipulation and includes economies in information acquisition and utilization. The information-husbanding consequences of the durability and directability of the association smack of the synergism on which the productivity of the firmlike association ultimately rests. These sources of productivity enhancement are what Alchian and Demsetz might have relied upon to justify their assumption that team cooperation can achieve economies not otherwise available.

The one-person firm can capture some of these advantages, but to a lesser degree. The one person in this firm, after all, masters a specialized trade and hence reduces the cost of knowledge acquisition. He also learns his habits, strengths, and weaknesses through long association with himself and thus becomes familiar with his capabilities. But he cannot specialize his knowledge base as much as can members of a team of workers, nor can he rely on others to perform those tasks that he has learned he does not do so well. The multiperson organization can capture these advantages better than the one-person firm, but only at greater costs of communication and agency.

As previously indicated, variability of the tasks to be performed by cooperating inputs is an aspect of production that is likely to influence the optimal degree of directability and durability. The more variable the tasks, the less productive is the durability of the association. This is because different tasks generally require different inputs; in the case of human services, different tasks require persons with different specialized knowledge and talents. The advantage of constituting new teams over shorter intervals of time grows as does the variability over time of the tasks to be performed. On this reasoning, continuity of the association should be shorter in cooperative arrangements that, for one reason or another, are likely to experience considerable task variability (i.e., are likely to demand greater flexibility).

The productive giving of directions requires confidence that these directions are carried out. This confidence is itself a function of organization. The main difference between organizations in this respect lies in the benefits and costs of increasing reliability. Reliability becomes more important to an organization as the productivities of its various parts become more interdependent. The military organization, at least during a war, is an outstanding example of important interdependence. When an officer orders infantry to take a heavily fortified hill, there is likely to be considerable reticence among the troops. Not taking the hill may create a major problem for the larger military campaign that is also underway. This interdependency creates a demand for discipline that is stronger than in organizations in which spillover affects like this are not so important. Reliability is secured by conditioning troops during training and by the considerable penalty that can be imposed on a soldier who refuses to obey an order. In the extreme conditions that can arise in military operations, the availability of heavy penalties can increase the overall productivity of the organization.[14]

Business firms are unlikely to demand so high a level of reliability because the consequences of failure to follow directions are not likely to be so severe or so undermining of the productivities of other parts of the organization, although to this general condition exceptions surely exist. In contrast to the military, the penalty for failure to perform is largely that of dismissal from the organization. (Dismissal might be welcomed by the infantry man who has just been asked to charge up the hill; so different penalties are necessary. Court martial, prison, even execution on the spot have been used to secure compliance.)

The firm as the central contractor

X enters into a contract with Y, and Y subcontracts part of the task to Z. Each of these two contracts may create durability and directability of the association between the contracting parties, but this cooperative arrangement is less firm-like than one in which X contracts bilaterally with both Y and Z. The second of these arrangements involves centrality of contracting of a sort that we

---

14. The productive function must be interpreted narrowly in terms of the objectives of the organization. These objectives can be thought by some to be good and by others to be bad; so "productive" carries no necessary message concerning the organization's output.

associate with firmlike organization. Two different kinds of reasons can be offered to explain the productivity enhancement obtained through the use of a central contractor. Centrality of contracting internalizes interdependencies between performance of different tasks; the information that is obtained from the performers of these tasks enters one decision center where comparisons, judgments, and adjustments can be made without as much confusion, conflict, or opportunism as would exist if several different contractors attempted the same task. The second type of reason is that reliance on centrality of contracting makes it easier to concentrate profit and loss incentives, thus reducing the central contractor's incentive to shirk in the performance of the monitoring task.

The larger the firm and the more complex it is, the more severe are the problems of controlling the interdependencies among its parts. This severity can become so great that the advantages of centrality of contracting are overshadowed by the inability of one or a few persons to attend appropriately to matters of importance throughout the organization. At this juncture, institutional arrangements tend to become less firmlike and more decentralized; multiple firms, each with its own central contracting, substitute for fewer firms. Centralized contracting is more important the greater are the task interdependencies involved in the firm's production and the more specialized is the knowledge needed to take these interdependencies into account, but these very conditions place limits on the size of the efficient organization. Centralized contracting approaches an overburdened condition more rapidly the greater is the extent to which different bodies of knowledge must be mastered to cope effectively with task interdependencies, so that economies of specializing in knowledge are again at work in influencing this dimension of the firm's organization. Broadly ranging considerations of the acquisition and uses of knowledge are involved. These extend considerably beyond what might reasonably be thought of as transactions or opportunism considerations, although the latter certainly can strengthen or weaken the productivity enhancement achieved through a central contracting agent.[15]

15. Oliver Hart (1989) draws attention to the role of asset specificity in influencing the identity of the central contracting agent. The owner of an asset that is very specific to the cooperative arrangement is in the greatest jeopardy of being taken advantage of opportunistically by cooperating agents. This owner would place a higher value on being the central contractor than would others. However, there clearly is an ignored weighting problem. An asset may be very highly specialized but not a very valuable portion of the assets involved in the cooperative arrangement. The owner of a specially designed wrench, suitable only to tasks in which this particular cooperative arrangement is engaged, is hardly likely by virtue of this ownership to become the central contracting agent. He is more likely to sell the wrench to the party who, for other reasons, is the better central contracting agent. Ownership of an asset is not predetermined. It should gravitate to the party who possess the specialized knowledge necessary to do a good job of setting the general goal of the cooperative effort and monitoring the degree

The exploitation issue

In neoclassical theory, no one (but a monopolist) exploits anyone. Competitive markets determine prices in an impersonal way, and everyone is viewed as responding to these prices in ways that maximize utility. No power or authority is exercised. Competition and full information lead to this characterization of a market-based system. The emerging theory of the management-theoretic firm, depending as it does on costly and imperfect information, introduces conscious interaction between suppliers and demanders of resources. Tactics, strategy, guile, and opportunism become viable behavior traits, and so do countervailing traits of honesty, openness, trust, and reputation. This creates new intellectual space for Marxist notions of exploitation, and available space seldom remains unoccupied. Old ideas of exploitation are already being dressed in new garb. Preliminary skirmishes on this intellectual front have already emerged. These revolve around a few central points.

The first is that the Walrasian, Arrow, Debreu equilibrium models of an economic system are very sterile, even though under specified conditions they demonstrate efficiency consequences from a capitalistic type of economic system. These demonstrations are interpreted by Marxist-leaning economists as roadblocks to critiques of capitalism. The relevance of imperfect information to the theory of the firm is seen as a way to breach these roadblocks, using the agency problem as the vehicle. Many economists, including those who hold quite different views about capitalism from those held by neo-Marxists, have expressed doubts about the usefulness of Walrasian-Arrow-Debreu general equilibrium. This skirmish may be set aside, not only for this reason but also because it lacks relevance to the theory of the firm.

The second point is that viable interactions between self-interested persons in an imperfectly informed world include guile and opportunism. This gives rise to *relational* behavior problems that cannot exist within the neoclassical informational framework. As Bowles and Gintis put it, "the self-interested behavior underlying neoclassical theory is artificially truncated: it depicts a charmingly Victorian but utopian world in which conflicts abound but a handshake is a

---

to which various owners of inputs accomplish their tasks. This suggests that a theory of the central contracting agent should entail a comparison between the cost of changing the identity of the owner of the specialized asset and the cost of acquiring the desired specialized knowledge.

Williamson (1970, 1971) uses a knowledge-based explanation of the advantages of different structures of the managerial hierarchy that firms rely upon. His emphasis is on reducing degradation in the quality of information as it moves between the top of the hierarchy and points lower down. He believes that the M-form hierarchal structure, in which a central office allocates resources among separate major divisions of the firm, is superior in yielding greater accuracy of information. This is relevant to the firm's organization, but it is not the same as the desire to take advantage of specialized knowledge.

handshake."[16] This misperceives neoclassical economics, and neo-Marxists are not alone in this. As discussed in the first commentary, the interest of neoclassical theory is not mainly to delve into personal interactions and the behavior that might result from these, but to examine a (price) system that makes such interaction impotent and therefore unimportant. Had neoclassical theory been interested in the managed control of resources, it would not have chosen as its centerpiece the perfect competition model. The neoclassical view of the price system *is* truncated, not because it takes a naive view of human behavior, but because it presumes full information in order to make the study of price coordination easier. In a full information world, guile and opportunism can yield no profit and have no substantive standing as viable tactics. To say this is not to deny them a role in imperfectly informed market exchanges. They undoubtedly play a part in market exchanges as well as in the conscious management of resources within firms and within the state. Duplicity is found in all forms of social organization, including the employee-owned firm, a new favorite of neo-Marxists (and one that violates no tenet of a market-based system). The modern university in its internal dealings is pretty much employee-controlled even if not completely employee-owned.[17] But, as all who read this surely know, duplicity is no stranger to the halls of academe.

If a handshake is not a handshake, neither is a dishonest handshake free. Fakery is costly to those who practice it as well as to those on whom it is practiced. The cost is in loss of reputational capital and future profitable dealings. But more than this is involved. Competition often makes fakery unprofitable even if it is never uncovered. Let every marketer of coffee fill its coffee cans with less than the amount of coffee advertised and recorded on the label. Competition between cheating manufacturers brings the price per pound of coffee to about the same level, its marginal cost, as if a full measure of coffee

---

16. See the *Journal of Economic Perspectives* (Bowles and Gintis, 1993) for an exchange of ideas between Bowles and Gintis, representing the neo-Marxist view that the role of power has been resurrected by the new theories of the firm, and Williamson, representing a transactional view of the firm. Stiglitz, presumably invoking the prerogative of editor, joins in the discussion; he tells Bowles and Gintis that they have not gone far enough in their critique but that no major revision of economic theory may be called for because the points raised by Bowles and Gintis have already been noted in the literature! The rejoinder by Williamson, in my opinion, is narrowly limited to a main point; this is that transactional economics at least offers testable propositions, something that remains to be accomplished from the "power" perspective of neo-Marxians. It takes testable propositions to make meaningful comparisons of theories (true enough), but this leaves the logic of the issues raised by Bowles and Gintis's attack unchallenged.

17. This is especially the case for private universities. These do respond to students, donors, and trustees, but their management is largely in the hands of faculty. State universities respond to similar constituencies, but also to state legislatures that provide much of their funding. These legislatures, or at least some legislators, have been known to intercede in the management of "their" universities.

were put into each can. Consumers need no scales by which to weigh their purchases, they are protected by competition. Similarly, competition between employers and between laborers, even if decisions are based on less than full information, tends to protect each from a wage that is exploitive in either direction.

Neo-Marxists assert that imperfect information conveys greater power to capital in its dealings with labor, and persons adopting this view often quote for criticism a point raised in the Alchian and Demsetz (1972) article on the theory of the firm. We assert there that the firm

> has no power of *fiat*, no authority, no disciplinary action any different in the slightest degree from ordinary market contracting between any two people . . . [The firm] can fire or sue, just as I can fire my grocer by stopping purchases from him, or sue him for delivering faulty products.

This quotation, it should be noted, is a mere aside in an article devoted to arguing the importance of shirking behavior and monitoring cost to a theory of the firm, but it is critiqued as if it were a central analytical point. In fact, employees can quit and can be fired. And persons can refuse to trade with others across markets also. The institution of the firm does not legally bind people against their will into conditions of servitude, although contemporary law seems to hold a firm to an employment contract more firmly than it holds employees. There is a point to be conceded. The costs borne by cooperating parties if their interaction should end are not necessarily equal, whether the interaction takes place within firms or across markets. The manner in which costs of disassociation vary across situations and institutions merits examination, but a point that is often ignored is that inequality in these costs gives rise to a compensating offset in the prices or wages at which the parties agree to cooperate in the first place. Prospective employees, in considering alternative places of employment, will ask wages that reflect their expectations of the costs they might bear should they lose their jobs. The prospective employer considering alternative employees will offer a wage in accord with the likelihood that an employee will quit. Imperfect information makes these compensations less likely to be on the mark, but it does not necessarily bias their levels. Examples of the exercise of power can be cited as helping either side of an employment arrangement, but the real issue is whether "capital" systematically exploits or is exploited by "labor," or neither.

Voluntary cooperative arrangements are made even though costs of separation loom should there be disengagement. Such arrangements are likely to involve the direction of some employees by others or of all employees by owner-managers, but this is voluntarily agreed to because of the desirable effects it has on joint productivity. Direction of some by others in a voluntary association arises precisely because information is imperfect, but the terms by which various parties participate in the arrangement reflect the protections afforded them not only by the legal system and explicit monitoring, but also by competition. Systematic, one-sided exploitation is not clearly the consequence of capitalism.

Because duplicity can be practiced if information is imperfect, a demand for measures to control or reduce the amount of duplicity arises. Neo-Marxists familiar with contemporary writings about the firm and labor management classify these measures into two categories: monitoring devices and incentive wages. The first is presumed to use real resources to police behavior. The second is presumed to rely simply on a transfer payment, such as a higher wage, to discourage employees from shirking or from behaving in some other opportunistic manner. Assume that the amount employers would need to spend to achieve a given reduction in duplicitous behavior is the same no matter which of these two methods is used. The employer, argue neo-Marxists, is then indifferent between these methods. Workers and society are not. The indifference shown by employers leads to the diversion of real resources into a monitoring effort when all that is needed is a transfer payment in the form of a higher wage. Workers, of course, prefer higher wages to being monitored; society prefers transfer payments rather than diversion of real resources. Hence, the capitalist firm, because of its alleged indifference, can be a source of inefficiency if information is imperfect. That is how some neo-Marxists see it. In the new Nirvana, incentive wages replace monitoring. The employee-owned firm triumphs because employee-owners surely will adopt higher wages instead of monitoring. Imperfect information has created a source of inefficiency in the capitalistic firm that is not based on simple externalities. Eureka!

This cannot be taken seriously. The reasoning is shallow. The party that is potentially subject to monitoring, in this case the employees, has an incentive to pay the person planning to do the monitoring to refrain from doing so and to choose instead the higher wage that accomplishes the same end. Both parties are made better off for this payment if the facts are as stated. If the employer truly suffers no higher cost from this arrangement, competition sees to it that the amount employees need to pay to bring about this happy state of affairs is infinitesimally small. So, when the facts fit, the capitalist firm in search of profit should not be indifferent between incentive wages and monitoring, and the concession in the wage, or in the side-payment to employers, that is required to eliminate indifference is made very slight by competition. Arrangements akin to this resolution exist. Sums paid to become a licensed member of a franchise usually exceed the cost to the franchise of accepting new members; this is a payment to the monitor. The franchise, in turn, allows franchise outlets to set mark-ups at levels that, in themselves and aside from the payment to be licensed, yield powerful incentives to work hard; this is the equivalent of the incentive wage. In labor markets, wages that rise over time more rapidly than does worker productivity, but which start at levels below worker productivity, are approximations of the same resolution of the problem. Workers choose to work hard because they wish to remain employed into the period during which they are paid in excess of their productivities.[18] But be careful. If there were no monitoring efforts, why should workers be fearful of losing jobs? The notion that incentive wages obviate the need for monitoring is wrong, and it is wrong even in the case of the employee-owned firm.

18. Yes, employers need to be put in a position that they will bear costs if they terminate worker employment merely to avoid paying these higher wages.

Enterprise control, wealth, and economic development

The control problem discussed in the second commentary has implications far beyond those that concern the firm itself. This is not generally appreciated, and the purpose of this commentary is to show the importance of this problem to broader social issues. The issues discussed here bear on questions of economic development, regulation, and the distribution of wealth. The connection of these to the firm's agency problem is lodged in the production function.

As long as societies differ in the principles of organization (e.g., socialist vs. capitalist) and in the wealth distribution on which they rely, they will not face the same production possibility frontier. This is so even if they have identical resources and technical knowledge. If the old Soviet Union could be endowed with the resource and knowledge base available to the United States, it still would not, and could not, turn out the same mixes of outputs if it were to rely on socialist techniques of management and preferences for an egalitarian distribution of wealth. The formalist will complain that wealth distribution, culture, institutions, and organizing principles must be counted as inputs if differences in output mixes persist. And this is precisely my claim. To be the equivalent of the United States, the Soviet Union would need to be the United States. My point simply is that development theory has at best paid lip service to the importance of wealth distribution and of organizing institutions when discussing the production possibility frontier. Only now, as East Europe tries to change, has the importance of these considerations become apparent. Their importance may very well exceed that of the variables stressed in neoclassical development theory – resource endowments and technology.

One would have thought that the production consequences of enterprise control and wealth distribution would have become analytically important once attention shifted from the analysis of a capitalist economy, in which the existence of a private property system is taken for granted, to the conversion of socialist economies to capitalist, in which the existence of capitalistic institutions cannot be taken for granted. It would seem that the analysis of a socialist economy, unlike that of a capitalist economy, cannot ignore to the same degree problems of control of enterprise and of the distribution of wealth. In neoclassical theory, these are resolved mainly by the workings of uncontrolled markets, and, as the prior commentary discusses, neoclassical theory essentially ignores the organizational problem of the firm. The theory of socialism, however, seeks to substitute managed coordination for price coordination. In principle, this would seem to make the problem of control within the enterprise a serious issue. The control issue arises in the writings of Oscar Lange, Abba Lerner, and others who were interested in promoting socialization of the means of production, but the organizational problem was slighted every bit as much as in neoclassical theory. The analytical work offered by these economists was essentially institution-free. They focused on the deduction of appropriate formal marginal equalities that managers of state-owned firms should use to guide their activities, equalities that mimic those that arise in the neoclassical analysis of the private economy. One possible reason for the absence of serious discussion of the control issue by these economists was that a key source of their fascination with socialism was its alleged ability to free wealth distribution from the imperatives of production, thereby allowing socialist society to pursue egalitarianism without the constraints implicit in the institutions of capitalism. This surely biased their analyses, making it difficult for them to recognize the various ways in which wealth distribution and institutions are important to production. The consequence of all this was that the control problem, as a problem of wealth distribution and institutional design, was ignored rather than studied.

The aspect of control of interest here is the agency problem, and especially the agency problem that we associate with diffuse ownership of large enterprises. This problem highlights the possible consequences of differences between the interests of owners and those of professional managers. It has a long history in economic discussions, but early references to it are noted for their superficiality. Smith, for example, raises doubts in the *Wealth of Nations* about the ability of joint stock companies to perform well in the service of their owners:

> The directors of such companies, however, being the managers rather of other people's money than of their own, it cannot well be expected, that they should watch over it with the same vigilance with which the partners in a private copartnery frequently watch over their own. Like the stewards of a rich man, they are apt to consider attention to small matters as not for their master's honour, and very easily give themselves a dispensation from having it. Negligence and profusion, therefore, must always prevail, more or less, in the management of the affairs of such a company. . . . They have, accordingly, very seldom succeeded without an exclusive privilege; and frequently have not succeeded with one.[19]
>
> . . . The only trades which it seems possible for a joint stock company to carry on successfully, without an exclusive privilege, are those, of which all the operations are capable of being reduced to what is called a Routine or to such a uniformity of method as admits of little or no variation.[20]

19. Smith, A., *The Wealth of Nations*, p. 741.   20. Id., p. 756.

The corporate control agency problem so clearly noticed by Smith plays no systematic part in his general inquiry into the sources of the wealth of nations. It is treated superficially in more recent writings also. In both Veblen's *The Engineers and the Price System* (1921) and Galbraith's *New Industrial State* (1967), technocratic managers wrest control from owners of firms and use the resources of firms in ways different from those that owners would have wanted. For Galbraith, the separation between ownership and control yields a private sector that is too large and a public sector that is too small. For Veblen, the separation causes a desirable increase in private sector output. These works use the control issue. They presume a shift of control to technocrats, and they postulate a technocrat culture that leads to output levels greater than would have been produced by owners of firms. However, they fall far short of providing substantive analyses of the control problem.

The more analytical part of the intellectual history of the control problem derives from the well-known book on the corporation by Berle and Means (1933), and the problem plays a central role in contemporary theorizing about the firm and in discussions of corporate takeovers and financial structures. In this contemporary literature, the degree to which the control problem is resolved turns on several considerations. Among these are the ownership structure of the firm, the compensation plan used to pay top management, the make-up of and the incentives faced by boards of directors, and the efficacy of hostile takeovers. These are important, but they share a common characteristic that makes their focus narrow. They view the control problem as springing only from *within* the firm. A central point of the present paper is that one source of the control problem lies beyond the firm's organization and even beyond the financial markets in which it raises funds. Two of its sources are found in the wealth of a country and in the distribution of this wealth across its population. A third source is found in a country's legislation.

The control problem at issue

Many control problems plague complex organizations. One is of particular interest here. This is the inability of the owners of a corporation that is very diffusely owned to be motivated or empowered to discipline the professional management that runs the firm. The applicability of this problem extends beyond the modern corporation. Socialism pretends to be a system based on citizen ownership of resources, but the hopelessly diffuse nature of a citizen ownership structure makes citizens powerless; the management of assets then becomes the task and privilege of state bureaucracies. These respond in their own unique ways to the control task facing them, giving rise to a control problem that reflects management insulation from tests of profit and market competition.

Studies of corporate takeovers, undertaken mainly in the United States during the 1980s, offer evidence that separation between ownership and control remains a problem in the West, although it is a considerably less severe problem than in socialist parts of the world. These studies show that shareholders of target companies benefit considerably from a takeover of their firm. Successful takeovers increase share prices of target firms by an average of about 30 percent (Jarrell, Brickley, and Netter, 1988). The increase may derive from several aspects of takeovers, but the dominant view is that target shareholder gains derive mainly from the removal of entrenched and inept managements.[21] It should be noted, however, that a very small fraction of all corporate assets have become the target of takeover attempts. This can be interpreted as statistical support for the proposition that most modern corporations are *not* seriously afflicted with the problem of separation between ownership and control.

The separation thesis is based on the belief that corporate ownership is hopelessly divided among thousands of separately owned small shareholdings. Contemporary students of the control problem aside, the many adherents of the separation thesis, from Smith to Galbraith, have accepted this belief as fact. That thousands of shareholders jointly own the typical large corporation is a fact, but recent studies (e.g., Demsetz and Lehn, 1985; Shleifer and Vishny, 1986) show that not every shareholder owns an insignificant number of shares. Describing the ownership of the large corporation as extremely diffuse distorts reality. In the typical situation of even the very large corporation a few shareholders own a relatively large fraction of the firm's equity. The ownership structure of the large corporation is more concentrated than serves the separation thesis well, and it is tempting to accept as a conclusion from this that the separation problem is not nearly as severe in capitalistic countries as one might suppose from a reading of Berle and Means.

For U.S. corporations as large as the Fortune 500, the fraction of equity owned by the five largest shareholders is about one-fourth. In Japan and several important European countries, this fraction is much larger. The average large corporation, then, is one in which a small number of shareholders have well focused interests because they own nontrivial blocs of votes. For the smaller corporation, ownership is even more concentrated. Facing such concentrated share holdings, professional management cannot be as unguided by shareholder interests as the separation thesis supposes, although there surely are cases in which ownership structure has become too diffuse to serve shareholder interests well. When ownership is too diffuse, restructuring should take place. The

---

21. Evidence to date seems to indicate that target company gains do not derive from wealth transferred from bondholders (Jarrell, Brickley, and Netter, 1988) or from most lower-level employees. Although management personnel are released in disproportionately large numbers from target companies when a takeover occurs, the mass of laborers are not.

corporate takeover and the Chapter 11 reorganization are two dramatic ways in which this happens. They accomplish a restructuring of ownership within a short time. Ownership is restructured less dramatically through the normal issuing and purchasing of equity shares.[22]

Concentration of ownership is not achieved freely. A few owners must be prepared to place a considerable portion of their wealth at risk in a single enterprise if its ownership is to be highly concentrated. If this cost is high, the ownership structure that is utility-maximizing for owners cannot look much like that of the single-owner firm. This is especially the case for very large firms because a high degree of ownership concentration in these firms requires that important owners put very large amounts of wealth at stake in a single enterprise. This would expose them to a great deal of firm-specific risk. The utility-maximizing ownership structure for important shareholders in large firms, therefore, is not a single-owner firm, contrary to what seems to be suggested by the agency problem. It is a more diffuse ownership structure because the cost of bearing firm-specific risk should be reflected in the optimal ownership structure. Nonetheless, this structure should be one in which enough shares are owned by very few shareholders to allow them to exercise more than a modicum of control over professional management. The data reveal precisely this – greater diffuseness in ownership structure for larger firms than for smaller firms but with ownership concentrated sufficiently to allow large shareholding interests to influence management.[23] This pattern of ownership suggests that ownership structure is not exogenous to shareholder decisions. Shareholders appear to choose ownership structures that maximize the utility value to them of their ownership stakes. This pattern of ownership has been confirmed for Swedish firms (Bergstrom and Rydqvist, 1990), Japanese firms (Prowse, 1991 [2]), and South African firms (Gerson, 1992). Considerations other than firm-specific risk and agency problems (such as tax considerations, the managerial competence of important owners, and assorted regulations, some of which are discussed later in this commentary), help to define the optimal ownership structure.

22. There are several ways by which professional management can be guided to serve shareholder interest in the modern corporation – concentrated ownership, the consequences of the capital market's measurement of management performance, legal proceedings, and compensation systems. It is improbable that all these mechanisms transform the modern corporation into a precise analog of the firm pictured in neoclassical theory, but they do raise serious questions about the Berle and Means thesis.

23. Data also give evidence that other aspects of shareholder interests are reflected in the ownership structure of corporations, but this evidence and these aspects are not discussed here. Corporate takeovers, like ownership structures, also are not random. Target firms usually are those that have unwisely acquired and retained assets through prior mergers (Mitchell and Lehn, 1990), and that have ownership structures too diffuse to link management behavior tightly enough to shareholder interests.

The role of wealth

We now reach a key consideration. The riskiness inherent in obtaining a controlling fraction of a corporation's stock is not only a function of the size of the corporation and its firm-specific risk. It is also a function of the wealth of the shareholder and of the time and knowledge available to them. A very wealthy person can own a sizable fraction of the shares of a very large corporation and still maintain a somewhat diversified portfolio of investments. Perhaps more important, a very wealthy person should be willing to accept the higher degree of firm-specific risk that accompanies the specialization of controlling investment in one or only a few firms. The corporate control problem can be significantly attenuated in a society that has enough very wealthy individuals to allow the ownership of its larger firms to be structured without much regard to firm-specific risk. The control problems that remain are due to the limited time and mental capability that owners can bring to the task of control. Very wealthy persons who seek to avoid all firm-specific risk may take controlling positions in the equity of many large companies, but in doing so the control they are able to exert will be weakened by restrictions on their time and capability.

The severity of the control problem, then, is partly a reflection of poverty, partly of wealth distribution, and partly of time and expertise. These become more binding the larger is the capitalization needed by firms if they are to be efficient. Poorer countries, if they are to resolve agency problems while reducing firm-specific risk, must forsake reliance on larger firms. If they choose to rely on large firms, they must accept less effective control of enterprise (by utilizing very diffuse ownership structures that avoid firm-specific risk), or they must have the owners of these firms bear considerably greater firm-specific risk than would be the case for wealthier nations.

Up to a point, inequality in the distribution of wealth enables a given total wealth to achieve more effective control over at least some large enterprises. But inequality can be carried too far. Extreme inequality *and* extreme equality in wealth distribution both reduce the degree to which effective control can be maintained. Consider, first, extreme inequality of wealth. Very wealthy persons hold wealth sufficient for them to take a concentrated ownership position in many large firms. If they take this position for a single firm only, or for very few large firms, they can exercise effective control of these enterprises. However, if they take this position in many large firms, their control of the professional managements of these companies is compromised by their time and knowledge limitations. These limitations cannot be avoided by having wealthy persons lend a portion of their wealth to others who, in turn, take controlling equity positions, for the loans themselves must be monitored and defaulters must be disciplined. Hence, extreme inequality in wealth can place so large a fraction of a nation's wealth in the hands of so few people that time and knowledge limitations undermine their ability to control professional management effectively. Inequality in the distribution of wealth that is great enough to allow individuals in the upper tier of the distribution of wealth to become less risk-averse and to take concentrated positions in only a few firms, so that time and knowledge constraints can be satisfied, offers a practical route to the effective control of large firms.

Solutions to the control problem are also undermined by extreme equality in the distribution of wealth. Consider the large U.S. corporation. Most of the 511 U.S. corporations in the Demsetz and Lehn study previously referred to were large enough to rank on a level with or just below the Fortune 500 largest corporations. During the 1975–80 period studied, these firms, on average, had ownership structures such that the five largest shareholders owned about 25 percent of outstanding shares. Some of these owners were institutional (about which more will be said). Set these aside. The five largest noninstitutional owners controlled slightly less than 10 percent of shares in the typical large United States corporation. Take as a working assumption that capital markets in the United States have provided us with a rough estimate of the noninstitutional ownership structure required to establish effective control of large firms. On this basis, the average large corporation should have 10 percent of its shares owned by no more than five noninstitutional owners.

Now, if net wealth in the United States in 1976 had been equally distributed across families, five families could not have provided funds anywhere near the amounts that were required to own 10 percent of the shares of these large corporations. The five largest noninstitutional owners, in aggregate, invested more than $100 million in the average large firm in the Demsetz-Lehn sample. If wealth had been distributed equally across families in 1976, the net wealth available to any one family for such investments would have been less than $10,000; so five families could amass among them a sum of only $50,000. Assuming that the price per share in 1976 fairly represented replacement cost plus good will, $50,000 would have fallen far short of the amount needed to establish adequate control. Even a country as rich as the United States must have wealth inequality if effective control over large enterprises is an important desideratum. Enough inequality must exist not just to allow enough groups of five owners to hold a 10-percent stake in the number of large firms in an economy, but to allow each such owner to attain an acceptable degree of diversification in his or her holdings. Resolution of the enterprise control problem, therefore, would seem to be more difficult if there exists extreme inequality or extreme lack of inequality in the distribution of wealth. Given the arithmetic implicit in U.S. data, no country is wealthy enough to have wealth make a maximal contribution to the solution of this problem without there being some nontrivial degree of inequality in its distribution.

Suppose there were enough wealthy families in the United States in 1976 to allow each of the 500 largest U.S. corporations to have $100 million of its equity owned by five families, with a different group of five families for each firm. Each of the requisite 2,500 families would have net wealth of $20 million. Assume the number of families in the United States was 60 million. Given that the average family in 1976 had net wealth equal to about $10,000, this translates into .004 percent of the families possessing 8.33 percent of the nation's net wealth. No allowance is made in this calculation for large equity positions that might be taken by mutual funds, insurance companies, etc.; these would reduce the degree of required net wealth inequality. But no allowance is made for portfolio diversification for the wealthy families with controlling interests, and the impact of a demand for diversification is to increase the required degree of inequality.

Reference here is solely to the control problem and not to other possible productivity consequences of wealth and its distribution. The distribution of wealth may affect investment in human capital and, in turn, economic progress. An egalitarian distribution of wealth among families in a poor country implies low but fairly equal levels of family investments in human capital. Unequal distribution of wealth implies higher levels of investments among wealthier families and lower levels among poorer families. Extreme inequality in the distribution of wealth means great disparities in human capital investment, greater than can be rationalized by the distribution of latent talent. Unless a capital market in human capital investments can be made to function, one that would require enforcement of paybacks from future earnings of those receiving loans, extreme inequality of wealth could lead to too little investment in the human capital of children of poor families. The distribution of wealth also affects the political stability of a nation, and this has important consequences for the productivity of an enterprise. Thus, wealth and its distribution impinge in many ways on productivity, often with conflicting consequences. It would be a mistake to believe that the only direction of impact on productivity is through the enterprise control problem, and I intend no such assertion. My claim is only that there is an ignored connection between wealth and the resolution of the enterprise control problem, and that this connection suggests that a nontrivial degree of inequality in the distribution of wealth, but not extreme inequality, strengthens the ability of a society to resolve the control problem.

Resource endowments, climate, and the state of technical art help – but only help – determine the lines of activities in which a country's comparative advantages reside. They are not sufficient determinants because they ignore the enterprise control problem and the role of wealth in reducing the severity of the problem. The theory of comparative advantage, as usually interpreted, does not explicitly acknowledge the importance of these. Firms that demand a large amount of capital if they are to be efficient can be controlled more effectively if they are located in wealthy countries, in countries tolerant of wealth inequality, and in countries also tolerant of foreign ownership, whereas firms that demand only small amounts of capital suffer relatively less loss of control for being in poor, egalitarian countries that bar foreign investment. Poor countries err if they attempt to force resources into economic sectors in which firms must use large amounts of capital to be competitive. The error is the more serious if accompanied by policies that maintain close approximations to equality in the distribution of domestic wealth and barriers to foreign capital.

The discussion that follows largely ignores foreign wealth. The practical control problems of particular nations are very much affected by their attitudes toward foreign capital, but the principles at issue are not. Instead of discussing the problem of wealth and its distribution at the level of a nation, for which foreign capital flows are important, we can treat the world as one large nation. Then there is no possibility of ameliorating control problems by importing capital, but the significance of wealth and its distribution for the control problem remains. To the extent barriers hinder the flow of foreign capital into equity positions of poor nations and nations with very equal distributions of wealth, these principles, of course, apply to nation states.

If control of enterprise were the only relevant problem – and it is not – a poor, egalitarian country would do well to avoid policies that encourage investment in activities that require large firms. Retail establishments, services, light commerce, and farming, if we suppose that these are activities that can be performed quite well with the capital, time, and mental capabilities of the typical citizen or of a small group of citizens, should be favored by poor countries who choose to rely on internally supplied capital and control. Only after investments in these controllable enterprises have had time to allow their owners to accumulate wealth, or only after a greater degree of wealth inequality becomes politically tolerable, can *controllable* investments be made in larger firms. From the perspective of control, large firms and the industries to which they belong are better located in countries with high per capita wealth and moderate inequality in its distribution.[24]

Firm size and transition to capitalism

Many size distributions, such as heights of people, are represented well by the normal frequency distribution. Relatively few observations have sizes that are very small or very large, and most observations fall in the intermediate size

---

24. Of course, the control advantage for poor countries of relying on small-scale enterprise can be outweighed by their possession of resource endowments heavily favoring industries in which large-scale enterprise is more efficient. My focus here is only on the control issue.

classes. Firm size, however, is distributed differently. Most firms are small, fewer are middle size, and very few are very large. The form of this distribution is much more log normal than normal (Gibrat, 1931; Ijiri and Simon, 1977). From the perspective of economics, the source of this distribution should be explained in terms of firm efficiency and profit, but there is no reason to believe that the neoclassical production function, depending as it does on quantities of inputs, favors firms of small size over those of intermediate and large size. In the absence of input indivisibilities, all firm sizes are equally efficient, and, although input indivisibilities call forth a U-shaped cost function, we have no reason to suppose, other than on an ad hoc basis, that this obtains its minimum at very small firm size much more frequently than at middle or large firm sizes. The control problem, whose solution reflects the role of wealth and wealth distribution, offers an explanation that is less ad hoc in nature.

Nations are too poor, and so is the world as a whole, to solve the control problem if there are more than a few very large firms. Small firms offer the best scale of production if the control problem is the only determinant of efficient size. Clearly, it is not, for there are a few large firms. Equally clearly, there are not many. Justification for the existence of these few large firms rests on a supposition that scale economies with respect to noncontrol inputs are so large that large firm size is advantageous in a few instances even if control costs are thereby raised. This supposition is ad hoc in nature, but the control and wealth considerations are not (or, at least, they are much less so). Even should we suppose that scale economies with respect to noncontrol inputs are such that these would call for equal numbers of small, medium-sized, and large firms, the problems of control and wealth insufficiency would pull firm sizes down, skewing them toward small firm size.

The problem posed by ownership structure is implicit in the difficulties now being faced by socialist countries seeking to privatize. They have little difficulty converting small-firm socialist enterprises into privately owned enterprises, usually through the simple device of auctioning off facilities to citizens. Poland, Hungary, and the Czech Republic have already converted a substantial fraction of small socialist firms into small private enterprises, and the process is being repeated now in Russia. The private sector of China's economy also began with small firms, either farms or business enterprises, and it has grown rapidly. The large state-owned enterprises present more difficult problems of conversion. China has no plans to convert its huge state-owned firms to private ownership, hoping instead to rely on joint ventures with foreign firms to invigorate its socialist sector. This course has been set, at least partly, for ideological reasons. But in China, and more so in East Europe and Russia, a major source of the problem is the lack of private wealth of a sort that stirs no resentment in the population at large. Although such wealth is emerging from China's rapidly growing private sector, a sector that is decades old if we include agriculture,

East Europe and Russia, which have not had a private sector of any significance for 40 to 70 years, have not yet had a similar experience. The private wealth that has been accumulated in these countries often has its sources in illegal black market activities and in the shady dealings of government officials. Citizens who have borne taxes, shortages, and the cost of bureaucratic self-enrichment for 40 to 70 years resist the acquisition of larger state-owned firms by those who have become wealthy in seemingly antisocial ways. A paralysis in privatizing large state-owned firms has taken hold. These firms still languish under socialist control unless they have been sold to foreigners. This does not help much to resolve the control problem; perforce of necessity, control remains with government bureaucracies functioning against a backdrop of the extreme diffuseness of "ownership" that characterizes "public" ownership.

A different precondition for the control problem

Wealth possessed in small amounts by many persons can be pooled into private domestic investment funds big enough to be used to establish controlling positions in the equity of even capital-demanding firms. To the extent that those who manage the institutional investment funds effectively represent the interest of these individual investors, these funds can exert considerable influence over the professional managements of the firms in which they have purchased large fractions of equity. The overall wealth of a country still sets a limit on how many funds can be financed adequately to undertake this control mission, but to some degree the institutional investor serves as a mechanism for aggregating the ownership interests of individual investors into coordinated investments in *controlling* positions. In this section, the strengths and weaknesses of the institutional investor solution are discussed, but, as prerequisite to this, it will be useful to highlight a generally ignored aspect of the agency problem.

A recognized condition for the entrenchment of management that is ineffective (from the shareholder's perspective) is the existence of a diffuse ownership structure, but there is another largely unrecognized condition. This is the inability of investors to force a firm to disgorge assets purchased with funds secured from the initial sale of stock. Essentially, this means the inability of investors to force the firm to repurchase outstanding shares of its stock. Assets made available to a corporation when investors purchase initial public offerings of shares become the *firm's* property. Shareholders acquire shares conveying rights to vote and to collect dividends, but not to claim (individually) the fraction of the firm's assets represented by their shares. The assets belong to the firm. Shareholders may sell their shares if they are dissatisfied with the firm's performance, and in combination with other shareholders they may vote to sell the firm. What they cannot do individually is insist that the corporation buy back their shares.

The absence of a repurchase condition gives professional management greater control over equity capital. The corporation, not the shareholder, has title to funds and other assets that have been secured from its initial sale of stock.[25] If shareholders could reclaim these assets, the severity of the control problem would be lessened. This lessening would take place even in the presence of a very diffuse ownership structure. Disappointed shareholders, acting individually but in large numbers, could demand payouts that strip management of corporate assets. Assets might be worth less because of poor management, but they could be rescued from management's control by disgruntled shareholders.

It is impractical from the perspective of being able to make business commitments to allow shareholders to reclaim their share of the firm's assets in the typical case. The corporation makes commitments to purchase materials and plant, as well as to supply goods and services. If these commitments are to be treated as reliable, the firm must have control of the assets it has secured through the sale of stock or bonds. It cannot be in continual jeopardy of losing assets to its disappointed shareholders. The typical corporation must be organized in a way that bars investors from reclaiming their fraction of the firm's assets in other than exceptional circumstances. The firm is, therefore, granted a life that is in important ways distinct from the lives and desires of those who supply it with capital and other inputs.[26] Only by a majority vote to sell the firm or to sell its assets, and not by independent individual decisions, can shareholders effectively force the firm to release the value of its assets to them.

This exercise of continued control over assets ceases to be prerequisite to doing business if time-based commitments are unimportant to the firm's suppliers and customers. The open-end mutual stock fund gathers capital from investors and uses its skill to invest in the shares of other corporations. The fund can sell these acquired shares on a moment's notice should it decide to do so, without jeopardizing its business commitments. The fund's business activity does not depend on the availability and continued deployment of specialized assets, as does the business of an automobile company. Capital placed at its disposal can be withdrawn by its investors without seriously compromising its commitments to others. The open-end mutual fund is obligated to "repurchase" prorata investment positions. Those that invest through such a fund are not the legal equivalent of shareholders. General dissatisfaction with the management of a fund can cause investors to deprive it of most of its capital, even though no single investor has invested a considerable sum. This disciplining force does

25. Sale of shares by shareholders has a depressing effect on the price of the corporation's stock if enough shareholders offer to sell. This has some disciplining effect on management because of the difficulty it causes in raising new equity capital, but, even so, the corporation remains in control of the assets it has acquired.
26. A similar point is made by my colleague Axel Leijonhufvud (1985) in an essay on "Capitalism and the factory system."

not depend on the existence of concentrated ownership. Because of this difference, the problem of control over management is potentially more severe in the typical corporation than in the open-end fund.[27]

Attenuation of the control problem in open-end funds can be transferred to attenuation of the control problem in the typical corporation if some of these funds take concentrated ownership positions in the stocks they purchase and if this reduces the probability that fund investors will withdraw funds. Financial institutions such as open-end mutual stock funds thus have the potential for reducing the severity of the corporate control problem. This can be important in facilitating enterprise control, especially in countries with low levels of wealth and egalitarian distributions of wealth. The funds can contain enough invested wealth to allow them to take concentrated positions in the ownership of some of the corporations in which they invest without thereby seriously impairing their ability to diversify. They can act somewhat as if they were very wealthy individuals.[28]

Investors in closed-end investment funds do not enjoy the same disciplining capability since they cannot insist on a return of assets from the fund. The financing of the closed-end fund is like that of the typical corporation. Once an initial sale of shares in the fund has been concluded, investors can realize cash by selling the shares in the open market, not by forcing the fund to repurchase shares at asset value. A sale in the open market does not directly reduce the resources available to the managements of closed-end funds, although it depresses share price and impairs the fund's ability to sell additional shares. The financial rules under which the closed-end fund operates give its management the ability to make investment plans without fear of being forced to alter them should investors become dissatisfied; these rules also eliminate an avenue of control over management that is accessible in the open-end fund even to diffusely organized investors. Of course, if the shares in which the open-end fund has invested perform poorly, asset value per investment unit is reduced and investors can redeem a unit only at a value lower than they paid for it. There is no gainsaying the fact that investors bear the cost of poor past investment decisions by the fund management, whether these investors have put their money into closed- or open-end funds, but only investors in open-end funds can deprive fund managements of the capital that still remains in the fund.

Suppose, contrary to present fact in the United States, that commercial banks are allowed to invest savings deposited with them in the equity of business firms. Unlike investors in the open-end fund, who purchase a share whose value is determined by how well the fund chooses the firms in which it invests, a bank promises to allow savers to withdraw the same dollar sum they deposited. A

27. Fama and Jensen (1983) recognize this characteristic of the mutual fund and its relationship to the agency problem.
28. The difference between the open-ended fund and the government, where government is viewed as a gatherer of taxes, is that the provision of revenues to the fund is voluntary and reversible.

bank's management that invests these savings unwisely, or that fails to pressure wisely the managements of the firms in which it invests, would not be able to maintain a competitive interest payment to savers. They would withdraw their funds, possibly transferring them to banks that have performed better. In this case there is an ability to withdraw investments whose values have not been reduced by the poor performance of bank investment departments. This differs from investors in open-end funds who will experience a reduction in the value of their investment units should the fund invest unwisely. However, it is not clear from this difference whether investors would be more or less willing to withdraw assets from fund managements than from bank management, nor is it clear that banks will continue to allow dollar-denominated withdrawals once they get into the stock investment business. What is clear is that, if dollar denomination is maintained, investor-savers will monitor the performance of their fund more continuously and closely than they monitor the performance of their bank. The forced imposition of deposit insurance, if applied to savings invested in stocks through banks, of course, would further undermine the monitoring of bank performance by savers.

Although the ability of investors to reclaim funds from an open-end invest-ment fund ameliorates the diffuse investor agency problem that otherwise would arise, it is not clear by just how much. The problem of controlling the fund's management is more effectively dealt with if capital is provided in a concentrated fashion to the fund itself, for this strengthens incentives to monitor and discipline the fund management. Such concentration, however, would make the fund less effective in coping with the wealth distribution problem that has brought it into the present discussion.[29] Even if the agency problem is reduced, there remains the problem of the constraints imposed by the limited knowledge and time of the fund's management. A fund that serves mainly to diversify the investments of savers eliminates firm-specific risk, but, like very wealthy investors who achieve a similar diversification on their own, it is unlikely that the fund will be able effectively to oversee and influence the managements of the corporations whose stocks it owns. Data seem to support the proposition that, on average, actively managed, diversified funds do less well than nonmanaged funds that simply buy a broadly based index of stocks. From the perspective of effective control, it would be better for managed funds to accept a significant amount of specialization in their portfolios, so that they can bring more knowledge and time to the task of influencing corporate managements. Legal institutions in the United States, based on fiduciary re-

29. However, a doctoral dissertation recently completed at UCLA (Clyde, 1990) gives some evidence that the managements of institutional investment funds behave much as do individual and family shareholders with respect to decisions they make about taking concentrated stakes in the equity of corporations. This dissertation called my attention to the variety of legal restrictions that impinge on the ability of institutional investors to take controlling positions in the equity structure of the firms in which they invest.

sponsibility, discourage this, not recognizing that individual investors, if they wish, can avoid firm-specific risk by investing in a portfolio of such funds.

If it is not possible for the closed-end fund to be deprived of its assets by disgruntled investors, a source of discipline for its management is absent. It is noteworthy that purchasers of the intial offering of shares in closed-end funds suffer from the emergence of a discount in the value of their shares from the value of the fund's portfolio. Perhaps closed-end funds expose investors to a more severe agency problem than do open-end funds. Still, closed-end funds seem to compete successfully with open-end funds in efforts to raise capital, and this implies the existence of some compensating advantage. Two possible compensating advantages come to mind. First, the open-end fund, precisely because it must stand ready to repurchase units on demand, needs a more liquid asset structure than does the closed-end fund. This allows the closed-end fund to put more of its assets to work on investments. Second, the closed-end fund may ameliorate its potentially greater agency problem by relying on a more concentrated ownership structure than the unit ownership stucture of the open-end fund. Both aspects of these two types of funds can be studied, and probably have been, but here they stand as conjectures. However, the ownership structure of the closed-end fund, should it turn out to be more concentrated, makes this type of fund less useful as an offset to the wealth and wealth distribution problems that confront poorer nations.

Finally, it may be noted that capital acquired through the sale of debt, although it creates an agency problem between equity and debt holders, reduces the amount of capital that must be supplied through ownership and thereby reduces the amount of capital needed to establish a concentrated ownership stake. Debt serves in much the same capacity as equity secured in small amounts from many investors; neither, unlike the concentrated ownership stake, normally creates the opportunity to control professional management, although both, in special circumstances can influence management behavior. Two agency problems are created by these sources of capital. Issuance of debt creates an agency problem between equity holders and debt holders. Acquisition of capital from diffuse sources creates an agency problem between majority and minority shareholders. But both debt and diffuse source equity, by reducing the amount of concentrated equity required to finance a firm, make it less costly for majority shareholders to discipline professional management.

There is a difference between debt and diffuse source equity, one that relates to the distinction between open-end and close-end mutual funds. Debt ultimately is paid off, so that bondholders reclaim their assets from the firm they have helped to finance. This reclaim privilege operates not continuously, as it does for the investor in an open-end fund, but periodically. A decision as to whether to replace old debt with new debt or with new equity, or at all, necessarily arises. At this juncture, professional management is subject to capital market disciplines that do not operate as compellingly during periods when debt is not being repaid. The issuance of debt is therefore different from the issuance of stock in that debt ultimately triggers a reclaiming opportunity.[30]

Institutional considerations

Differences in ownership concentration across nations indicate that institutional arrangements, as well as wealth, matter in regard to control problems. For given values of variables that sensibly influence the ownership structure of corporations, such as firm size and firm-specific risk, ownership is significantly more diffuse in U.S. corporations than in Japanese, European, and South African corporations (but not more diffuse than in English corporations). The typical large corporation in the United States exhibits an ownership concentration ratio equal to about one-fourth of outstanding shares for the five largest ownership positions, but most corporations traded on the South Africa's Johannesburg Stock Exchange have ownership concentration ratios in the neighborhood of 50 percent (Gerson, 1992). Similarly high ratios are found in Sweden and Germany (Sundqvist, 1986), while Japan's large corporations have ownership concentration ratios of more than one-third of outstanding stock (Prowse, 1991[2]). If a five-shareholder group owning one-fourth of the voting equity of the typical large corporation is a suitable ownership structure in the United States, why is it too unconcentrated to be suitable in other countries? A plausible source of this difference lies in the variation across nations in regulations impinging on ownership structure. This possibility has only recently attracted the attention of scholars (Prowse, 1991[1]; Roe, 1991; and Gerson, 1992).

For over 60 years, the Glass-Steagall Act has barred banks from directly owning equity in U.S. corporations. There is no counterpart to this law in South Africa and in much of Western Europe, and only recently has Japan adopted a similar law. Glass-Steagall forces corporations to raise equity funds from other sources, whereas banks would seem to be low-cost conduits of equity capital. In fact, banks play important equity roles in other nations, where they supply enough equity to own sizable positions in corporate ownership structures. In the absence of the Glass-Steagall Act, U.S. banks could perform the same function as open-end mutual funds in loosening the connection between wealth distribution and resolution of the control problem.[31] U.S. laws also

---

30. I am indebted to Professor Dave Butz for pointing this out to me.
31. However, since banks make loan commitments to borrowers, it might be desirable for there to be some limitations on depositor withdrawal rights. Depositors might have the right to choose between an account from which they would be fully entitled to withdraw their funds and from which the bank would secure funds to purchase stock in other corporations, and an account that would limit rights of withdrawals and from which the bank could make time commitment loans to borrowers. Presumably, the second account would earn more interest for depositors.

hamper the degree to which insurance companies and pension funds can establish and maintain controlling ownership positions. These laws generally pressure institutions to maintain diversified portfolios and to avoid taking large positions in a single company. It is also true that West European countries and their organized stock exchanges allow nonvoting stock, whereas the major stock trading market in the United States, the New York Stock Exchange, has insisted since late in the decade of the 1920s that the corporations it lists rely only on one-share, one-vote common stock. Nonvoting shares reduce the cost of establishing controlling equity positions in a company because only voting shares must be reckoned with when considering the direct control of management. Nonvoting shares, like debt, offer a medium by which funds can be raised without diluting voting equity.[32]

Public interest arguments can be made to support and oppose reliance on voting shares to obtain equity capital. Similarly, arguments pro and con can be made in regard to the various legal hurdles that keep important conduits of capital from easily accessing the equity markets. Whatever the truths in this regard, I do not believe that the impact of these legal hurdles on ownership structure and control has adequately been taken into account when evaluating their social desirability. The problems they create for control offer a novel downside to their use.

The protection afforded shareholders by the legal requirements of corporate and security laws also bears on ownership. To the extent that dominant shareholders can undertake unilateral actions that result in the transfer of wealth to themselves from minority shareholders (or from bondholders), difficulties in accumulating capital from diffuse sources will arise. This will cause firms to be smaller so as to reduce exposure to firm-specific risk, since small firms require less wealth per degree of control purchased. U.S. laws reduce the risk borne by minority shareholders in their implicit dealings with majority shareholders. Dividend payouts must be the same, majority approval of mergers is required, derivative law suits are allowed, standard accounting methods are required, etc. These requirements make it easier for large firms to tap diffuse sources of capital without requiring proportionate increases in the capital

32. Since holders of small positions in the voting equity structure of even NYSE-listed corporations do not play an active role in corporate governance, their stock is de facto nonvoting stock under normal circumstances. But there always exists the potential for a contest for control, and, when one takes place, the voting privilege latent in noncontrolling shareholdings becomes a problem for controlling owners. Because of this, the presence of diffusely owned voting shares raises the cost of maintaining a controlling position in the ownership structure of the corporation, a cost that would not be borne as heavily if a portion of the firm's equity could be raised through the sale of nonvoting shares. The value of the vote will reflect itself in a difference in price between voting and nonvoting shares, and to the extent of this difference the cost of owning voting shares is increased even if equity is also raised through sale of nonvoting shares. Even so, the existence of nonvoting shares makes it possible to maintain a controlling position more cheaply in large corporations under normal circumstances.

provided by dominant shareholders. This allows large firm ownership structures to be less concentrated than would otherwise be required, and perhaps contributes to an explanation of the relatively low ownership concentration found in large U.S. corporations. A good system of security laws, therefore, helps poorer countries maintain larger firms than would be possible if minority shareholders were left at the mercy of dominant shareholders.[33]

Wealth possession vs. wealth acquisition

The control problem imbues wealth with a source of productivity different from that which is usually recognized in economic literature. The possibility of *acquiring* wealth is recognized to be a powerful incentive, one that encourages people to put forth effort and bear risk, but in principle this should be distinguished from the productivity of simply *having* wealth. Properly designed compensation systems, including incentive wages for management and retention of profit-loss residuals by owners, are methods by which the acquisition of wealth helps to solve control problems. Yet the acquisition of a dominant equity position in large firms in the face of firm-specific risk requires that some persons already have considerable wealth. If there are enough such persons, small groups can be formed that are numerous enough to allow a country to utilize many large firms yet have the managements of these firms influenced significantly by their owners. This productive function of the possession of wealth derives from the control empowerment of owners and not necessarily from the pursuit of wealth. Normally, dominant owners are guided by the pursuit of wealth when they exercise control, but this is not necessarily the case. Control can be exercised to use the firm to pursue goals different from profit maximization for as long as the wealth of dominant shareholders allows them to engage in this form of on-the-job consumption. Wealth as an existing input serves an analytically distinct role from that served by the seeking of wealth.[34]

33. A legal system protecting minority shareholders cannot be taken for granted. Argentina, for example, lacks such a system. Dominant shareholders hide their company's profit from both the local internal revenue service and minority shareholders. Cash dividends are rarely paid, and the difference between true profit and dividend payout seems to be going into the pockets of majority shareholders. Small investors have become reluctant to make their funds available, resulting in severe financing problems for firms that need to be large to compete. The capital needed by these firms must come from investors large enough to be able to protect their interests. In the absence of corporate and security laws that protect the small investor, greater firm-specific risk raises the capital acquisition cost.

34. The productivity of wealth in ameliorating the control problem is similar to wealth's role in reducing the risk-averseness that characterizes the choices that people make. Wealthy persons, for example, presumably because only a small fraction of their wealth is involved, are more willing to experiment with new products. Because of this reduction in risk-averse purchasing behavior, wealth produces information that is of use to others, and especially to the not-so-wealthy, about new products. Without the wealthy, society presumably would have a more difficult time evaluating new products.

The *having* of a particular distribution of wealth also bears on productivity in a way that is different from the possibility of *acquiring* more wealth than one's fellow citizens. Distributions that are "too unequal" or "too close to egalitarian" impair a society's ability to have enterprises controlled effectively. The functional relationship between the amelioration of the control problem, as the dependent variable, and the distribution of wealth, as the causal variable, is shaped as an inverted U. An index of the overall level of control that is exercised should increase as inequality in wealth increases, reaching its maximum at some intermediate level of inequality; then, at a point where inequality becomes so great that the very wealthy few are overburdened by their inability to carefully oversee their investments, the function decreases.

This special source of the productivity of having wealth, as well as of a particular distribution of wealth, means that policies toward wealth cannot be discussed intelligently without reference to production. This bears on J. S. Mill's assertion that policy may be applied in two conceptually separate compartments. One of these deals with the allocation of resources to competing ends. In this compartment, Mill asserts, policy is constrained by fixed laws of production. In the second compartment, pertaining to wealth distribution, policy is unconstrained because the personal distribution of income is not subject to fixed economic laws. Mill is wrong, and not just because the incentive effects of the acquiring of wealth are important to production. He is wrong also because the having of wealth is important to the control of enterprise. Wrong for the same reasons are Joan Robinson and other neo-Ricardian Cambridge economists who took Sraffa (1960) more seriously than they should have and argued, like Lange and Lerner, that the distribution of wealth, unlike the production of wealth, is purely a political question.

The two avenues by which wealth affects production possibilities are sometimes competitive. It is widely recognized that a tax policy designed to bring forth an egalitarian distribution of wealth has adverse incentive effects, but so has a policy designed to increase inequality in the distribution of wealth. Both give and take from persons without regard to their productivity. Both conflict with the incentive effects of allowing work effort and ingenuity to determine income and thereby wealth. It is not clear whether the distribution of wealth that would arise from the functioning of purely private markets would be too unequal or too egalitarian from the narrow perspective of achieving adequate resolution of the control problem. If we suppose that all persons are equally competent and hard working, their efforts might result in too little inequality to resolve the control problems found in large firms (although chance events might introduce substantial inequality in the face of equal competence). If we suppose that all persons differ considerably in productivity, a very few being vastly more productive than most, a very skewed distribution of wealth would result, and this is likely to be too skewed to resolve the control problem of large firms adequately. (However, if some persons are so wealthy that they cannot adequately supervise the uses made of their funds, they, or their families, are unlikely to be able to maintain their relative wealth positions over time and generations. "Shirt-sleeves to shirt-sleeves in three generations" is the applicable saying.) For both cases, setting aside the considerations mentioned parenthetically, if better resolution of the control problem is desired, a redistributionist tax policy might be called for. In the first case, this policy would create more inequality, and in the second case it would create less. Both policies would distort the market-provided incentives to acquire wealth, leading, in the first case, in which policy exacerbates inequality, to too much effort and, in the second case, to too little effort. These distortions may be so costly to a society that it would prefer to avoid them, rely entirely on market-determined wealth, and forego large firms or improved solutions to their control problems. Yet, in principle, the gain from improving resolution of the control problem could make some distortion of market incentives acceptable.

The productive role of insider trading

Great wealth allows an investor in equity to maintain a diversified portfolio even though concentrated ownership positions are taken in several large firms. Only a few persons have such wealth. More persons have enough wealth to reduce but not to eliminate firm-specific risk upon their taking concentrated ownership stakes. The firm-specific risk they still bear is an impediment to reducing the severity of the control problem even more. To help reduce this impediment, a method by which the acquisition of wealth can be linked to the bearing of firm-specific risk would be useful. Highly organized markets tend to undermine the establishment of this linkage. Rates of return to stock ownership may be linked positively with systematic risk but not with firm-specific risk. Portfolio diversification reduces the firm-specific risk that shareholders bear, and such diversification is easy enough to achieve that all reward for bearing firm-specific risk should be eliminated. Based on this reasoning, the return to shareholders holding small equity positions in several companies contains no compensation for firm-specific risk, but shareholders holding controlling equity positions trade at the same market prices as do minority shareholders; hence, dominant shareholders are not compensated for bearing firm-specific risk.

However, there is a compensation method that establishes an appropriate linkage, but which does not operate in the open. Shareholders who have dominant positions in the equity of their firms enjoy privileged access to inside information, access that is denied to outsiders and minority shareholders. Based on this special knowledge and the importance of timing in stock transactions, dominant shareholders can time purchases and sales of stock so that they receive a higher return than outsiders and minority shareholders. To be able to acquire wealth in this fashion, investors need to own important stakes in equity, and to acquire these stakes they need to have wealth. The incentive system offered through insider trading allows the acquiring of wealth and the having of wealth to reinforce each other and to increase the degree to which the control problem can be ameliorated. (Demsetz, 1986.) There is no gain without some cost. Toleration of insider trading creates an agency problem between minority and majority shareholders. The resolution of this problem, however, may tolerate a positive amount of insider trading. Suppose, hypothetically, that minority and majority shareholders devise a corporate constitution in full recognition of all the effects of insider trading. These effects include the agency problem between majority and minority shareholders and the agency problem between shareholders and corporate management. The efficient constitution generally will not contain a "corner solution" in which only one of these agency problems is ameliorated but not the other. Some tolerance for insider trading will be included, for, from the perspective of minority shareholders, it is worth losing something to majority shareholders, who trade on inside information, in order to reduce the severity of the professional management agency problem.

Profit maximization
and rational behavior

Do real firms maximize profit? The answer to this question is sure to please some and disappoint others. Those who see unhealthy greed in profit maximization are unlikely to react to an answer in the same way as those who see healthy incentives. As we have seen in the first commentary, profit maximization is a logical consequence, under conditions of full knowledge of prices and technologies, of assuming that firms produce only for outsiders. Maximizing profit in this context makes no claims about the degree to which owners of firms behave in charitable, altruistic fashion when making decisions from within their households. The lack of desire to maximize profit and/or the failure to maximize profit require that the firm not be a specialized production unit or that it not have full and perfect information available to it. Outside the rarified context of the perfect competition model, and surely in the firm of the real world, these requirements would seem to be met; this makes the question of profit maximization raise issues of substance.

These issues are important too. Attacks on profit maximization carry implications that extend beyond pure science. Normative issues are imbedded. The influential book by Berle and Means (1933) has as its full title *The Modern Corporation and Private Property*. Private property is tagged on to the title because Berle and Means believe that profit maximization supplies the social justification for private property and that the corporation, in failing to maximize profit, undermines this justification. From the perspective of neoclassical economic theory, the private ownership of firms creates powerful profit-linked incentives that guide owners to minimize the cost of producing any given quantity of good; this minimal production cost benefits all society because competition between private owners of firms forces prices down to the levels of these costs. In this way, the efficiencies achieved within the firm in pursuit of profit are passed to and throughout the larger society by competition. Cost minimization is less successful if the profit motive is weakened. Competition loses its force and sense of "social direction." Noncapitalistic economic systems may suffer from greater defects than this, but nonetheless the significance of the debate about profit maximization (and competition) is seriously underestimated.

In the first part of this commentary, I discuss a few of the more important critiques of the profit maximization assumption. In the second part, my discussion ranges more broadly to consider some recent attacks on the assumption that behavior is rational. Problems inherent in the measurement of profit are discussed in a later commentary.

Profit maximization and the agency problem

The main concern of Berle and Means was with the separation between ownership and control that they perceived to exist in the large modern corporation. The agency problem that we associate with diffuse ownership was recognized well before Berle and Means wrote their book. In *The Wealth of Nations,* as I have already noted, Smith writes:

> The directors of [jointstock] companies, however, being the managers rather of other people's money than of their own, it cannot well be expected that they should watch over it with the same anxious vigilance with which the partners in a private co-partnery frequently watch over their own . . . . Negligence and profusion, therefore, must always prevail, more or less, in the management of the affairs of such a company.

The theme reappears in 1921 in Thorstein Veblen's *Engineers and the Price System.* Veblen believed he was witnessing a major transfer of control of the leadership of the corporation from financial interests, which he identified with the banking community, to engineers. It is not clear from his book whether Veblen thought of bankers as legal owners or as de facto controllers of firms to which they have provided capital, but it is clear that he approved of the asserted transfer of control from bankers to engineers because of his sociological judgment of these two groups. To Veblen, the culture of the bankers leads to collusion and output restriction in the search for profit; the culture of engineers leads to more output and to greater efficiency. While there is an agency control problem implicit in the transfer of control from owners to engineer-managers, it is not a social problem insofar as Veblen's preferences constitute the test.

Veblen's view of process, but not his preference for outcome, is shared by Galbraith. *The New Industrial State* (1967) borrows heavily from Veblen. In it, Galbraith describes the shift in control as passing to the technostructure. His argument is much the same as Veblen's. Guided by training and culture, the technostructure increases output, but by too much. It sells what it produces, not because of the intrinsic value of its output but because of the power of advertising to entice people to buy what they might not otherwise want. In Galbraith's judgment, the private sector becomes too large and the public sector too small. Berle and Means, who wrote in the period between the appearances of Veblen's and of Galbraith's works, espouse a view of the corporate control problem much like Smith's view and not much like Veblen's and Galbraith's.

Yet all these views share the common presumption that the control of the large corporation is beyond the reach of its shareholders' interests.

These writings were assertedly normative and theoretically speculative, not essentially empirical, although Berle and Means reference data. The treatment of the topic in recent years includes both formal models of agency and empirical investigations. Notions of shirking, monitoring, and compensation system, as well as the linkage between these (discussed in the prior commentary), influenced the important article by Jensen and Meckling (1976). Jensen and Meckling formalized the agency problem in the context of the firm and then went on to examine the implications of this problem for financial structure. From the middle 1970s to now, there have been three major lines of investigation. Each explores a different facet of the alleged separation between ownership and control. The first deals with the structure of corporate ownership, the second with corporate takeovers, and the third with executive compensation.

Corporate takeovers have been studied in detail over a long period by financial economists and accountants. The history of this investigation is long enough to make beginnings difficult to isolate. Manne (1965) wrote an insightful conjectural paper calling attention to the role and importance of the market for corporate control. Early empirical investigations began with the study of the effect of mergers on stock prices (Mandelker, 1974). The technique of investigating stock price behavior flowed easily into the study of takeovers (Dodd and Ruback, 1977; Bradley, 1980) and continues to now. Executive compensation has been examined in attempts to uncover the strength of the linkage between corporate performance and managerial rewards (Lewellen, 1971; Jensen and Murphy, 1990). The relevance of the ownership structure of corporations to the agency problem became a topic of research (Demsetz and Lehn, 1985). All three of these lines of investigation bear directly on control. Is ownership concentrated sufficiently to guide management to serve the interests of owners? When management fails to be disciplined by owners, do hostile takeovers reestablish the linkage between ownership and control? Do executive compensation systems work well enough to substitute for concentrated ownership and hostile takeovers? Definitive answers cannot be given, but progress has been made.

Two findings stand out from the work on the structure of corporate ownership. First, ownership of even the largest U.S. corporations is more concentrated than Berle and Means' discussion of the separation issue would lead one to believe. Together, the five largest shareholding interests of Fortune-500–size corporations own, on average, slightly more than one-fourth of all outstanding shares. This fraction tends to be even larger for Western European (but not U.K.) and Japanese corporations. Ownership stakes like these are important enough to influence the way professional management does its job. Ownership structure of specific corporations varies around this average, and the second finding of this work is that ownership becomes more concentrated when the benefits to owners of concentrating ownership plausibly outweigh the costs. Ownership structure is thus influenced by endogenous considerations, and its pattern is consistent with the pursuit of profit. Prior literature had treated the alleged diffuseness of ownership structure as an exogenous fact that was simply taken as a given. Ownership concentration of the sort that enhances the control exercised by owners comes at a cost, primarily that of bearing firm-specific risk. As a consequence of recognizing this, it is proper to discard the notion that complete control by owners yields cost minimization. Taking account of the risk implications to the wealth of owners, owner utility is maximized if owners exercise less than full control over the very large firm. True minimzation of the cost of production should take account of this risk component. Absence of full control over management does not in and of itself undermine the social attractiveness of a private property system.

In addition to significant concentration of ownership in even the large corporation, there is an active market for corporate control by which professional management may be controlled. The theory that currently dominates explanations of the empirical findings about corporate takeovers is that they are corrective responses to situations in which a poorly performing professional management has become entrenched. It should be noted that one important consequence of virtually every successful takeover is the restructuring of ownership, making this structure much more concentrated than it was prior to the takeover. In this respect, the corporate takeover is not an alternative to a tight ownership structure; it is a method for achieving a concentrated ownership structure quickly in the face of opposition.

Takeovers produce sizable gains in share prices of target companies, gains on the order of 30-plus percent. These are thought to reflect the displacement of entrenched management and the restructuring of the firm. Restructuring often involves the sale of assets that have not yielded much profit but which nonetheless had been retained by the prior management. Other theories have been marshaled to explain the large premium paid to target company shareholders. One attributes the premium to the revision of the claims on target company profit, a revision that benefits shareholders at the expense of other stakeholders. Another attributes the premium not to the displacement of an inefficient management but to the discovery of firms whose managements have been doing a better job than the market had realized; this information, which leads to an upward revision in the price of the misjudged company, is revealed to the market by the takeover attempt. Finally, a third alternative sees the "winner's curse" (Roll, 1986) as the explanation for target share premiums. Firms that succeed in acquiring other firms over the potential or actual competition from other acquirers do so because they overestimate the value of the target. This overestimate is reflected in the high price paid for target shares. We do not yet possess a great deal of evidence about the strength of these alternative explanations of the data surrounding hostile takeovers.

The next line of defense after concentration of ownership and hostile takeovers is the compensation plan that is used to motivate management. The study of management compensation is still underway (for example, see the commentary on management compensation in this volume). The limited studies done so far indicate that the linkage between corporate performance and executive compensation is weak. Only small fractions of changes in shareholder wealth filter through to changes in executive compensation, although these small fractions translate into more significant percentage changes in executive income. Buried within the average or typical relationship between performance and compensation is considerable variation across corporations. An index of the sensitivity of executive compensation to performance correlates with the degree to which firm-specific risk is present (Murdoch, 1991), suggesting that the less stable the environment in which the firm operates, and therefore the more difficult and the more important it is to monitor and discipline management effectively, the more sensitive to performance is the compensation system used. This is consistent with the fact that ownership also tends to become more concentrated as firm-specific risk increases. Concentration of ownership and sensitivity of compensation system correlate as if they are complementary tools in the guiding of professional management.

The fine-tuning of executive compensation systems to serve shareholder interests is, however, more difficult than one might think. Share prices fluctuate for reasons that have little to do with the quality of management. They respond to changes in interest rates, weather, peace and war, political elections, etc. Establishing a close tie between executive compensation and share prices exposes management to variations in compensation attributable to forces beyond management's control. Management is exposed to a riskier compensation flow, and might require higher average salaries to compensate for this greater risk. Moreover, the team structure of management makes it difficult not only to partition performance rewards to individual members of the management team, but also to partition rewards between management and shareholders. The management team has been selected by important shareholders through their board of directors. Some fraction of the value of good (or poor) performance should be received by controlling shareholders to provide them with incentives to choose top management carefully. Finally, the idea that CEO compensation should be, or is designed to be, linked to the actual productivity of the CEO may be wrong. The literature on tournament compensation suggests that, even if top management does nothing, it may be wise for shareholders to pay the CEO a high level of compensation in order to give lower management incentives to work harder in the competition to succeed the present CEO.

All this said, executive compensation systems in large corporations seem weak in their relationship to firm performance. They seem poorly designed even when one of the objectives is to link compensation to performance. For example, compensation is often tied to stock price without regard for how well the stock is performing relative to the stock of other firms in the same industry. By normalizing the stock price on performance of rival firms, the compensation system of a firm would be able to escape some of the variation in price attributable to forces beyond management's control yet give recognition to unusual performance by its own management. I shall return to some of these issues in the Sixth Commentary, "Management Compensation and Tournament Theory."

Profit maximization in the absence of the agency problem

There appeared between 1940 and 1970 three noteworthy critiques of the profit maximization assumption, those of Simon (1947), Alchian (1950), and Leibenstein (1966). Leibenstein's concept of X-efficiency and Alchian's application of natural selection are discussed in the present section. Simon's introduction of bounded rationality is considered in broader context in the next section. No one of these economists takes note of the work by Berle and Means, even though the agency issue raised in this work is an attack on the profit-maximizing assumption.

In neoclassical theory it is the individual who maximizes, but what the individual maximizes seems to depend on is whether he or she is cast in the role of head of a household or owner of a firm. The owner of a firm maximizes profit, but the head of a household maximizes utility. The preceding commentaries defend the usefulness of this dichotomy in a debate about the merits of decentralization, such as that which was started by the argument between Smith and the mercantilists. To allow the owner of a firm to be a significant consumer of the output of the firm – i.e, to allow profit to be sacrificed for some utility-conferring objective of the owner – is to introduce a measure of self-sufficiency into the economizing problem and to reduce the degree to which persons depend on mechanisms such as the price system to coordinate the interdependent activities of specialists.

Reserving profit and utility maximization, respectively, to heads of firms and to heads of households serves the purpose of understanding the price system but distorts our views of what goes on inside firms. Clearly, individuals involved in owning, managing, and working in *real* firms maximize utility. If one is interested in agency problems within the firm, it is useful to take note of differences between utility and profit-maximizing behavior in regard to professional management. But this should not be confused with utility-maximizing behavior by *owners*. Agency problems are not involved when owners maximize utility rather than profit. All that is involved is the fact that consumption by owners may be more efficient when carried on within the firm rather than within the household.[35]

This consideration plays a role in evaluating Harvey Leibenstein's 1960 X-efficiency critique of neoclassical theory's assumption that firms maximize profit. Unlike the critiques of Simon and Alchian, which were written earlier than Leibenstein's, Leibenstein claims not that owners of firms *cannot* maximize profit but that many of them *do not* in fact maximize profit. For Leibenstein, owners of firms fail in their pursuit of profit to a degree large enough to require this fact to be taken into account if we are to understand the functioning of the economy. He attributes this failure to owner-manager incompetence.

Although neoclassical theory does not explicitly treat competence problems, the perfectly competitive model on which the theory's main conclusions rest uses assumptions implying that all owners are fully competent in their pursuit of profit. Owners are assumed to possess complete knowledge about prices and technologies, to employ errorless logic, and to be motivated equally strongly to seek maximum profit. Competence is not treated as a capability that can vary in quality from person to person. Variations would derive largely from a lack of knowledge, inferior thinking ability, and differential motivation, but the theory assumes these possibilities away. Profit maximization is uniformly and consistently assumed to be the motive of business owners, and the knowledge that is needed to maximize profit is assumed to be possessed by all.

Defenders of the relevance of the theory will and should point to the usefulness of its predictions, even if these are derived from factually incorrect assumptions. The selection criterion of evolutionary processes, for example, may account for the survival of profitable firms and the failure of unprofitable firms (a proposition that will be discussed more fully), but the pattern of success that results may nonetheless comfortably fit the predictions of the neoclassical price-theoretic model. It should be recognized, however, that this model was

---

35. The confusion about this goes as far back as an influential note written by Scitovsky (1943), in which he points out that a firm's output is likely to be less than what is required to maximize its profit because utility maximization by typical owner-entrepreneurs will often lead them to indulge somewhat their taste for leisure. When the owner does not devote "full time" to the firm, the firm ostensibly realizes less profit than it would yield if the owner took no leisure. Clearly, this is an incorrect deduction. Part of the profit realized from the firm comes to the owner in the form of the leisure time taken. Since he or she prefers this leisure time to the money profit sacrificed, the sum of the value of leisure time and the smaller money profit realized adds to more than the sum of no leisure and a larger money profit. In essence, the owner is "selling" (by not producing) some of the firm's potential output in order to consume more leisure in a way that is efficient by comparison to acquiring leisure through the sacrifice of other uses of his or her time.

not constructed to predict the success and failure of firms; it was constructed to facilitate the understanding of the coordinating role of the price system. To fault the theory for assuming the full competence by owners of firms is to misinterpret its field of application. The theory sheds light on the mystery of the coordinating mechanism of a decentralized society, not on the information-knowledge base of the individuals whose actions are being coordinated. Once the proper field of application of the theory is abandoned, its usefulness is likely to diminish, and this is so especially in regard to *managed* coordination. Still, the Great Debate is about decentralization vs. centralization, and there is no reason to suppose that the coordinating work of the price system is fundamentally different or fundamentally impaired relative to centralized control simply because decision makers act on imperfect information.

Differences in the competence and performance of owners is a fact that is obvious to all who would observe real firms. It is surprising, therefore, that Leibenstein could take the price-theoretic assumption that owners of firms succeed in profit maximizing to mean that real owners of real firms actually always succeed. Leibenstein is struck by studies offering evidence of differential performance by firms. These studies contain evidence that profitability and productivity vary across firms and even across firms that seemingly produce the same or highly similar goods.

He uses these studies to justify a rejection of neoclassical theory, noting that this theory identifies the source of inefficiency as divergence between price and marginal cost, divergence that might stem from monopoly, tariffs, and other impediments to competitive output rates, but not from the failure of businesspersons to pursue profit competently. While this is quite true, the inference to be drawn from it is that the theory does not seek to analyze the behavior of businesspersons within their firms but rather to analyze the workings of the price system. Monopoly, tariffs, and the like are impediments to the functioning of the price system. That is why they play a prominent role in the theory's deliberations. Leibenstein shows that inefficiency deriving from these impediments is small in comparison to that deriving from the failure of businesspersons to adopt the best available technologies and work place methods. Neoclassical inefficiency, which arises from inappropriate output rates given the use of the best technology, is labeled by Leibenstein as allocative inefficiency. Inefficiency attributable to the failure to adopt the best technology and work place methods he labels *X-inefficiency*. X-inefficiency results from the failure of businesspersons to realize the lowest possible cost functions for producing their goods, and this can account for wasted resources even if an industry is highly competitive and free of tariffs and other regulatory barriers to allocative efficiency. That X-inefficiency seems to be much more important than allocative inefficiency *is* of interest; it establishes the importance of competency to economic performance. Apparently, some firms do not adopt known technologies and work place incentives even though these presumably would yield substantial increases in productivity.

Now, errors in adopting technology and work place methods are to be expected from rational behavior in the real world of imperfect information. Positive information cost implies mistakes of this sort. No one takes perfect information as an accurate description of the decision-making context. However, the studies used by Leibenstein suggest that more is involved than shortlived, randomly occurring error, and this raises doubts about the suitability of perfect competition theory for a study of what goes on inside the firm.

Beyond a defense of perfect competition theory based on using it for purposes for which it is appropriate, there are two other types of defense. One is that the theory's critics misunderstand what the theory has to say about the treatment of incompetence. The other is that they misinterpret the evidence.

Misunderstanding the theory arises if we suppose, as Leibenstein and most of us do, that it implies that competition quickly weeds out incompetence. The theory has no dynamic message, but even in static equilibrium incompetence can survive. The theory claims that those who err bear the cost of their incompetence. Bearing this cost reduces incompetence, but it may not eliminate it completely. Owners of firms may willingly bear the cost of their incompetence if it is a necessary adjunct to accomplishing other objectives that serve their interests. Since these other objectives are properly thought of as on-the-job consumption, we are brought to the substitution of utility maximization for profit maximization once we turn to a consideration of the inner workings of the firm. A person may derive considerable utility from being her own "boss" even if she runs her business poorly, and she can indulge this preference as long as her wealth permits.

Taking this case farther, we can consider the owner's activity across *two* dimensions: product produced for others and product (being one's own boss) produced for consumption by the owner. We cannot conclude from the existence of incompetence in regard to the first product that the owners are incompetent in the totality of their behavior. Incompetence in producing what others are to consume may be the cheapest way for owners to purchase the pleasure of being their own bosses. The business assets of such owners may be worth less than they would be if owned by others who are more competent in making business decisions. However, if they continue to be owned by those who run the business incompetently, it may be *inferred from* the assumption of rational (utility-maximizing) behavior that these assets are nonetheless being put to their highest valued use. It is thus possible to argue that the appearance of business incompetency is deceiving and that inefficiency vanishes once all the ramifications of business behavior are understood. Assets should pass into the control of those who can wring more profit from them for a given amount of on-the-job consumption or more on-the-job consumption from them for a given amount of profit, but neither passing implies the necessary end of incompetence.[36]

There are two sources of depressed market values of those firms that are used to further on-the-job consumption by their present owners. These are, first, the prevalence among *potential* owners of a stronger taste for profit than guides the behavior of present owners and, second, the possession by present owners of sufficient wealth to allow them to persist in on-the-job consumption. Once the utility-conferring possibilities of business assets are recognized, it is easy to see that the market values of such firms can be depressed in equilibrium without violating neoclassical rational behavior assumptions. All that neoclassical theory requires is that those who consume on the job bear the cost of their consumption.

Since "incompetently" run firms may be producing an unrecorded output – the owner's on-the-job consumption – their productivities will be underestimated by conventional measurements. These focus on output that is produced for sale to others. Indexes of productivity, such as physical output per unit of input, will incorrectly give evidence of inefficiency because they fail to give weight to the utility derived by owners from continuing to run their own firms. These owners would be pleased to be more competent *if only they could do so without giving up control of these firms*! Measurement error arises because the world is not as specialized as neoclassical theory implicitly assumes in setting forth its model of perfect competition. A degree of self-sufficiency exists. Not all consumption takes place outside firms and in households; some of what the firm produces is not sold to others but is consumed by owners on the job.

I have emphasized on-the-job consumption by *owners* quite purposefully. As perviously mentioned, employees, including hired management, may also find it efficient to consume on the job, but theory asserts that they, unlike owners, pay for this consumption through lower wages. When deciding whether to offer one's services to this firm or that, a prospective employee considers the working conditions associated with alternative jobs. Such knowledge is important because real workers spend enough of their lives on the job to make it worthwhile for them to take firm-provided amenities into account. Consumption on the job well may be more efficient for them than consumption in the household. Would-be employees become actual employees only if reductions in the wage

---

36. Stigler's (1976) criticism of the X-efficiency concept carries a similar message. He does not refer to the utility of owner-managers but to the production of amenities for workers and society. However, it is incorrect to believe that amenities provided to workers and to society at large, rather than to the owner, can account for the appearance of inefficiency. The value of these amenities should be reflected in lower wages, if workers receive amenities, and in greater cooperation from the State, if the firm provides social services. If they are so reflected, these amenities should not be a source of biased downward rates of return on the firm's assets.

bill compensate the employer appropriately for the cost of providing improved working conditions to workers. A wage earner who seeks out better working conditions, accepting lower wages, is in fact consuming in the firm and not at home. Owners of firms provide amenities to workers when this lowers wage costs and/or increases productivity sufficiently to cover the cost of the amenities. Consequently, there is no reason to expect on-the-job consumption by employees to bias recorded profit downward.

Much of this reasoning is also applicable to on-the-job consumption by owners. One way to conceptualize this is to view owners as maximizing the difference between revenues and the amounts paid for inputs owned by others, and then to view them as spending some of this profit, now their personal wealth, to purchase on-the-job amenities, much as if they took this profit to their homes and consumed it within their households. Viewed this way, on-the-job consumption by owners does not impair the usefulness of assuming that owners seek to maximize profit. But this view works easily only if owners' on-the-job consumption is independent of how the firm is used to produce and market goods. It presumes that profit maximization leads to utility maximization. The only difference is whether fine art gets put on the walls of the owner's home or office.

Some on-the-job consumption is secured not simply by using (earned maximum) profit in-house, but by altering the way the firm's assets are constructed and used and by the nature of the product the owner of these assets chooses to produce. An individual who owns a newspaper might derive utility from influencing the political tastes of readers. (There is evidence for this.)[37] Catering to this preference may come at the expense of profit, for readers might not relish continued exposure to the owner's political philosophy in the news and editorializing given to them, and it certainly will alter the content of the newspaper as compared to one designed simply to maximize profit. If the owner yields to this preference, his newspaper, as a business, will not perform as well as it might. Nonetheless, the reduction in the firm's profit and the different uses made of the firm's assets will be utility maximizing if the owner gains sufficient utility from affecting the political views of the readers. Owner on-the-job consumption is served not simply by raising the firm's cost in order to put fine art on the walls of management offices but also by altering the firm's marketable product. Utility maximization that requires manipulation of the firm's resources and product is involved, and if the profit-maximizing assumption is applied to situations such as this it may mislead. Put differently, the firm does not only print news and advertising, the output on which its measured profit is based; it also persuades political opinion for its owner. The implicit

37. See Chapter 17, "The Amenity Potential of Newspapers and the Reporting of Presidential Campaigns," in my *Efficiency, Competition, and Policy* (1989), pp. 245–62.

revenue derived from this persuasion by the owner (i.e., the value of the utility derived from it) should be taken into account when reckoning true profit. Recorded profit overlooks this implicit revenue because it is not tracked by the explicit revenue that flows into the firm. The owner who enjoys on-the-job consumption is required by competition, as in the case of his employees, to supply services at lower costs, but, since his reward is received as profit, this just means that he is willing to accept a smaller profit to own the firm.

Yet it must be admitted that it is easy to create a utility-maximizing rationale to explain away apparent incompetence. We are unable in convincing fashion to place many restrictions on the utility function and its arguments. Nothing in principle bars incompetence even with regard to attempts to maximize utility! If incompetence is extensive in human behavior, predictions drawn from the assumption that behavior follows profit or utility maximization guidelines will be off the mark frequently. "Incompetence" cries for a definition. It cannot refer to errors that arise only from the fact that information is costly, for a proper application of maximization principles should predict these errors. They should be more severe or more frequent, the more costly it is to acquire good information.

Alchian's critique of the profit-maximization assumption has little to do with incompetence. It is based on the impossibility of knowing the profit-maximizing solution beforehand. The profitability of a management decision is linked to a probability distribution of states of the world. No specific state is sure to materialize, and different decisions can yield identical outcomes under different states of the world. Given this, Alchian can make little sense of thinking that any given decision is maximizing profit when viewed *a priori*.[38] It is possible for many different policies, each appealing to a different management group, to be described by that group as profit-maximizing.

Alchian argues the case for substituting natural selection for rational behavior as the arbiter of success and failure. The selection criterion he adopts is positive profit. Even if owner-managers of different firms make different business decisions, no one of which can be described convincingly as rational maximizing on an *a priori* basis, or for that matter even on an *ex post* basis, the business environment selects for survival those that yield positive profit. That life is full of great risk and uncertainty is not in doubt; nor is the fact that many successes and failures are unanticipated. The economic system does select winners and losers. Profits and losses are made. If success and failure could be predicted perfectly there would be no failure and there would be only normal

---

38. Knight would describe the difficulties that Alchian points to as *risky*, not as inherently *uncertain*. In Knight's view, there is sense to the notion that businesspersons maximize *expected* profit. Alchian wrote after Knight did, but before Bayesian decision making returned the topics of risk, uncertainty, and subjectivity to the forefront of discussions about decision making.

returns to success. Natural selection, as distinct from rational selection, is at work, but rational behavior in the face of imperfect information is not thereby excluded.

Positive profit as survival criterion has the ring of plausibility to it. Firms that enjoy positive profit are not compelled to fail. They survive to play the economic game yet one more time. Still, firms enjoying positive profit have been known to go out of business, presumably because they *foresee* dismal prospects. And firms with low positive profit rates have more difficulty than those with high profit rates when it comes to securing capital and other resources because the probability that they *will* go out of business is believed to be greater by those who own these resources. Hence, despite Alchian's reliance on positive *realized* profit as the relevant selection criterion, the business environment seems to make resources available more readily to firms on the basis of *forecasts* of the magnitude of future profitability. All the italicized words in this paragraph hint at least of attempts to behave rationally. Owners of resources behave as if they seek higher profit, not just positive profit. Capitalism's selection criterion seems to be the expectation of greater profit, not merely the realization of positive profit. Of course, the forecasts made by owners of resources need not make much more sense than the attempts by firms to maximize profit, and, I suppose, Alchian could claim that resource owners who (accidentally) happen to make better forecasts amass greater amounts of resources, while the resources of others are depleted.[39]

The selection system of capitalism, be it greater profit or positive profit, should not be thought of as the selection system of evolution. The analogy between a natural organism and a business organization is appealing, but defective. Applied to organisms, natural selection imposes a survival filter that in the main is exogenous to the behavior of the organisms. An ice age, drought, volcanic disturbance, or the like forces the selection of certain types of plants and animals and rejects others. The selection criteria wrought by these events are highly independent of the organisms that are affected by them, and it is the organisms, not their institutions, that evolution selects. Alchian's positive profit criterion is not exogenous and it is a characteristic not of the human but, rather,

39. It is important to recognize the limits set to the discussion if we adopt the business environment as the survival filter. If the environment were widened to encompass political institutions, we could plausibly add other survival criteria – size of firm, for example. The Chrysler Corporation, the Continental Bank, and the Pennsylvania Railroad succeeded despite negative profits because they were bailed out by a political mechanism that refused to tolerate the failure of such important firms. Now, one might claim that these bailouts constituted sources of profit and that some firms exhibited characteristics that turned out, luckily enough for them, to attract politically provided funds. But this becomes quite tautological. Anything that promotes survival is called a lucky outcome. It is more useful to recognize that political institutions give characteristics of firms different weights from those applied by pure market tests; the issue then becomes one of the survival of competing political institutions.

of the capitalist system. It emanates from human decisions made by those who own, control, and supply resources to firms.

As to the criterion itself, what causes owners to adopt positive profit as the guide for their decisions? Why do they refuse to make resources available to firms experiencing negative profit? Here, at decision levels deeper than those focused by Alchian, there lurks nonrandom and quite possibly maximizing behavior. To eliminate this sub rosa maximizing behavior, we would need a selection criterion that is not itself implicitly reliant on rational calculation. If positive profit is to be the selection criterion, it is necessary to give some argument as to why persons with a preference for positive profit have been selected by a nature-determined exogenous condition. More than this; the condition must have faced the human race long enough to inbreed this preference for positive profit through the natural selection process. In the absence of evidence relating to such a condition, or in the absence of cogent (rational!) reasoning about this, one could just as well assume that the condition for survival called forth a preference for greater, not just positive profit.

If we suppose that typical resource owners (or customers) do not favor positive profit, but that they make resources available to supplicant firms on a random selection basis, then implicit rational behavior on their part is avoided. Unfortunately, then we are left without reason for supposing that only positive profit firms survive.[40]

Alternatively, we may suppose that some resource owners favor positive profit supplicant firms and that others favor negative profit firms, thus setting aside the notion of a "typical" resource owner. It is possible to argue that the first group of resource owners, if they are investors, are more likely than the second group to augment their resources. The second group, it might be argued, is more likely to go without the return of its investments. But to suppose this requires us to make the further unwarranted suppositions: (1) that a positive profit firm this period is more likely to be a positive profit firm next period, and (2) that there exists the equivalent of bankruptcy laws, each of which reintroduces the possibility of implicit rational behavior.

Analogizing business firms to natural organisms runs into yet another difficulty. In the biology of natural selection, surviving individuals bring offspring into the world. This results in the transmission of genetically carried characteristics of the parents, including those that enabled them to survive the applicable natural selection filter. Business firms possess no analogous reproduction process. We can expect some business firms to meet the test of the environment, and we might further suppose that there is a conservancy of the

---

40. Alchian insightfully discusses the way in which random choice might lead to particular patterns of survival, but these patterns seem to depend on the existence of a positive profit filter.

culture within a *given* business firm over time (Nelson and Winter, 1982). Successful firms retain their characteristics through time. Yet we have no reason to expect successful firms to be replicated through a process similar to the bearing of offspring.

We know that resources, usually in the form of entrants, move into profitable markets rapidly and that they tend to take organizational forms like those that have in the past been successful in these markets. This looks like propagation, but it is not. How does one account for this inflow of resources? Alchian relies on *imitative* behavior, meaning that firms imitate success as measured by the positive profit criterion. But imitative behavior seems pretty much like rational, goal-seeking behavior (although it might be simply a biological propensity of persons to emulate success). It seems to require prediction and logic, not a random choice of which firms to imitate (chaos theory aside). Again, at another level of calculation than that focused on by Alchian, there is the strong suggestion of rational behavior.

My intent is not to reject the usefulness of evolution theory to an understanding of the business firm. Alchian's insights about this helped to break an uncritical reliance on the belief that permeates neoclassical theory that rational behavior is the guiding consideration for economic behavior. His early recognition of the applicability of the evolutionary process motivated work by many others, and it deserves high praise. Nonetheless, the use of evolution in this context usually rejects too quickly the natural selection potential of (what we identify as) purposeful behavior. Often, some substitute criterion is adopted without subjecting it to critical examination.[41]

For example, Becker (1962) demonstrates that budget constraints imply that demand curves will be negatively sloped even if buying behavior is not rational. The role of the budget constraint is to divide the choice set into feasible and unfeasible compartments. If product prices are allowed to vary, consumer purchases will reflect the law of negatively sloped demand because consumers cannot purchase bundles of goods that would cause them to violate the budget constraint they face, not necessarily because consumers apply rational behavior axioms to their choices. It is a well-drawn demonstration of the power of budget constraints. Yet, as a demonstration of the unnecessary luxury of using rational behavior in our models, it is not fully convincing. It suffers from sub rosa maximizing like that which seems to be present in Alchian's analysis.

In fact, consumers violate their budget constraints, buying on credit that extends their debts beyond their incomes. No natural law bars such behavior. Ultimately, the economic system imposes its discipline, limiting extravagant

---

41. Knight, like Alchian, also suspected the ability of rationality to explain much human behavior, but, unlike Alchian, he believes that behavior in business is the one arena where rationality might count for something.

behavior such as this, but when doing so it functions as if it were guided by purposeful behavior seeking to limit loss. The "constraint" in the budget constraint is a product of the economic system, and the economic system is itself a product of individual behavior. The constraint is present because people will not make goods available to those who cannot pay for them, and they will not offer loans to those who cannot repay them. When charitable and government redistributive forces are at work, the budget is no longer a binding constraint. The effective constraint seems to depend on the protection of narrowly defined self-interest.

Ultimately, of course, an aggregate budget constraint based on the natural supplies of resources limits the opportunities available to a society and its members. The constraint is not entirely exogenous, since wants and preference also affect the definition of supplies, but nature has nonetheless cast an overarching limit to what can be done within a given state of technology. Certain types of individual behavior drain a nation's resources more than do other types, or they fail to augment these resources as much. Ultimately, this results in a situation in which the "inefficient" types of behavior no longer can be sustained. On this basis, one could predict the ultimate cessation of inefficient behavior.

Russia and East Europe have just experienced a situation remarkably appropriate to the issue being discussed. The organizational methods these nations had used in the past relied on a set of (soft and subsidized) budget constraints different from the (hard) budget constraints that tend to prevail in capitalist societies. The conditions that established and defined these soft budget constraints permitted gross subsidization and redistribution of just the sort required to undermine the disciplining force of hard constraints. The political-economic organizations that gave birth to and maintained "Eastern-type" budget constraints failed because productivity was reduced, even if productivity is defined and measured by behind-the-Iron-Curtain preferences for goods. Finally, the resource bases of these societies eroded faster than people who lived with them were willing to tolerate.

The failure of these economies may be interpreted as an inability to produce the goods that people wanted, but the rejection of the system was not simply automatic, as is the failure of a species to survive an ice age. Nothing barred the East from continuing to absorb reductions in living standards. Increasing poverty could have been sustained for many years. Rational choice, or evolution's equivalent, does not preclude error. Once a course of action is set upon (whether this is determined by persons or by natural selection), the action subsequently might turn out to be less satisfactory than another selection might have been. Societies that chose to start down the path to Communism may have viewed this course of action as better than the alternatives they saw facing them at the time. Once started, the cost of altering the path may have become greater than it was before the choice had been made. The time dependency of the set of feasible choice options may give rise to regrets at not having struck out along different pathways, but regrets signify neither that the initial choice was wrong when it was made nor that it pays now to alter this path. Commitment may continue for a considerable time before the costs of continuing on a path become so large that a shift to an alternative path becomes feasible.

Nothing is necessarily irrational or inefficient about having made choices that give rise to regrets, but the regret emotion is difficult to interpret other than as a reflection of (an evolutionarily created) desire to behave rationally. Failure leads to *dissatisfaction,* and dissatisfaction motivates the search for change. Often, this search seeks out an alternative that is worthy of imitation. The capability for being dissatisfied and for attempting to do something to alleviate dissatisfaction, possibly by imitating others, may be the product of evolutionary forces, but these responses are quite consistent with what we mean by rational behavior. If they are, it is no great disservice to social science to proceed on the assumption that people have the capacity to, and frequently do, indulge in rational choice.

As evolution culls out losers and selects winners, the criterion it employs in the case of humans might very well be the ability to look back and see regularities in relationships between phenomena, and then to use these regularities for similar but not necessarily identical phenomena. If this ability is associated with inheritable traits, it would be augmented through succeeding generations and come to be known as rational behavior.

Rational behavior more broadly considered

Rational behavior is a topic so much written about, and in so many different contexts, that its many facets cannot possibly be covered in one section of a single commentary. I focus here first on Knight's uncertainty and Simon's bounded rationality, finding these to be unhelpful guides to behavior or to the analysis of behavior. I then suggest what I believe to be a more useful way to view the decision problem when information is seriously lacking. Finally, I give rebuttal to recently offered evidence that behavior is irrational.

Knight and Simon

The earliest significant challenge to rational behavior put forward by an economist came from Knight. His *Risk, Uncertainty, and Profit* emphasized the impact of uncertainty on decision making. He uses uncertainty to rationalize the existence of profit in a not fully informed (but somehow still) competitive equilibrium. Uncertainty is defined by decision situations so lacking in background experience as to make probabilistic estimates of possible outcomes impossible. Without these probabilities, rational calculation becomes impossible. Decisions nonetheless must be made even under uncertainty conditions. Knight substitutes human emotions for rational calculation under these circumstances, relying on psychological dispositions such as optimism and pessimism to guide choice.[42]

A position similar to Knight's was taken by Herbert Simon a quarter of a century after Knight wrote. Unlike Knight, who blames lack of experience for the impossibility of rational calculation, and Alchian and Leibenstein, who attribute nonmaximizing behavior, respectively, to inadequate knowledge and poorly designed incentives, Simon, in his *Administrative Behavior* (1947), reasons that nonmaximizing behavior is a necessary consequence of the limited capabilities of the human mind. He calls this limit *bounded rationality,* and describes it as coming into play if decision problems are so "complex" that their rational resolution requires more mental ability than humans possess.

In his earlier work, Simon tends to treat rules of thumb and organizational arrangements as devices by which rational solutions to complex problems are approximated at acceptable cost. This makes these arrangements rationally calculated responses to complex problems. But in later work he interprets bounded rationality differently. We may call this interpretation *strong-form bounded rationality,* and the immediately following discussion concerns only this strong-form. Strong-form bounded rationality claims that our inability to rationally solve complex problems leads us to substitute *satisficing* for the maximizing decision criterion. Satisficing behavior is reflected in the willingness of decision makers to settle for outcomes that fall short of being optimal but that exceed a subjective standard of minimal acceptable satisfaction.

Maximization relies on known principles. Stationary values obtain when first derivatives are zero, and maxima obtain when these stationary values are accompanied by negative second derivatives. No principles like these define satisficing. What is or is not statisficing is a matter of psychology and emotion, and Simon's substitution of satisficing for rational maximization is therefore much like Knight's substitution of emotions for rational calculation. Rational calculation implies the examination of options in a principled way. Practically, this may be a difficult exercise, involving as it does comparisons of costs and benefits. But conceptually it is possible for the owners of firms to state their expected cost and revenue functions as they judge these to be, and from these we can determine whether they have acted in a manner consistent with utility or profit maximization. It cannot be ascertained on the basis of similar theoretical principles whether realized outcomes that fall short

---

42. Beyond this, Knight claims that only a small fraction of human behavior is to be explained in terms of rational behavior. Much is to be explained as game playing. However, these claims are not reinforced with evidence, nor are they developed theoretically. I pass over them without further comment.

of achieving full maximization have resulted from the substitution of emotion or satisficing for rational calculation. This makes it rather difficult if not impossible to construct an empirical test that in principle can be used to refute the assertion that decision makers substitute satisficing or emotions for rational calculation.

Refutation is made all the more difficult because neither Simon nor Knight provide clear empirical guideposts by which to determine when rational behavior, which must reflect costly knowledge, is abandoned. For Knight and Simon, rational calculation is the preferred method for reaching decisions, and it will be used if uncertainty and complexity do not complicate the decision problem; decisions made by emotion and satisficing are predicted only if the decision problem is of the complex or uncertainty varieties. But what criteria allow us to determine when this case is controlling?

Knight and Simon treat decision problems differently from how they would be treated if one simply tried to take account of the cost of acquiring additional information (as did Stigler, 1961) or if one tried to take account of the cost of making greater mental efforts to reach a solution. A perspective of decision making that relies on the cost of acquiring information would make decision error smaller if more resources are put into solving a problem. Better rules of thumb (theories) would result. The perspectives adopted by Knight and Simon impose discontinuities in human behavior that preclude this. For Knight, the discontinuity occurs when experience falls below the threshold required to calculate risk; at this point emotional response substitutes for rational response. For Simon, it occurs when the line between simple and complex problems is crossed, at which point satisficing substitutes for maximizing.[43]

Knight's distinction between risk and uncertainty is sharply drawn. Risky events involve outcomes to which, by virtue of our experience, probabilities can be assigned, and uncertain events are those for which they cannot. Uncertainty attaches to completely novel events. Simon adopts rational calculation as the problem-solving method if problems are simple, but requires satisficing behavior if problems are complex. Of course, persons can and do form expectations about events that seem in nature to be close to those that Knight calls novel and Simon calls complex. Otherwise, decision makers would be frozen into inaction, and even inaction can be interpreted as a reflection of expectations concerning the merits of doing something vs. the merits of doing nothing. Since expectations are in fact formed, perhaps through reliance on emotions,

43. To be consistent, we should recognize that rationality is ruled out when theorizing about decision making. Those who analyze behavior and who agree with Knight and Simon are in jeopardy of doubting the rationality of their theory of decision making. They are as much at sea without a rudder as those whose behavior they study, for the problem on which they work is sufficiently complex and possibly sufficiently devoid of experience so as to call for analytical decisions that are of the satisficing and emotional variety described by Knight and Simon.

Knight cannot be supposing an expectations "vacuum." He must really mean that expectations bear no necessary relationship to the real but unknown underlying probabilities that attach to outcomes for which we have no experience. In contrast to this, Knight treats a risk decision situation as if an *accurate* calculable statistical frequency can be assigned to it on the basis of past experience.

The presumed convergence of expectations to reality in experience-rich decision situations implicitly presumes the existence of some unspecified suitable mechanism for bringing expectations into agreement with correct underlying probabilities. This applies also to Simon's view. Rational solution is possible for simple problems, but there is no specification of a mechanism by which convergence of expectations to reality is brought about. Dichotomous treatment of decision situations bars Knight and Simon from introducing a plausible convergence mechanism, for such a mechanism would force them to view decision making along a continuum much like that which would represent an analysis based on information cost. More experience and simpler decision problems would then reduce the relative role played by emotion and satisficing in decision making, just as lower information cost plausibly reduces the role of error in decision making. Formulating a model for decision making in this way would reduce the significance of the contrast they wish to make between risk and uncertainty and between maximizing and satisficing. This puts their analyses in an uncomfortable position. Surely Knight would want to say that expectations are held with less confidence as experience becomes thin, and Simon would want to say that maximizing becomes more difficult as problems become less simple. What is there to disrupt this continuity and make the decision process suddenly abandon all maximizing calculations?[44] Are we to believe that experience is so lacking for some business problems, or that complexity is so great, that more time, effort, and resources cannot improve expectations? If there are such problems, they surely are very rare by comparison to those whose solutions we believe are likely to be improved (but not necessarily to be more profitable) through the commitment of additional resources. The dichotomies relied on by Knight and Simon clarify concepts, but they are not very useful for characterizing real decision situations. Hardly any decision situations – none really – are such that experience is totally absent and rational analysis totally unproductive. But it is also true that we do not enjoy the luxuries of being able to count on expectations that *surely* equal the underlying correct probabilities or on rational analysis that *surely* yields the best solution.

44. There is some difficulty for Simon's case in interpreting a changing emphasis on maximizing and satisficing as problem complexity increases. One possible interpretation would be that as satisficing becomes relatively more important, and maximizing relatively less important, the number of outcomes that pass the (subjective) satisficing filter becomes larger.

Emotions play a larger role in decision making when experience is thin and problems are more complex, but there is no conflict between this and rational behavior. Rational behavior conserves on rational effort if situations make such effort more costly, and emotions may reflect hidden rationality. But however we interpret emotional responses, they clearly play a role in decision making, and they are likely to play larger roles in contexts burdened with inexperience and complexity. What prediction about behavior does this observation yield? If inexperience and/or the complexity of problems could be measured, one would think that larger values, as measured across a set of decision problems, imply greater differences in the solutions selected by a set of decision makers, these differences reflecting variation in the emotional responses of decision makers. But even this prediction is suspect. Analytical abilities, as well as emotions, differ among decision makers, so that we are dealing with two sources of variation in decisions. If the variance in emotions across persons is smaller than the variance in analytical abilities, then the larger weight given to emotions in situations where experience is thin and problems are complex would make for smaller differences in decisions; emotionally influenced behavior may be more moblike in its uniformity. Suppose inexperience and complexity are carried to extremes that make uncertainty and bounded rationality the operable conditions facing decision makers. In what other ways would this fact affect decisions? If interest rates are higher in one scenario than in another, would we not still expect decisions to be more conserving of capital inputs in the first scenario? That is, emotional and satisficing behavior may add an unexplained larger random element to decisions, but wouldn't they be affected on average by the high interest rates? Ah, but the reader might observe that the knowledge of the role of interest rates on the profitability of investments is evidence that our experience is not so lacking and that the bounds of our rationality are not so strained as is necessary to have uncertainty and bounded rationality to control the decision process.

Exactly! Decisions are never made without any knowledge, nor are they so complex that rational analysis can make no contribution. And if for reasons of pure hypothetical speculation we are willing to assume that uncertainty and bounded rationality govern decisions, well, then, this does not help us say much more about decisions. It is more useful to avoid the categorical extremes set forth by Knight and Simon. They generate conundrums but not answers. Conundrum: Only a problem that does not exceed the bounds of rationality merits the investment of analytical resources, but this cannot be determined without first investing these resources.

Simon's ideas are of help in understanding the decision-making process not through application of the strong-form bounded-rationality constraint but by forcing us to recognize that the act of thinking is not costless. Consider classical sampling techniques. These treat the knowledge problem as the inference of stable characteristics of an unknown underlying population from sample data drawn from it. They take account of the cost of sampling, as in search theory, but they treat knowledge as though it is no different from any other input that goes into a decision problem. Just as another unit of labor services adds to cost and contributes to productivity, so does another sample. In some respects, knowledge and labor services do not differ, but in other respects they do. Of particular importance is that facts, the building blocks of knowledge, must be *interpreted*. Classical sampling theory ignores the cost of mentally "digesting" the data that sampling brings forth. The costs of thinking about data, of ascertaining how they bear on the decision problem, and even of designing the search process itself are ignored. The theory implicitly assumes that the cost of interpreting data is zero or somehow irrelevant. It treats information as if it or its source of productivity is wholly external to our minds and, although costly to acquire, once acquired, freely converted to maximizing solutions. Simon has clearly spotlighted the idea that facts alone do not yield solutions and that the use of the mind is not free. Improvements in decisions can be secured by more intensive thinking as well as by more data gathering.

Improvements in knowledge thus entails two kinds of costs. So as to underscore the difference between emotional and logical-analytical thought, we may label the second of these as the *cost of comprehending*. Opportunities to use the mind for emotional purposes, such as loving, hating, and enjoying, as well as to put it into sleep mode, are foregone when it is used to comprehend. To these foregone nonanalytical opportunities must be added the foregone opportunity to think logically about *other* analytical problems; these define the cost of giving mental time and energy to understanding how a particular inflow of data bears on a particular problem.[45]

Perfect competition and classical search theory both treat comprehension as if it were free. Knight and Simon, in their concepts of uncertainty and strong-form bounded rationality, go to the other extreme, treating comprehension as if it were infinitely costly. These starkly contrasting extremes – zero and infinite comprehension cost – are much less interesting than the case that lies between them, in which comprehension is costly but not so costly as to bar the possibility of improving our understanding. The intermediate case brings comprehension within the framework of economics by treating it as an activity that has manageable scarcity value.

A neoclassical economic theory of this scarcity value, were it to be constructed, would be cast in terms of the demand and supply of the requisite

---

45. Nonlogical thinking activities can impinge on the effectiveness with which the mind performs its calculating function; the mind calculates better when rested, when not experiencing a sudden change in time zones, when not preoccupied, and when not laboring under the burden of a psychosis. The interrelationship between rational and nonrational uses of the mind is complex and not simply one of substitution.

mental activity, and it would seek to determine the equilibrium amount of comprehension. Equilibrium would depend on more than just the nature of the data being sampled and the technology of collecting data, as it generally does in classical search theory. Comprehension cost is affected by a person's intelligence, by the time value of preoccupying a person's mind, and by the amount of mental capital already acquired in dealing with similar data. Some minds are brighter than others, some offer superior calculating abilities, and some are more sensible interpreters. Others are more demanding of sleep or emotional feelings. There is no reason to expect different persons to comprehend equally well or to produce equally good solutions even though the same universe of data is being searched with the same data collection technology to resolve the same problems.[46] These personal differentiating variables are largely ignored in statistical decision theory, which, since it attaches no cost to mental inference, implicitly assumes all searchers are equally good at comprehending already acquired data.

Personal differences such as these raise a question about the meaning of the evidence given by Leibenstein in support of X-efficiency. Differences in the comprehension abilities of owners of firms can yield differences in profit and productivity data of the sort that lead Leibenstein to claim that some firms create inadequate incentives to pursue profit-maximizing strategies. The data are consistent with Leibenstein's claim, but not only with this claim. Let us suppose that the supply of superior comprehension abilities is limited. Further assume that attempts to digest large amounts of data, especially different types of data, strain the comprehension skills of even those possessed of superior abilities. Then, *ceteris paribus,* only the firms *owned* by those who possess superior comprehending abilities will exhibit low average cost and high average productivity. Since, by assumption, these abilities are housed in the minds of controlling owners, not professional managers, their existence is recorded in high profit rates, not in high management compensation. Other firms, relying on owners who have only inferior comprehension skills, will exhibit high average cost, low average productivity, and low profit rates. These different outcomes can persist in equilibrium if demands for goods produced by these firms exceed the production capabilities of firms headed by superior comprehenders, even though, contrary to Leibenstein's thesis, incentives are such that all persons succeed in maximizing profit to the fullest extent of their (varying) abilities.

---

46. The considerations germane here are related to, but still different from those discussed by the articles of Grossman and Stiglitz (1976), Conlisk (1980), and Haltiwanger and Waldman (1991). The authors of these papers recognize that some decision makers are better informed or brighter than other decision makers, or that they possess different psychologies, but their focus is on how this may generate externalities across these different groups or on the importance of each group to the characteristics of equilibrium.

Perception

The fact of costly comprehension assures productive roles for rules of thumb in (rational) decision making. The incentive to rely on these arises from the greater cost of undertaking careful, detailed reasoning. But rules of thumb make up a category of reaction to costly comprehension that is much too narrow. Broadly conceived *perceptions* are also involved. Careful, detailed reasoning may be called the *calculating machinery* of decision making. I distinguish this from the *perception machinery* of decision making. The application of perceptions to the task of interpreting data allows decision makers to economize on the use of their calculating machinery.

Perception is to be thought of as the judgments people develop about "how the world works." Perceptions develop from the exposure of particular personalities and mental facilities to particular life experiences. In fine detail, each perception is unique to each individual. It informs an individual about the extent to which strangers may be trusted, about the extent to which persons behave altruistically, about the general reliability of climate, political processes, and products. How many generations does it take before another major war erupts? How likely is it that the medical treatment recommended today will be discarded tomorrow? How likely is it that inflation will dominate deflation over the decades to come? What probability should be attached to a job change during the next decade? People act on the basis of answers that emerge from the perceptions they possess, perceptions created from the unstudied interaction between their minds and their life experiences. The more costly it is to use the calculating machinery of the mind, the greater is the reliance that is placed on perception when making decisions.

Readers may agree that classical theory decision making assigns no decision role to perception, but may object that Bayesian statistical decision making does. The subjective element in Bayesian statistical inference distinguishes it from classical statistical decision theory, but this distinction is more formal and less substantive than might be supposed. Bayesian theory does not seek to understand perceptions and how they might emerge from experience and be different for different persons or for the same person over time. This seems to be an issue best left with psychologists, sociologists, economists, and biologists. The concern of Bayesian analysis is how a *rational calculator* might modify ad hoc initial subjective estimates (perceptions, if you will) when new data are acquired; it is not with the subjective views we hold to begin with. Bayesian theory neglects those forces that govern the perceptions we hold – our life experiences and the mental filter through which these pass and are interpreted. Optimists hold expectations different from those held by pessimists, and they probably revise their expectations differently also. Persons who have experienced abject poverty most of their lives are hardly likely to interpret data as would persons who have enjoyed wealth for most of their lives. Someone who has specialized in one line of activity is unlikely to hold the same perceptions as is a person who has specialized in another line.[47]

Tolerance of error and experimental findings

A person uses both calculating and perception decision-making machineries when facing a real decision problem. Nonetheless, the modes of operation of these machineries differ, especially with respect to their tolerance for runs of similarly signed errors. Perception machinery, to achieve its potential, must treat problems as if they are the same when in some respects they are likely to differ. This stance requires the users of perception machinery to tolerate longer runs of similarly signed errors before revising their perception or reducing their reliance on it. Similarly signed errors must be interpreted more persistently as the product of innocent statistical noise. To change perception frequently, or on slight cause, is equivalent to abandoning the use of perception as an aid to decision making.

Error is more tolerated when decisions are being made about matters in which we are inexpert, and it is in regard to unfamiliar matter that we are most likely to find it advisable to rely a good deal on perception. Experts are prepared to give a problem within their specialty a more thoroughly studied appraisal. For perception to be productive, the sum of errors it generates for the lack of studied appraisal must be less costly than is the effort to become more expert about unfamiliar decision problems. A perception is productive when it copes fairly well, on average, with frequently encountered situations about which a person neither is nor seeks to become a specialist. Productivity is enhanced if the underlying conditions generating these situations are stable, for this makes it more likely that our perceptions offer suitable reactions and are less in need of revision.

Although the degree of error toleration surely varies from person to person,

47. Attention has been given by a few economists to differences in the perspectives of classes of persons. Schumpeter (1939) lays great stress on the atypical willingness of entrepreneurs to invest in the midst of a recession after input prices have fallen. Knight, in his ad hoc fashion, describes businesspeople as having optimistic perspectives, and he does so to the point that he believes that they overinvest and consequently receive negative returns on their investments. Hayek, in his classic discussion of the role of market prices as conveyers of information, emphasizes differences in personal knowledge that arise from the special circumstances in which each person finds himself or herself. Indeed, the generally accepted position of economists, which is to deny meaningfully objective interpersonal utility comparisons, ultimately rests on unshared personalized knowledge of one's tastes. These insights notwithstanding, there nevertheless has been little systematic examination of the implications of the prevalence of different perspectives.

it should also vary systematically with respect to certain considerations. Pervasive toleration of error is an interesting matter for investigation. Since the reconsideration and reformulation of perception machinery with each new batch of information is uneconomic, toleration is quite rational.[48] Recognition of this is important to an assessment of empirical studies that have challenged the rationality of decision making.

Reconsideration of evidence of error

Consider the influential Ellsberg paradox (1961), in which Ellsberg distinguishes between uncertainty and probability in the following way. Urn 1 contains 100 balls of either red or black color but with the numerical division between these colors unknown. Urn 2 contains 50 balls of each color. Players are told that if they bet on a specific color and that color is drawn from the urn they receive $100, but if the other color is drawn they receive $0. Most people are found to be indifferent between betting on red and betting on black when confronted by *either* urn, which suggests that they attach a .5 probability to either color being selected from either urn. But when asked which urn they would prefer to have the ball drawn from, most people chose urn 2. This seems to imply that they believe they have a higher probability of drawing the color they chose from the urn with known proportions than from the urn with unknown proportions, and this is inconsistent with their previously revealed belief that the probability of drawing the chosen color is .5 for both urns. They prefer the less ambiguous situation, if we define "less ambiguous" to correspond with the possession of more information about the proportion of balls in the urn.

This outcome has been interpreted as revealing a degree of irrationality, rationality being defined to require consistency. The same things (probabilities equal to .5), then, should be treated the same way. (Of course, Ellsberg's second choice problem does not really confront players with the same things; it confronts them with two urns about which they have different information.) Alternatively, the experiment's outcome may be interpreted as revealing a preference for more knowledge over less knowledge, but this also seems to imply irrationality because the additional knowledge, which in practice would come at a cost, does not in this case beneficially affect the expected payoff to be received; knowing that urn 2 contains 50 balls of each color does not allow players to improve the payoff they expect to receive.

Suppose players are offered the choice of playing either of the urns at no fee

48. To the extent that perception arises from genetic endowment, change in perception is likely to require periods of time long enough for natural selection to work its ways. Even if genetics is not involved and perceptions are viewed as *our* creation rather than as a result of natural selection, persistent commitment to perceptions serves a productive function.

to them, as in the preceding experiment, or alternatively of buying more information about the content of urn 1 before playing. Clearly, it would be entirely rational for them to offer some positive amount for this information before they play the game, for urn 1 might contain balls predominately of one color. The additional information might be of positive value. The Ellsberg experiment is constructed in such a way that knowing only the information provided within the context of the experiment does not make one urn a higher payoff choice than the other, but in the more general run of cases upon which persons build their perception machinery, there *is* a positive payoff to learning more about one's choices.

The Ellsberg experiment presents an unusual choice problem for most persons, one about which they are not expert. They *rationally* should deploy a *perspective* garnered from the sum of their past experiences with unfamiliar choice problems, especially since the payoffs involved are too small to entice them into becoming more expert about this particular choice problem. Put in the position of nonexpert, and unwilling to devote studied time to the choice set offered in the Ellsberg experiment, persons are quite rational to rely on a rule of thumb that has served them well in the past. When confronted by choices that seem the same but about which you know differing amounts of information, choose the alternative you know more about. This choice perspective derives not so much from aversion to "ambiguity" as from the many occasions on which persons have experienced disadvantaged dealings when interacting with others possessed of superior information. Given the perspective that arises from such experiences, it would be irrational to choose the more unknown urn in Ellsberg's experiment, or even to treat the urns as equally attractive without giving the proposition and the person offering it a great deal more consideration.

Virtually all experiments that yield apparently irrational choice outcomes are of this nature. They confront persons with decisions involving comparisons that are not obvious or familiar, and requiring comparisons entailing calculations of expectations based on probabilistic outcomes. These not only raise suspicion in the chooser's mind about what really is going on, they also invite arithmetic errors. Tversky and Kahneman (1981), for example, asked undergraduate students to consider the following two decisions:

> *First decision:* Choose between (A), a sure gain of $240, and (B), a 25 percent chance to gain $1000 combined with a 75 percent chance to gain nothing.
>
> *Second decision:* Choose between (C), a sure loss of $750, and (D), a 75 percent chance to lose $1000 combined with a 25 percent chance to lose nothing.

For the first decision, a large majority of students chose (A), while for the second decision a large majority chose (D). A risk-averse attitude is revealed for the first decision but a risk-preferring attitude for the second. To the investigators, this implies an inconsistent and hence irrational difference in attitude between essentially similar decision situations.

What it suggests to me is that, since this was a hypothetical choice in which the students neither received nor paid actual (large) sums of money, they did not choose to waste their time becoming experts in the arithmetic of the choice problem. Their rule of thumb is that, since the choice matters hardly at all to them, a very rough guess is all that is warranted. Rather than leading them to calculate correctly the expected payoff of (B) as $250, this rough guess led a majority of them to calculate the payoff to (B) as $250 for one-fourth of the plays and $0 for three-fourths of the plays for an expected payoff of $62.50. This led them to choose (A) with its sure payoff of $240. A similar mistake makes (D) appear to be a smaller loss than (C). Hence, the preference of most students was for (A) and (D). This interpretation seems all the more plausible because the majorities that chose (A) and (D), 84 percent and 87 percent, are so close in number that these results demonstrate a consistent attitude about when it pays to tolerate error.

It strikes me as peculiar that investigators, when judging rationality, pay greater attention to choice in complex situations than in simple situations. A choice between $1000 for sure and $0 for sure is a clearer test of whether someone needs psychiatric help than is the same payoff expectation couched in arithmetic manipulation. Yet the latter type of choice is given precedence over the former when evaluating rationality. The more complex situations seem to be chosen to get at the question of attitudes toward risk, but even for this purpose simpler comparisons are available. Do you prefer equal chances of $50 and −$50 or equal chances of $500 and −$500? To put the issues so simply gives us greater confidence that rationality is not hidden by lack of incentives, calculating problems, and suspicions about what is *really* at stake in the game.

On the other side of the ledger from the evidence offered in these experiments, there is an almost infinitely long list of experiences in which people purchase less when price is raised, seek out higher-interest checking accounts, put jackets on when temperatures fall, have more children when society subsidizes the having of children, and consistently respond in the same reasonable way to repeated versions of life's choices. What is to be learned from a study of both sides of the ledger is that it is a mistake for investigators to presume that full comprehension of every choice problem is rational behavior. It is even a mistake to assume that rational behavior rules out a run of mistakes of the same sign or a pattern of mistakes common to many individuals.

Recognition of this makes it more difficult to assess rationality, but it also suggests more reasonable ways to approach the assessment problem. The larger are the stakes, and the more frequently encountered is the choice situation in which they are embedded, the less error there should be. The cost of comprehension requires this to be true for rational decision makers. Irrational are those who strive to err no more frequently when stakes are small than when they are large and when choice situations are unfamiliar and complex.

As a final example of evidence of irrational behavior, consider the fairly well-documented apparent inconsistency in behavior revealed when persons alternatively face bid and ask prices (Knetsch and Sinden, 1984; Hoffman and Spitzer, 1987). The experiment seeks to determine whether the price that persons pay to acquire an asset is approximately equal to what they would take to sell the same asset, where possession of the asset has not resulted from underlying preferences or from search among opportunities. One group of students is given possession of lottery tickets, which the investigators then attempt to repurchase; students in another group, that had not been given lottery tickets, are asked what they would be willing to pay to acquire identical lottery tickets. This second group was willing to pay, on average, $1.28, whereas the first group, on average, asked $5.18 for the tickets they already possessed.

This result, in different experiments, has been substantiated, and an "explanation" has been offered for the apparently irrational behavior shown in the disparity between bid and ask prices. People are alleged to deal with real decision problems by reliance on "mental accounts" (Thaler, 1985). These contain categories of expenditures and income that give different weights to costs and benefits than would be assigned by rational decision makers, and these categories are not easily altered once they are set up. Thus, if an asset is physically possessed, it is reckoned as more valuable than if it has not yet been acquired. This "explanation," it seems to me, is merely a way of describing the outcomes of these experiments, at least until it has been formulated in a way that allows it to be tested outside this small body of experience.

We know from other experiments (V. Smith, 1991) that this apparent irrationality diminishes as experience with the decision problem grows, and we also know that these experiments involve such small sums that error is relatively unimportant. Can anyone doubt that the spread between bid and ask prices will narrow if very large sums are involved in frequently recurring decision situations? Which outcomes are the most relevant for establishing rationality, those involving small sums and infrequent exposure or those involving large sums and frequent exposure? Is rationality to be tested by confronting small numbers of hardly interested students with buy and sell opportunities, or by observing the behavior of investors of large sums on the major stock trading exchanges of the world.[49]

Moreover, it is a delusion to believe that the persons confronting decisions in an experimental setting view the experiment on the same terms as those conducting the experiment. The subjects of the experiment might believe that

---

49. For the first study of the systematic, rational forces operating on the bid-ask spread recorded on organized stock exchanges, see Demsetz (1968a).

it has not completely ended once bid and ask prices have been established. Students might think that they will have been judged as performing better than their fellows if they can demonstrate the ability to realize larger profits. If so, they would ask for higher prices than they are willing to bid, and this would be fully consistent with rational behavior once the suspected "hidden agenda" of researchers is taken into account. How easy is it for researchers to establish the agenda they want the students to believe? Not easy at all, but the impact of the hidden agenda problem probably is reduced if large sums are involved in repeated exposures.

These searches for evidence of irrationality, I believe, are wasteful. More worthwhile would be a search for perceptions and rules of thumb that help to explain, presumably on the basis of (evolutionarily produced) rational behavior, the outcomes we in fact observe, and then to follow this search with empirical tests. A disparity between decisions actually made and those that would be made if knowledge were perfect can be met by rejecting rationality or by explaining the rational basis for the disparity; the second course of action seems to me the more productive.

Recent studies of stock prices pose such a puzzle, and a consideration of the findings of these studies offers an example of what I have in mind. These indicate the presence of an overshooting phenomenon. Stock prices seem to vary more widely than the present value of future dividends or earnings per share. Since stock prices presumably represent the value discounted to present of dividends and/or earnings, this is taken to represent overshooting and possibly irrational investor behavior. Alternatively, one can interpret overshooting as evidence of the (rational) use of a rule of thumb based on comprehension cost.

A rule of thumb such as this would be contrary to Knight's belief, which is that calculated probabilities yield expectations in accord with underlying probabilities for risk situations (about which we are rich in experience). But it is also contrary to the theory of stock prices, which is based on the propositions that (a) prices reflect the present value of expected future share earnings and (b) expectations are unbiased. In the present instance, stock price theory would assert that investments should be in accord with correctly calculated probabilities of stock price changes. Overshooting should not take place. But consider the following two empirical assumptions:

1. *Most* changes that take place in nature occur slowly when set against the time frame of a person's life or of a society's collective memory of its history.
2. Natural selection has encouraged the development of human capabilities for (a) recognizing past trends and (b) utilizing these to guide future actions.

If assumption 1 holds, then survival probabilities will be higher for persons who act in accord with assumption 2, given that the cost of comprehending is significantly positive. Natural selection, then, favors persons who abide by the second assumption in the *usual* case (in which change is slow). People, we may suppose, look backward and simply extrapolate what appear to them to be trends, and their reliance on these extrapolations persists in the face of (runs of) error because comprehension cost is high. Since, by assumption, most trends posed by nature change only slowly, these extrapolations will not always or usually be grossly in error. In those rarer circumstances in which conditions change abruptly, error will be more significant.

Overshooting of the sort previously described could be a case in point. This would follow if expectations about future stock prices are based on extrapolations of past trends in stock prices. Stock prices that have been rising (falling) are expected to continue rising (falling). Stock prices continue to rise even after earnings have stopped rising, or continue to fall after earnings have stopped falling. The resulting relationship between prices and earnings will produce an overshooting phenomenon, for, in the case at hand, the stock price patterns, reflecting both rising and falling price trends, will yield prices that overshoot earnings. The significance of overshooting should relate positively to the cost of comprehending that fundamental changes in earnings are taking place in the market. Can this be what market analysts mean when they say "a correction is overdue?"[50]

Attempts by experts to respond more quickly or more frequently to fundamental changes in market conditions do not necessarily improve their investment results as compared to going along with current trends. It all depends on when they leap from the bandwagon. However, the leap by experts should be delayed longer the greater is the weight of nonexperts in determining market supply and demand conditions.

I do not mean to press the case for this particular explanation of overshooting, but only to argue that there is more payoff in searching for a rational explanation of what appears to be error than in quickly accepting this appearance as a factual demonstration that behavior is irrational. By testing such speculations about investor perceptions against data, it should be possible to assess their merits. This assumes that perceptions are important when discussing errors and that rational explanation becomes possible when this assumption is accepted. This seems more interesting to me than using error to refute rationality. But, then, each to his own preferences.

---

50. Note that analogous reasoning can yield undershooting. Suppose either that rising stock price trends combine with changes in earnings trends to cause earnings to rise by more than would be justified by past experience with price trends, or alternatively that falling price trends combine with changes in earnings trends to make earnings fall by more than would be justified by the price trend. Both conditions cause greater variations in observed earnings than in observed stock prices. Whether we should observe overshooting or undershooting depends on the direction of fundamental changes in earnings relative to the earnings that can be justified by past price trends.

The use and abuse of accounting profit data

It is one thing to question the sensibility of assuming that businesspersons seek to maximize profit, but there can be no doubt that business profit is a widely used index of performance. The government, investors, and people in business all pay attention to profit as measured by accountants. And so do economists. Accounting profit rates play important roles in assessing the national economic condition, in forecasts of business investment and tax revenues, and, as discussed in the prior commentary, in assessing whether stock prices overshoot earnings performance. In attempting to test the market concentration doctrine, economists consistently examine the relationship between market concentration and accounting profit rates or some derivative of these rates. These are only a small fraction of the uses to which accounting profit data are put. Reliability, or the lack thereof, of these data has important and extensive consequences.

Doubts about our ability to measure profit rates accurately are long standing. Adam Smith's theory of the decentralized economy put the theoretical role of profit at the center of the allocation mechanism, but he was skeptical about our ability to measure profit accurately.

> It is not easy, it has already been observed, to ascertain what are average wages of labour even in a particular place ... We can ... seldom determine more than what are the most usual wages. But even this can seldom be done with regard to the profits of stock. Profit is so very fluctuating, that the person who carries on a particular trade cannot always tell you himself what is the average of annual profit. It is affected, not only by every variation of price in the commodities which he deals in, but by the good or bad fortune both of his rivals and of his customers, and by a thousand other accidents to which goods when carried either by sea or by land, or even when stored in a warehouse, are liable. It varies, therefore, not only from year to year, but from day to day, and almost from hour to hour. To ascertain what is the average profit of all the different trades carried on in a great kingdom, must be much more difficult; and to judge of what it may have been formerly, or in remote periods of time, with any degree of precision, must be altogether impossible.[51]

51. *The Wealth of Nations* (The Glasgow Edition, Ed. Campbell and Skinner, 1981), 105. Smith is not easily deterred by even his own doubts, for he then proceeds to describe a method for determining the general level of nominal profit across nations and across time.

> It may be laid down as a maxim, that wherever a great deal can be made by the use of money, a great deal will commonly be given for the use of it; and that wherever

The problems he recites relate chiefly to the time period over which profit is measured. He did not anticipate many contemporary concerns about the measurement of profit. And there should be concern about accounting profit rate data, but not so much concern as to lead us to ignore this source of information.

For some analytical problems there is no good substitute for accounting data, even if such data are very imperfect. The chief rival measure of profitability is that which is derived from the behavior of stock prices. The stock-market-measured rate of return is superior to accounting measures of profit rates for some purposes but not others. Management chooses to merge its firm with another, or the government changes the allowed tax procedure for valuing inventories. These events affect the *prospects* of firms in different ways, and the behavior of the stock-market-measured rate of return at the time these events take place is a good way to judge the market's evaluations of future consequences of events such as these. But suppose we seek confirmation of the market's judgment? Since the market functions to equalize risk-adjusted stock returns, future observations on stock-market-measured rates of return no longer reveal the impact of past events; firms that have been adversely and beneficially affected should reveal equal market-measured rates of return for future observations. Stock prices, after all, are forward looking market *guesses* that can be wrong.

Accounting-measured profit rates, on the other hand, are intended to reveal how well a past period has gone for a firm. They are not completely free of forecasts of the future. When accountants depreciate assets, they make implicit use of a forecasted (perhaps by tax authorities) life span of the assets, and if assets are acquired from other firms, perhaps as a result of a merger, the value assigned to the transferred assets by accountants is sometimes different from their actual purchase price. But accounting procedures are fairly standardized across firms and are scrutinized by tax authorities, and their main concern is with past performance, not with guesses about future developments, however necessary some guesses may be to calculate the evidence about past performance. Much of the information underlying these data comes from past sales, committed deliveries, and market-determined prices received and paid during the past accounting period. A comparison of the pre- and postmerger accounting profit histories of a firm can help determine whether a past merger has been profitable. Of course, many other things might affect these histories, but many other things might also affect stock-market-measured profit rates.

Those seeking evidence as to whether a particular firm enjoys monopoly

little can be made by it, less will commonly be given for it. According, therefore, as the usual market rate of interest varies in any country, we may be assured that the ordinary profits of stock must vary with it, must sink as it sinks, and rise as it rises.
Smith obviously had greater faith in interest rate data than profit data.

status do not look to market-measured rates of return, as they would if seeking to evaluate the consequences of an event that is believed to have created monopoly status. If there is no such single specifiable event, as there would not be if the firm has for a long period enjoyed a dominant market position, or if such an event occurred too long ago to be recorded in available stock prices, an event study of stock prices would not be informative or possible. Firms that enjoy monopoly status should record the same stock-market-measured rate of return as do firms that face stiff competition, simply because stock prices have adjusted to any differences in the conditions that these firms may face.

There are, of course, difficulties in interpreting accounting profit data. These derive mainly from the durability of some business assets. Accounting procedures have strongly favored the valuation of assets at historical rather than replacement cost. Two firms that have purchased identical assets at different times may record different profit rates today because depreciation charges are higher for the firm that purchased assets when price levels were higher. Two firms that use different mixtures of advertising and equipment may record different profit rates simply because the intangible capital created by advertising, unlike the tangible capital created by equipment purchases, is not treated as a durable asset by accountants. These well-known problems may account for some of the profit rate differences that exist across firms. They may even explain some of the correlation between profit rates and market concentration, since firms in concentrated markets tend to rely in greater degree on advertising expenditures.

Accounting data are less suitable for some questions than for others. In attempting to gather evidence for Smith's proposition about the equalization of profit rates across investment opportunities, one would want the value of all durable assets to be measured at replacement value, not historical value, for this informs the analysis as to the profit rates available from alternative allocations of resources. But if one is interested in judging management performance, then data derived from the historical value of assets are more appropriate, since management that has been sufficiently lucky or wise to have purchased assets at deflated prices just before an inflation occurs has done a better job than management that has waited too long. Similarly, pure economic rent, although it should not be included in profit if the analysis were judging Smith's proposition, is quite properly counted as profit if judging an owner-entrepreneur's decision to enter a positive-slope supply curve market *before* demand for this market's product has grown.

There is no surprise in claiming that the question asked has much to do with the type of data collected, but the point has not received the emphasis it deserves when assessing the usefulness of accounting data. Its neglect is revealed in a frequently cited article rejecting the usefulness of accounting data for economic analysis. The subtleties involved in matching profit data to the question are important enough to take as our first substantive task the reconsideration of the attack on accounting profit rates mounted by Fisher and McGowan (1983).

The Fisher and McGowan attack on accounting data

Fisher and McGowan do not base their analysis on the usual sources of accounting data imperfection. Their claim is the much bolder one that the very nature of accounting profit data makes these data useless as a gauge of economically relevant profit. Their critique is quite general in its nature, but their narrow concern is with the relevance of accounting data for ascertaining the presence of monopoly pricing power. Empirically, one of the most intensely studied propositions in economics is the market concentration doctrine that relates market structure to monopoly power. A very large majority of the studies undertaken reveal a statistically significant positive relationship between these if accounting profit rate is used as an index of monopoly power. Explanations for this relationship other than monopoly have been given. These include not only the superior efficiency of large firms in concentrated industries, but also accounting artifact explanations relating to the accounting treatment of advertising capital. I do not discuss these here, but it is useful to note that the statistical relationship exhibited between market concentration and accounting profit rate seems to reflect more than noise in the data. The relationship is found repeatedly, at least during the period of time covered by most of these studies. Either there is something to the market concentration doctrine or there is something to plausible alternative explanations, but the accounting data seem to be telling us something systematic.

Moreover, the world does not treat such data as if they are worthless for measuring the true profit record of firms. Accounting data are produced at great cost, and a substantial part of the demand for these data comes from those who will use it analytically to guide their deployments of assets. Large sums are spent to collect and analyze these data, and even larger sums are wagered partly on what these data are believed to reveal about investment opportunities. True, much demand for accounting data derives from government reporting statistics, but no one can doubt that profit data similar to what is now being produced would be sought even in the absence of these requirements. Either users of data are foolish or Fisher and McGowan are mistaken. Their discussion clearly demonstrates that it would be pure happenstance if the accounting profit rate were to equal the economic rate of return, *even when measurement problems are set aside.* I have no quarrel with their demonstration, only with the conclusion they draw from it.

Their argument is based on the time profile of an investment's net revenue stream. This profile can, and is likely to, generate a series of annual accounting

Table 5.1. *Fisher and McGowan table – after-tax accounting rates of return*

(1)	(2)	(3)	(4)	(5) (6) Beginning-of-year assets		(7) (8) End-of-year assets	
Year	Gross profits (cash flow before tax)	Depreciation	After-tax profits	Assets	Rate of return	Assets	Rate of return
1	23.3	28.6	(5.3)	100.0	(5.3)	71.4	(7.4)
2	44.1	23.8	11.2	71.4	15.7	47.6	23.5
3	51.9	19.0	18.1	47.6	38.0	28.6	63.3
4	40.5	14.3	14.4	28.6	50.3	14.3	100.7
5	20.2	9.5	5.9	14.3	41.3	4.8	122.9
6	7.8	4.8	1.7	4.8	35.4	0	Infinite

profit rates quite different from the underlying rate of return it implies. The point can be grasped easily by utilizing one of the examples they use. Table 5.1 is adapted from their article. In constructing this table, Fisher and McGowan assume a $100 investment whose benefits begin immediately, last for six years, and take the time shape shown in column 2. Using sum-of-the-years'-digits depreciation and a profit tax rate of 45 percent, they have chosen the numbers in column 2 so that after-tax profits, shown in column 4, yield an economic rate of return equal to 15 percent (i.e., 15 percent is the percentage that, when applied to column 4's after-tax profit to calculate the present value of this profit stream, yields the initial investment of $100). The remaining columns in the table use the after-tax profit column to report annual accounting profit rates on the basis of beginning-of-the-year and end-of-the-year asset values. These accounting profit rates never equal 15 percent, nor do they average out to equal 15 percent.

By changing the time profile of gross profits (column 2), yet constraining it to yield a 15 percent economic rate of return, one can produce a wide variety of accounting profit rates that also compare poorly to the true economic rate of return. Although particular time profiles of gross profits can be constructed to make accounting profit rates look better, nothing in the nature of investment payouts makes such profiles more likely than others. Proportionate increases in investments in continuing projects are needed to bring accounting rates of return into closer accord with economic rates of return. Fisher and McGowan's demonstration, which is more general than the example they discuss, that there is no necessary correspondence between accounting profit rates and economic rates of return is convincing. Yet the conclusion they draw from it – that accounting profit rates are useless for analytical purposes – is not.

Their demonstration supposes that we know the economic life of an investment and its profit profile over time. With this knowledge we can calculate the rate of return that will have been earned once the investment project has run its course completely. They know the investment illustrated in their table lasts for six years and yields a profit profile calibrated to equal a 15 percent economic rate of return on the $100 investment. However, the annual data they use to calculate this 15 percent are the same data as would be available to accountants (absent accounting measurement problems) *after* an investment has run its full course, and accountants using these data would, if asked, report to the management that over the life of the investment it yielded 15 percent. Neither the data nor the accounting procedure causes discord between measured and economic rate of return. It is the special nature of the question that Fisher and McGowan ask of the data and their assumption of perfect foresight.

Accounting profit statements (as distinct from special analyses prepared for management) are reports on how well things have gone during the past *accounting period*. They are not reports on how well already completed investments projects have worked out, nor are they forecasts about the outcome of on-going investment projects. The answer to the question asked of accountants is not likely to yield a flow of reported profits over time that approximates an answer to the question Fisher and McGowan are able to ask of data they have produced with perfect foresight over the entire life of an investment project. However, this does not make these reports irrelevant, as the question asked of accountants is not meaningless. One wonders how Fisher and McGowan would answer it for each year from the data they have assumed.

That the numbers produced by accountants in answer to the question put to them are not the same as the numbers produced by Fisher and McGowan in answer to a different question, whose resolution requires full knowledge of the future, is not surprising. What is surprising is to have this difference interpreted as a demonstration that the information provided by accountants is useless.

Suppose we set aside the imperfection in depreciation rates (since this is not the target of Fisher and McGowan's analysis), and allow depreciation charges to correctly value the annual decline in the investment assets market value. Suppose the specific investment project described in the text table were to fail, or suppose it were to be abandoned, after one year. The economic rate of return on the project would then be reckoned by accountants as a loss of 5.3 percent plus the undepreciated value of the $100 investment, and this would be correct under the circumstances. Suppose, instead, that the project were to be allowed to run a second year. How well did it do during the second year? To answer this, we would calculate the profit after depreciation and taxes during the second year and divide this by the value of the assets at the beginning of the second year, since these assets could have been sold had we not continued the project for the second year. The answer – 15.7 percent – is precisely that which is given by the accountants when they use end-of-(first)-year depreciation. This does not inform management about the rate of return that will be earned if the project is allowed to run a full six years, nor does it inform management about the rate of return earned over the first two years of the project's life, although this could be calculated. It correctly informs management about the rate of return received as a result of allowing the project to continue for a second year rather than abandoning it. This information will not be responsive to every question that can be asked of a firm's performance, but it is not irrelevant to the sensible question that has been asserted here.

The rate of return on an investment can never be known, even in principle, until a project ends. The concept of the economic rate of return, as used by Fisher and McGowan, is therefore not very useful for determining how things are progressing in a world full of uncertainty and in which investment projects are being allowed to continue. Periodically calculated accounting profit rates of the sort depreciated by Fisher and McGowan can be useful to management if they are interpreted correctly, although the fact that they are calculated may have more to do with the reporting requirements of governments than with the management of assets. Management in search of guidance asks accountants to prepare analyses that are more appropriate to the questions management wishes to address.

The blind use of annual profit rates by antitrust authorities merits Fisher and McGowan's criticism. Recorded annual accounting profits, combined with the depreciated values of capital, will not equate to the rate of return (calculable from the same data) after a firm's investments have run their full course. However, antitrust proceedings are not likely to be held in abeyance while all on-going projects are completed (and after barring all new projects), so that assessments of a firm's performance in the investments it has already made can be calculated more accurately! For large firms with many on-going projects, comparisons of accounting profit rates – although these do not equate to economic rates of return – probably give a usable *ranking* of rates of return, and this may be useful for judging some issues relevant to antitrust.

Investors know that accounting profit rates are imperfect representations of how well firms are doing. That is why they make efforts to interpret accounting information and to correct for imperfections. Importantly, these efforts place accounting information *in context*. A new and innovative biotechnology firm is not expected to yield positive profits during its first years. The investment community expects to experience losses initially, and these will be reported in accounting statements. Positive profits are expected to follow in later years. The profit profile revealed by accounting data is useful because it can be compared to these expectations. Suppose the market expects such a firm to realize a 15 percent rate of return over the first six years of its life, but also expects severe early losses to be followed by robust profits. If early accounting profits are positive, or if losses are merely moderate rather than severe, the firm's performance can be judged highly successful and likely to yield more than 15 percent. This judgment requires information about progress to date, which is what accountants attempt to provide when not constrained by the reporting demands of the government. Accounting profit rates cannot be taken at face value, but they cannot be discarded either. They need to be adjusted for expectations, if the information they contain is to be used wisely. An antitrust investigation of a company such as our hypothetical biotech firm, if the investigation is to be sensible, must see that later profits have resulted from the bearing of early losses, and that this is the common pattern of competitive invention in the biotechnology industry.

For large, complex on-going enterprises, carrying on many projects in different stages of their expected lives, reported accounting profit rates may be taken as closer approximations of the underlying performance of a firm. Special circumstances might still exist, and these may excuse a poor recorded performance or undermine an apparently excellent one. The firm might be in cyclical lines of business or in defense industries, and the economy might be in a cyclical trough or adjusting to a surprising crumbling of organized communism across the world; the firm might have undertaken a new, very large investment project. Such known special circumstances aside, large well-established firms, as compared to entrepreneurial "upstart" firms, are likely to find their unadjusted annual accounting reports carrying more weight in the investment community.

If the usefulness of accounting profit rates cannot be judged by a standard borrowed from a world of perfect foresight, such as is Fisher and McGowan's true economic rate of return, neither can it be judged by a standard borrowed from a world in which the only thing investors know is the accounting profit rate. Whether or not accounting profit measurements are useful can be judged only by a standard appropriate to the world in which they are used, one in which more is known than the accounting numbers but one in which the future is unknown and the past only imperfectly known. This is the world for which information is produced and exchanged. If we find accounting profit data in demand over long periods of time and in a wide variety of circumstances, the premise must be that they serve useful purposes. However, other evidence of usefulness can be provided.

Evidence of the usefulness of accounting profit data

Accounting scholars have conducted several studies of the information content of accounting profit data. They judge the relevance of these data by whether they cause appropriate changes in a stock's market rate of return, as measured by changes in stock prices (and dividends). Ball and Brown (1968) offered the first systematic study of the reaction of stock prices to atypical earnings announcements. Follow-on studies have looked at different aspects of the issue (see, for example, Beaver, Clarke, and Wright, 1979; Kormendi and Lipe, 1987; and Cornell and Landsman, 1989).

This literature relies on event study methodology so popular with finance scholars. The *event* is an atypical accounting earnings report, usually judged to be atypical by the fact that it does not conform to past trends in earnings. Atypicality of earnings is relied on to judge the relevance of accounting profit data because the test of relevance in event studies is conditioned on change. Accounting profits in line with past trends are thought to be already impounded in stock price and therefore to offer no cause for change in stock price. Systematic risk aside, stocks should yield the same rates of return before and after the event if only the expected has happened. The heavy reliance on atypical earnings, I shall explain, not only is unnecessary, but it also imparts a downward bias in judging the information content of earnings reports. Nonetheless, all these studies show that stock prices respond in statistically significant ways when earnings reports are atypical, and in the direction to be predicted by assuming that accounting profit data are meaningful. Either the investment community throws away large sums on these reports or they contain information thought to be relevant.

Users of the event study approach tend to (1) neglect some methodological problems and (2) ignore the information content of typical (unsurprising) accounting profit reports. Both tendencies probably cause event studies to underestimate the information content of accounting reports. The methodological problem is to assume that expectations are gauged only by (trends from) past accounting data. A frequently used method is to make a linear extrapolation from past accounting earning reports and to measure the information content of a new accounting report by how much it deviates from this extrapolation. While not unreasonable, and certainly better than ignoring past data, this method presumes that accounting data are the sole source of information. The market could have been led by other information to expect an earnings report differing from extrapolated earnings. In this case, the actual announcement of an atypical accounting report, if it is in line with what the market has come to expect because of its other information sources, should be greeted by little change in the stock's rate of return. Belief about the pattern of reported earnings that is to be expected need not come from news releases or investment advisors; it can come from theories that investors hold. Perhaps one's expectations about the likely success of business firms are founded on Alfred Marshall's belief that firms go through a life cycle of early growth, stability, then descent. This belief might be interpreted to predict rising, stable, and falling profit rates, so that the expected time path is not linear but an inverted U. An earnings report that conforms to a linear extrapolation of past earnings might then be unexpected and likely to impact stock price.

There is no reason in principle why event studies cannot take other sources of information and states of beliefs into account, but in practice very little is done in this respect. Usually, there is an attempt to uncover something else that is going on at the same time that the event is revealed, so that the presence or absence of a stock price change may be attributed in part to this other event. This type of adjustment is laudable but hardly sufficient to deal with the complex conditions that surround and influence expectations, not only at the time of the event but before and after as well.

This suggests a much more general problem. Suppose accounting profits truly are at expected levels. The event study methodology attaches no informational value to these accounting reports, and correspondingly there should be no change in stock-market-calculated rate of return. Earnings reports that confirm expectations, however, are not without information value even if changes in stock prices do not take place. At the least, there is value in knowing that expectations are being fulfilled. But more than this is missed. Assume that accounting earnings reports contain no surprises. The issuing of these reports should produce no change in market rates of return to owning stocks, and, save for systematic risk, all stock prices should be such that they are expected to yield the same rate of return. Yet the information contained in these reports about likely earnings, cash flows, and dividends is the basis upon which the *levels* of stock prices (not rates of return to owning stocks or changes in stock price) should rest. One stock price exceeds another because expected share earnings, cash flow, and the like of this stock exceed the equivalents for the other stock. Typical (as well as atypical) earnings reports help to establish the hierarchy in share prices. Expected earnings per share can be higher for one stock than for another because one firm generates a higher cash flow or because its equity is represented by a smaller number of shares. In either or both situations, price per share of one stock should be higher than for the other stock, because expected earnings per share are higher. A correlation, across stocks, between share price and accounting earnings per share should arise from this "steady state" experiment if accounting data are meaningful, and, of course, there factually is a more than a rough correlation between stock price and earnings per share. This correlation is weakened by other expectations. Earnings per share for one stock that are twice as high as those for another stock may produce more or less than a doubling of price depending on expectations regarding the future pattern of earnings for these two stocks. Nonetheless, the correlation between share earnings and share price is strong, and deviations from strict proportionality correlate with differences in the patterns of short-term future earnings.

These facts are exhibited in Table 5.2. The table shows a matrix of rounded-off *t* statistics. These have come from least square estimates of linear regressions in which the dependent variable (shown by the vertical tab) is an end-of-year price per share of stock and the independent variables (shown by the horizontal tab) are annual share profits as measured in accounting reports over the period 1962–81. Stock prices are drawn from the CRSP tape for a sample of 489 manufacturing firms, chosen because they remain in the sample over the entire period and use the same fiscal year. By ignoring firms created during this period and firms that have disappeared through merger or exit, this sample biases the selection of firms in favor of those that are less likely to present investors with surprises. The accounting profit data come from the Compustat data base. Price and profit are adjusted for stock splits and stock dividends. The annual reporting of profit rates becomes public sometime during the first quarter of the next year; so share price for year *i* is recorded from one to three months before share profit for year *i*. However, since quarterly earnings reports during year *i* have already provided investors with some information about likely annual share profit, we may treat price and profit for year *i* as if they are observed at the same time.

Each row reports results for a single regression equation. The set of annual accounting share profit figures remains the same across rows, so that different columns report different *t* statistics because the dependent variable – end-of-year share price – differs across rows. Thus, the first row shows *t* statistics from a regression equation in which share prices for the end of 1962 are regressed on share earnings for the years 1962, 1963, ... , 1981. The second row regresses share prices recorded at the end of 1963 on the same earnings data, but in this regression 1962 earnings are lagged relative to 1963 prices. The last row regresses 1981 share prices on share earnings, all of which are lagged behind price except for 1981's share earnings. The consequence of this is that the ratio of lagged to future accounting reports increases as you go down the rows in the table. The main diagonal in this table shows the *t* statistics for same-year price and accounting data; the *t* statistics on this diagonal have been boxed. The *t* statistics for share earnings lagged one year lie on the diagonal just below the main diagonal; those for share earnings leading by one year lie on the diagonal just above the main diagonal.

A stock's share earnings in one year should approximate share earnings in adjacent years, and this suggests a multicollinearity problem in apportioning regression coefficients between adjacent years. In any case, the *t* statistics along the main diagonal clearly dominate those along any other diagonal, which is to say that differences in contemporaneous share profit across stocks explains more of the differences in the level of stock price than do lagged or leading share profit. A negative, significant *t* for main-diagonal values of *t*, indicating that share earnings are negatively correlated with stock prices, runs contrary to

Table 5.2. t statistics from regression across stocks of stock price on accounting profits per share (measured for each year from 1962 to 1981)

Stock Price year	α	62	63	64	65	66	67	68	69	70	71	72	73	74	75	76	77	78	79	80	81	R^2
62	7	7	5	1	2	2	0	1	-1	1	0	-1	0	-1	-2	1	0	-2	2	-0	1	0.46
63	2	0	13	-1	3	4	-1	-0	-1	2	2	-2	1	0	-2	0	-0	-1	2	-1	1	0.52
64	6	2	0	7	4	4	-1	2	-2	1	3	-3	1	0	-2	0	0	-1	2	-0	-0	0.51
65	8	-0	1	-3	9	3	2	3	-1	1	3	-6	0	0	-1	-0	0	-1	3	0	0	0.31
66	14	-1	1	-3	4	6	-0	5	2	1	0	-5	-1	1	-2	1	-1	-1	2	0	2	0.24
67	16	-0	0	-0	4	-0	6	-0	4	3	-1	-2	-2	1	-3	1	-0	-2	1	1	2	0.23
68	12	0	0	0	4	-1	-1	6	4	6	1	-3	-2	0	-2	0	-0	0	1	1	1	0.28
69	7	-0	-1	1	3	0	-0	2	2	4	2	-1	-2	-1	-3	1	1	-2	0	0	1	0.37
70	8	-0	-1	0	3	0	-1	2	2	7	2	-0	-2	-0	-3	2	1	-0	3	-0	1	0.29
71	10	-2	3	1	3	-1	1	-0	1	3	5	-2	-1	-1	-2	3	1	-2	3	-1	1	0.18
72	8	-1	3	1	1	1	2	0	-0	2	2	2	-1	-1	0	2	1	-3	2	-2	2	0.16
73	3	0	2	1	2	0	1	-1	-1	2	2	-1	-0	-2	0	2	2	-2	2	-1	1	0.21
74	5	0	2	1	2	0	2	1	-2	2	1	-1	-0	-2	0	5	2	-3	3	-2	1	0.28
75	3	-2	5	1	1	1	2	-1	-1	2	2	-1	-0	-3	-1	4	2	-2	2	-1	1	0.38
76	5	-1	2	1	1	-0	2	-0	-0	1	2	0	-1	-4	0	4	2	-1	2	-1	1	0.49
77	8	-1	2	1	1	-0	1	-0	-0	0	2	0	-1	-3	-0	2	2	-1	3	-1	1	0.44
78	9	-1	1	1	1	-1	1	-0	-0	1	2	-1	-1	-2	0	1	0	2	4	0	1	0.48
79	10	-1	0	1	2	-0	-0	-1	-0	1	-1	-1	-2	-2	-0	3	1	-1	4	-1	3	0.42
80	8	-1	1	1	3	1	-0	-2	1	1	-1	-2	-0	-3	-1	1	1	-1	2	1	4	0.55
81	8	-1	1	1	2	2	-2	-1	2	-2	0	-0	0	-2	-2	1	1	0	1	0	4	0.46

Year of accounting profits per share

expectations, but only one out of 20 of these t statistics is perceptibly negative.[52] Overwhelmingly, contemporaneous accounting profit per share influences stock price in the expected direction. The signing of off-diagonal coefficients is less constrained. Today's price may correlate less well, even negatively, with accounting share profit recorded, say, three years later. The recorded profit three years later may be above or below today's expectations of future profit, and it is today's expectations that influence today's stock price. And inter-temporal collinearity in accounting profits creates some ambiguity in signing. Clearly, the main-diagonal coefficients dominate in explanatory power (and these are generally quite strongly positive), but it is possible to find negative t statistics appearing in the relationship between stock prices and leading-year and lagging-year earning reports. The algebraic sum of the t statistics lying on the main (contemporary data) diagonal is 93 (and only one of the 20 coeffic-ients is negative). For the one-year lag, the algebraic sum is 8, but for the one-year lead it is 22. Thus, although contemporaneous accounting data impact stock price more than do leading or lagging accounting data, the one-year lead seems much more significant than the one-year lag. Stock price seems to exhibit some predictive power in regard to next year's earnings. These data indicate that stock prices reflect investor forecasts of performance more than past earnings performance.

Table 5.3 repeats the methodology used to construct Table 5.2, except that changes in stock prices between years are regressed on changes in share earnings between years. This helps circumvent multicollinearity problems. Also, as with event studies, this captures the impact of atypicalness in account-ing earnings. If it is assumed that expected price next year is this year's actual price,[53] the change in price becomes an index of new information, judged here by atypicalness in share earnings. Table 5.3 shows adjusted R-squares smaller than those shown in Table 5.2, but the dominance of the main diagonal t statistics remains quite significant. All the t statistics are positive on this diagonal (as compared to one that is negative in Table 5.2), and none has a value lower than 2. The algebraic sum of t statistics for contemporaneous earning changes is 151 (and is 93 if the large t statistic for 63–64 is dropped). The sum of the t statistics for one-year lagged-earnings changes is only 2, while for one-year lead-earnings changes the sum is 19. Again, these results can be explained on the basis of believing (1) that contemporaneous accounting re-ports have considerable information content for stock prices on relative share prices and (2) that the relative share prices also reflect attempts by investors to

---

52. There are several ways to explain this negative correlation. For example, it might be explained by developments that led to revisions of expectations concerning "high-flyer" and "low-flyer" stocks, such that stocks with low earnings now are expected to yield higher future earnings while stocks with high earnings now are expected to yield lower future earnings.
53. This adopts a random walk perspective of stock price movement.

Table 5.3. *t statistics from regressions across stocks of change in stock price (δS_t) on change in accounting profit per share, 1963–81*

Change in stock price year	Year of change in accounting profits per share																				R^2
	α	63	64	65	66	67	68	69	70	71	72	73	74	75	76	77	78	79	80	81	
63	-1	7	-1	2	1	-1	0	2	2	1	0	2	2	0	-0	0	1	-1	-1	-0	0.18
64	-1	-1	11	3	2	1	1	-2	-1	0	-1	-1	-1	-0	-0	-0	-0	0	0	-1	0.28
65	-4	2	0	9	4	5	2	1	-0	-0	-1	1	1	2	1	1	2	2	1	0	0.20
66	2	1	0	-0	5	2	4	1	-2	-2	1	-1	0	0	1	-0	1	1	2	1	0.12
67	2	-1	0	-2	-2	5	-1	4	2	-0	1	-1	-0	-0	1	0	-0	0	1	0	0.16
68	-4	-1	-1	-2	-1	-1	5	-1	3	0	-1	-1	-0	-1	-0	1	1	-2	-1	-1	0.12
69	-9	-1	1	0	1	-1	-1	3	3	3	1	-2	-2	-1	-1	-3	-3	-1	-1	-0	0.11
70	9	1	0	1	1	2	1	2	2	-1	0	1	1	1	2	2	1	2	-1	0	0.01
71	-0	1	-1	-2	-2	-1	-3	-1	0	-1	-1	2	-0	-0	0	0	1	2	-1	0	0,11
72	-6	-1	-1	-2	0	-1	-1	-2	0	4	3	2	-0	1	-1	-2	-2	2	-1	0	0.08
73	-6	-1	-1	-1	-2	-1	-2	-1	-1	-1	-0	2	-1	2	2	-0	-1	-0	-0	-1	0.09
74	4	0	-0	0	0	0	1	0	1	1	2	2	2	2	0	1	1	0	0	1	0.17
75	-0	2	-0	0	1	1	-0	1	1	1	0	0	0	1	0	-1	1	-0	0	-1	0.03
76	-1	-0	2	1	1	2	2	2	0	1	1	-1	0	-1	1	1	2	1	0	-0	0.05
77	-1	-0	-0	-0	-1	-0	0	1	-0	0	0	-0	0	-1	-0	1	3	0	0	0	0.11
78	-2	-1	-0	-0	-1	-0	-0	-0	-0	-1	-0	1	1	1	2	2	3	1	1	-0	0.16
79	0	-0	0	1	0	-0	-0	0	0	0	-1	1	-0	-0	1	0	-0	3	0	1	0.17
80	0	1	0	0	-1	-2	-0	0	-2	-2	0	1	-0	-0	2	2	2	1	3	1	0.18
81	-3	-0	-0	-1	0	-1	1	-0	-1	1	0	-2	-2	-2	-1	-1	-1	-1	-1	1	0.16

forecast future earnings on the basis of more information than is provided by past earnings records.

Imperfection in accounting profit data

Although accounting data are useful to investors in valuing securities, such data, as already indicated, are far from perfect. Much discretion remains in the hands of accountants and management when using the basic elements of expenditures, receipts, costs, and depreciation to construct summary measures of performance. Accounting profit can be raised or lowered somewhat within the scope of acceptable procedures. The ability to do this does not imply frequent attempts to mislead, nor, if such attempts are made, does it imply that they will be successful. Considerable amounts are spent by interested parties to ascertain whether accounting reports distort the underlying conditions of business firms. Moreover, the incentive to exaggerate profit this year is tempered by the exaggerated loss it is likely to bring forth next year. Purposeful misrepresentation of a firm's situation, however, is not the issue here. Rather, it is the inability of accountants to forecast the future perfectly. This inability impairs the information quality of accounting reports and makes their evaluation by interested parties more difficult.

Business expenditures may be divided into those expected to yield their services within the period of time encompassed by the accounting period and those expected to yield their services over longer time spans. "How did the firm do last year?" is easier and more accurately answered the more a firm's expenditures are of the first type. Without carry-over from year to year in costs or revenues, the problem highlighted by Fisher and McGowan could not exist, and a much more accurate appraisal could be made of the economic rate of return by using accounting data. Moreover, note that, in the extreme, if all expenditures were to yield their services during a year's period, the equivalent of a new firm would come into existence each year. Buried within this durability issue are implications for the theory of the firm, but discussion of these would carry the present commentary beyond its desirable boundaries.

Because much of a firm's expenditures are on assets and activities whose economic life is longer than the accounting period, no such easy reckoning is possible. Long-lived expenditures will have their costs allocated across accounting periods according to rules and judgments made to cope with government reporting requirements and with forecasting problems. Forecasts will be in error most of the time, and severely in error some of the time. Well-known measurement problems of allocating expenditures between present and future accounting periods come into play. "Identical" assets purchased at historically different prices are valued differently today. Estimated life spans of tangible assets, by which depreciation charges are calculated, are noticeably arbitrary.

Expenditures on intangible and tangible assets are treated differently even though their economic life spans can be the same; the prime example of this is the "expensing" of advertising and research expenditures, treating these as if their services are received completely within the accounting period.

The more serious are these measurement problems, the more uncertain is the information contained in accounting reports. As between two firms, the first of which spends mostly on inputs whose services are received during the same accounting period and the second of which spends heavily on the creation of tangible and intangible capital, the first firm will have the less speculative and more reliable accounting report. This conclusion can be tested.

There have been earlier attempts to correct reported earnings for the differences in treatment accorded tangible and intangible assets, but heroic assumptions and/or questionable estimation techniques have been used to judge the depreciable life of intangible assets. Much of this work estimates intangible capital depreciation rates with regression analyses that regress today's sales on lagged values of intangible capital expenditures. Estimates have conflicted significantly. Some studies estimate the life of advertising dollars to be several years, while others derive life spans that easily could fall within one or two accounting periods.[54]

The objective of these studies has been to determine whether the correlation between accounting profit rate and a firm's reliance on advertising, as measured by advertising expenditures taken in ratio to sales, is due to the accounting practice of expensing advertising expenditures rather than capitalizing them. This issue is somewhat different from that being addressed here. The accounting treatment of advertising (and research and development) expenditures may lead some firms to record higher profit rates than others, but this "fact" may be recognized by the investment market and hence not impair the information quality of accounting reports. Here, the issue is the potential for impairing information quality, not the potential for over- or understating "true" profit rates.

The method used here to judge whether information content is impaired is novel. No estimate of the life span of intangible assets is made. Instead, the analysis is based on correlations, calculated for each stock over time, between reported earnings and stock prices. These are used as indexes of the information content of accounting earnings, the theory being that higher levels of information content should cause these correlations to be stronger. Thus, lower correlations signal poorer quality information. Next, these correlations are regressed across stocks on variables (1) expected to influence the quality of accounting

---

54. The author has published one of these studies. Although it does not attempt to estimate depreciation rates, its methodology rests on strong assumptions regarding uniformity of these rates across firms. It concludes that advertising expenditures creates an upward bias in measured accounting rates of return. See Demsetz (1979).

Table 5.4. *Share price and share profit correlations regressed on measures of advertising, research and development, and capital expenditure intensities and on indexes of the time trend pattern of share profit*

Explanatory variables and R^2	$C(t, t)$	$C(t, t + 1)$	$C(t, \text{Ave}: t - 1, t, t + 1)$
Intercept	0.364	0.235	0.247
	(8.29)	(5.64)	(4.83)
Advertising/sales	−0.142	−0.536	−0.586
	(−0.48)	(−1.92)	(−1.72)
(R&D)/sales	−0.787	−1.562	−1.076
	(−1.21)	(−2.53)	(−1.43)
(Capital goods expenditures)/sales	−0.562	−0.626	−0.696
	(−2.40)	(−2.82)	(−2.56)
Absolute slope	0.539	0.876	0.649
	(1.53)	(2.68)	(1.62)
Mean square root	0.023	0.012	0.047
	(0.525)	(0.30)	(0.93)
Adjusted R^2	0.36	.124	.072

information and (2) expected to influence price-earnings ratios for reasons independent of information quality.

Table 5.4 shows the results of OLS regression estimates using three correlation coefficients, $C(t, t)$, $C(t, t + 1)$, and $C(t, \text{Ave}: t - 1, t, t + 1)$, as the dependent variables. $C(t, t)$, for each stock over time, measures the correlation between share price at time t and share earnings at time t. $C(t, t + 1)$, for each stock over time, measures the correlation between this year's share price and next year's share earnings. $C(t, \text{Ave}: t - 1, t, t + 1)$ uses as the dependent variable the average of three such correlation coefficients: between this year's share price and last year's share earnings, between this year's share price and this year's share earnings, and between this year's share price and next year's share earnings.

The explanatory variables expected to reflect the quality of accounting information are advertising expenditures, research and development expenditures, and capital goods expenditures, all measured in ratio to sales. The more important are advertising and R&D expenditures, the more important should be the intangible capital problem; the more important are capital goods expenditures, the more important should be the role of historic asset acquisition costs. Negative coefficients on these variables are to be expected if use of these inputs increases the difficulty in interpreting accounting reports.

The relationship between share price and share earnings also should be affected by anticipated time trends in share earnings, since stock prices are forward-looking indexes. A stock whose earnings per share are expected to trend upward, or alternatively downward, should exhibit a stronger correlation between today's price and tomorrow's share earnings than it does between today's price and today's share earnings, by comparison to nontrending stocks. The absolute value of the slope coefficient of the trend in share earnings is calculated for each stock and included as an explanatory variable. Since a given share-earnings-slope coefficient is more important the lower is the average level of share earnings, a last variable, the mean square root (since some earnings will be negative) of annual share earnings, is included in the set of explanatory variables.

Table 5.4 gives the results of regressing each of the three correlation coefficients on the five variables previously described. The number of observations is much lower than for Tables 5.2 and 5.3, because only firms with the complete reporting of advertising and research and development expenditures are used in Table 5.4. For all three correlation coefficients, the values of adjusted R-square are very low, so that the strength of the relationship between share price and share earnings, if it varies systematically across stocks, must depend on variables not included in the present study. However, some statistically significant coefficients are reported, especially for the $C(t, t + 1)$ and $c(t, $ Ave.$)$ regressions, and the algebraic signs of the coefficients on advertising, R&D, and capital expenditure ratios are uniformly negative. Capital expenditures/sales seems to be statistically the most surely negative in its impact on price-earnings correlations, but R&D, although statistically somewhat less surely negative, seems to have the largest average negative impact on these correlations. The greater the absolute slope of earnings time trend, the stronger is the correlation between share price at time t and share earnings at time $t+1$, and this is to be expected from stock prices that are determined in a forward-looking manner. The mean square root of earnings, however, has no impact on the price-earnings correlations.

Tables 5.2, 5.3, and 5.4, considered in total, offer evidence that accounting earnings are interpreted as meaningful by investors, that the impact of accounting information is fairly localized in time, and that the quality of this information is somewhat impaired when firms use inputs of a type that are more difficult for accountants to value. Have accounting data been unjustly maligned? Criticisms of these data based on problems of intangible capital and historic acquisition costs seem merited, but accountants face problems of forecasting the economic life and measuring replacement cost of assets that make improvements in these respects difficult. Improvements, however, are not impossible.

Management compensation and tournament theory

It is my purpose here to join the current debate about management compensation, giving special emphasis to the tournament theory explanation of high CEO compensation. Except for work on tournament compensation theory, most current studies of management compensation set aside questions about the *level* of CEO compensation. They consider instead questions about the sensitivity of CEO compensation to firm performance [Lewellen (1971); Jensen and Murphy (1990); Murdoch (1991)].[55] Their technique, consequently, has been to investigate the statistical association between *changes* in firm equity value and *changes* in CEO compensation, using the former as a measure of CEO productivity. The present study examines the *level* of CEO compensation and the *structure* of compensation within the management hierarchy, but a few words may be said about the sensitivity of CEO compensation to firm performance.

Some issues related to the sensitivity of management compensation to firm performance

The discussion to this point should have revealed just how difficult it is to measure productivity. Certainly, firm performance is an important aspect of this measurement insofar as top management productivity is concerned, but gross oversimplifying is involved in studies that take stock price measures of performance so seriously as the sole arbiter of CEO productivity. The working assumption used by the more important of these studies is that a dollar change in performance should translate to a dollar change in CEO compensation if proper incentives are to prevail. The assumption strains credulity. Interdependence between the productivities of team members, including leading shareholders and members of the board, argues against a dollar-for-dollar translation. But beyond these considerations is another. Measurement of productivity by firm performance is likely to bias the findings against a showing of performance sensitivity because of the impact of purely exogenous events on mea-

---

55. These studies find that (1) CEO compensation is not, on average, very sensitive to firm performance (Jensen and Murphy), (2) sensitivity of CEO compensation varies considerably across corporations (Murdoch), and (3) sensitivity is industry-specific but it also correlates with firm-specific risk (Murdoch).

110

sured performance. The CEO of a large oil company usually can bring about only a small change in equity value. The coming of a war can bring about a large change. It is unreasonable to expect that, as an act of rewarding performance, shareholders would want to change CEO compensation by an amount that is a large percentage of the change in the firm's equity value effected by the war. A sensible compensation plan would try to attenuate the impact on compensation of events that are exogenous to CEO decisions, even while it tries to transmit a large fraction of changes in equity value that are attributable to CEO actions. Failure to distinguish these sources of changes in equity value causes the statistical work on the sensitivity to firm performance of CEO compensation to underestimate the reaction of CEO compensation to equity value changes for which management is responsible.

Studies of the impact of performance on CEO compensation recognize this in one respect: They normalize changes in the stock prices of particular firms on changes in the value of a market portfolio. Such normalization is reasonable since the actions of CEOs of specific companies do not influence the value of the market portfolio. Variations in firm performance, as measured by variations in the price of a stock (plus variations in its dividends), therefore, should be purged of price variations associated with general movements of the stock market. However, exogenous events not reflected in stock market averages are not similarly purged by these studies. Instead they are ignored. Implementable compensation plans cannot cleanly separate causes of equity value change for purposes of rewarding or penalizing the CEO. It would be impractical, non-committal, and error-prone, for example, to use a compensation board to review nontrivial changes in stock price to determine what fraction of the change has been wrought by CEO decisions and what fraction by someone else's action or by some completely exogenous event. Consequently, the compensation plan designs a sensitivity factor into the compensation package that is smaller than it would be if it could be applied only to those performance changes attributable to CEO decisions and actions. It is this smaller sensitivity factor that is being estimated.

Compensating CEOs with stock options ties compensation to the stock market performance of their firms whether such performance results from CEO decisions or from exogenous events. Straight salary compensation eliminates the error of letting exogenous events affect compensation but commits the error of not changing compensation when performance is the result of CEO decisions. Practical compensation systems surely attempt to balance these errors, and one way of doing this is to base part of CEO compensation on straight salary and part on changes in equity value. The weight given to these two parts of the compensation plan should reflect, among other things, the degree to which a firm's market value has been, or is likely to be, susceptible to exogenous shocks and the degree to which a CEO can be expected to affect market value. Firms for which CEOs can have a large impact on equity value and that are not subject to much exogenous shock should weight stock market performance heavily in determining CEO compensation. Those with the opposite configuration, in which CEOs cannot have a large impact but exogenous events can, should weight stock market performance lightly in setting compensation. Those with a mixture of these configurations should weight performance moderately. The fraction of changes in equity values transmitted into changes in CEO compensation should vary across firms according to considerations such as these, but both high and low fractions of changes in equity are quite consistent with compensation plans that attempt to reflect productivity.[56]

The part of CEO compensation that is more or less insulated from short-term changes in stock price can be influenced by (expected) productivity even if it is not linked directly to stock price. A person's performance record is examined at the time he or she becomes the CEO. This history, considered along with the problems likely to face a firm, surely influences the size of the salary component of the compensation plan. Attention is also given to the position itself and, in particular, to the size of the firm. Size of firm offers an index of both the difficulty and the responsibility associated with performance of his tasks; so larger firms will tend to pay higher salaries. Yet there are offsetting benefits to the CEO who leads a larger firm, such as business and social prestige as well as personal satisfaction, and it is not clear just how size of firm should affect CEO compensation.

That part of the compensation plan tied to share price will bring rewards to the CEO if performance is exceptionally good and losses if it is exceptionally poor, even if performance reflects events beyond management control. The awarding of stock options, however, is a decision made anew at one-year intervals, and, if performance is excessively colored by exogenous events, the use of stock options can be reduced. This gives a short-run quality to this part of the compensation plan and makes it less mechanical than it might appear at first. The salary component also can be adjusted on a year-to-year basis, but adjustments to salary are more likely to be marginal in nature. The bulk of the salary component has a longer lasting, more stable quality to it.

The riskier the situations to which the CEO's reputation, career, and income are exposed, the higher should be the compensation received, at least if risk averseness is part of the psychological makeup of the typical CEO. It is not

---

56. These considerations can generate testable hypotheses. For example, a firm whose stock exhibits very high systematic risk, which usually is a reflection of the industry to which the firm belongs and not a reflection of CEO performance within the industry, should favor compensation plans that lightly weight the absolute level of the price of the firm's stock. This same firm should give greater weight to the price of its stock relative to that of other firms in the same industry. A firm whose stock exhibits low systematic risk and/or high firm-specific risk should give greater weight in its compensation plan to the level of the firm's stock price.

clear, however, in which of the two parts of the compensation plan the risk premium is to be found. Normally, it would be expected to be reflected in the salary component, but it also might be reflected in the component tied to short-run performance of the firm. An asymmetrical linking of this component to stock price can reflect compensation for the bearing of risk. Stock options, for example, have a floor to their value – $0 – but they have no ceiling. This asymmetry could represent the payment of a risk premium, and it could be large enough to result in a lower market-clearing salary component of compensation. The salary component, in this case, might correlate inversely with riskiness of situation even if CEOs are risk-averse, the premium for bearing risk being found in the asymmetrical tie of compensation to firm performance.

Firm size and the level of CEO compensation

The dominant statistical relationship is the positive one between size of firm and CEO compensation. This has been revealed in several studies. Justification for it in terms of CEO productivity can be given. The larger the firm, the greater is the responsibility of the CEO and the greater the probability that a very able person will be needed and, on average, will be chosen. Prospective and currently active CEOs establish their ability rating in several ways, but undoubtedly the most important of these is by successfully managing other firms. Normally, the CEO progresses up the ability reputation ladder by managing small firms, then somewhat larger firms, and then much larger firms. Presumably, the complexity of task and the importance of accomplishing the task well correlate with the size of the firm. The failure of a family-run grocery store may be quite serious for the family, but the failure of a large corporation carries with it consequences that are much more significant. Considerations such as this establish a productivity link between size of firm and compensating differentials in CEO compensation. But heading a large firm carries with it special rewards of prestige and power, and this argues against as strong a link between firm size and compensation as would exist in the absence of the prestige-power factor.

There is, however, an additional productivity explanation of the correlation between firm size and CEO compensation. High salary can be a device by which to establish and clarify the locus of authority in the firm. If the CEO and the vice-presidents receive the same wage, doubt will exist about who possesses authority. If it is thought desirable to place the power of command at the disposal of the CEO, it is also useful to have CEO compensation at a level considerably in excess of what is received by the next in command. A society in which *station* and *rank* carry little distinction is one in which larger pay differentials may be needed to establish authority. According to this reasoning, pay differentials should be (and are) less in countries such as Germany and Japan than they are in the United States, a country in which title means less.

Pay differences should also be greater in larger firms. In the large firm setting, authority is more likely to be divided and its true loci obscured by complex hierarchical structure. Pay differentials can guide one to the more important centers of control.

Thus, there are good productivity and compensating differential reasons to expect larger firms to pay higher levels of compensation to their chief officers. This relationship, however, does not necessarily imply an equally strong correlation between a CEO's salary and the performance of the firm. The on-the-job discipline is at least partly achieved by demotion, retirement, or outright separation of a poorly performing CEO from the corporation, while CEO salary remains roughly the same, as it waits for the new CEO to come aboard. Yungsan Kim, in his (1993) doctoral dissertation shows the existence of a statistically strong relationship between the probability of loss of job by the CEO and the poor quality of firm performance. Earlier studies had uncovered a relationship but not as strong as that which Kim finds. This is because the earlier studies measured performance largely by examining contemporary firm performance. Kim includes a measure of contemporary performance, but he also includes a measure of past performance, and this combination considerably strengthens the correlation between firm performance and probability that the CEO is let go. To the extent that this form of discipline is operative and useful, it is unnecessary to rely on as strong a linkage, over time, between firm performance and CEO salary to achieve an efficient degree of disciplining of CEOs.

Rosen (1982) uses a different explanation of the link between CEO compensation and firm size, one based on externalities. He argues that firm size and CEO productivity are related because there is a ripple or "multiplicative" impact of a CEO's performance throughout an organization and because the market assigns more able administrators to larger firms, presumably to capitalize on this multiplicative aspect of CEO productivity. Hence, the correlation between firm size and executive compensation is seen as an implication of the productivity theory of wages. The multiplicative impact of the CEO explains the higher salary levels received by those who command larger firms. However, Rosen does not seem to be entirely of one mind about this. His article with Lazear (Lazear and Rosen, 1981) puts forth a theory of tournament compensation that separates CEO compensation from the productivity of the CEO.

Tournament theory

In tournament theory as articulated by Lazear and Rosen, CEO compensation is a prize awarded to the person who becomes the CEO, not because this person's productivity is of value to match this prize but because the competition to win the prize brings forth more effort from all second-level management personnel. At a superficial level, the conflict can be resolved. The multiplicative aspect of CEO performance explains CEO pay differentials across firms of different sizes, while the tournament aspect of CEO compensation explains pay gaps within a firm's compensation structure. Yet CEO compensation is determined by CEO productivity in the one case and not in the other. Moreover, there is good reason to treat the difference in CEO compensations between a larger and a smaller firm as a tournament incentive to perform well when heading a smaller firm. The conflict between the multiplicative and tournament explanations of high CEO compensation aside, other difficulties with the tournament explanation merit more discussion.

Lazear and Rosen put forward a tournament explanation of management compensation for two reasons: The large amount received by the CEO of a large corporation seems to them to require an explanation that is independent of CEO productivity, and, it seems to them, the person chosen to be CEO is not significantly more productive than are other persons in the second-tier manager cohort group from which the CEO is chosen. Since the talent in the cohort group is able to perform CEO tasks about as well as the person chosen to be the CEO, any large gap between CEO and next level manager compensation should be competed away. The existence of CEO compensation high enough to create a large gap, therefore, calls for an explanation of compensation different from that offered by straightforward productivity theory. The issue is clearly stated as a motivation of their article:

> It appears as though the salary of, say, the vice-president of a particular corporation is substantially below that of the president of the same corporation. Yet presidents are often chosen from the ranks of vice-presidents. On the day that a given individual is promoted from vice-president to president, his salary may triple. It is difficult to argue that his skills have tripled in that one-day period, presenting difficulties for standard theory where supply factors should keep wages in those two occupations approximately equal. It is not a puzzle, however, when interpreted in the context of a prize. The president of a corporation is viewed as the winner of a contest in which he receives the higher prize . . . . His wage is settled on not necessarily because it reflects his current productivity as president, but rather because it induces that individual and all other individuals to perform appropriately when they are in more junior positions.[57]

This also bears on the relevance of firm size to compensation. If simple productivity theory cannot account for the large increase in compensation that accompanies promotion from a second rank to a top position, then neither can it account for the large increase in CEO compensation that accompanies promotion from a smaller to a larger firm. Presumably, the ample supply of good

---

57. Lazear and Rosen, p. 847.

substitute CEOs impacts wage differentials between larger and smaller firms as well as within firms. Hence, Rosen's "multiplicative productivity" theory of the positive associations between firm size and CEO compensation would seem to be jeopardized by Lazear and Rosen's tournament explanation of the gap between the compensation of a CEO and that of the second in command.[58]

Lazear and Rosen view rank-order compensation as a method for avoiding information cost that would be borne if compensation were to be based on measured productivity rather than on who does *best*. If information about productivity could be obtained at no cost, wage plans could be offered to second-tier management so that no further inducement to be productive, such as that which comes from the prospect of winning the CEO compensation prize, would be needed. Efficient levels of effort from second-tier management could be obtained with the CEO still paid according to his productivity. Rank-order promotion, combined with CEO compensation higher than CEO productivity, is viewed by them as more effective in achieving desired outcomes because information about productivity is difficult to obtain.

I harbor little doubt that there is a tournament prize aspect to CEO compensation, whether for reasons of avoiding opportunism or reducing information cost, but the underlying rationale and the quantitative importance of tournament-style compensation are open questions. The correct spread between the wage of the CEO and the wages of managers competing for the CEO position, assuming risk-neutral preferences, would be dictated by marginal productivity considerations *if* productivity could be measured costlessly. It is not obvious that the optimal spread becomes larger (or smaller) if information cost reduces the accuracy of productivity calculations.

The firm, in equilibrium, ultimately pays the cost of efforts and human capital investments made by competing managers (as Lazear and Rosen rec-

---

58. Malcomson's (1984) view, more recently stated than Lazear and Rosen's, offers a different explanation for tournament-style compensation. It is a method of assuring employees that there will be no reneging by employers on promised payments for services delivered. The need for such assurance arises because employees cannot know with confidence the productivity estimates on which management decides wages, and they therefore have difficulty in knowing whether an implicit agreement to increase wages on the basis of productivity improvement is being honored by the employer. Promotion of, say, a certain fraction of an employee group, such promotion being based on rank-ordering of performance rather than on absolute productivity, is seen as a way of providing an observable and enforceable wage process. Enforceability, in turn, implies the conveyance of work incentives to employees. The ability of rank-order compensation to attenuate opportunism problems is a source of enhanced productivity in the firm, but it is not productivity that is reflected in any single wage, such as that of the CEO. Rather, it presumably raises the entire wage (and dividend/earning) structure above what it would be if a different wage setting process were used. Malcomson's rationale for this type of compensation system does not immediately translate into unusually high wages for CEOs. Instead, it offers an explanation for the coupling of rank-order compensation and promotions.

ognize). Its interest is not served by encouraging excessive effort and investment by those who provide it with labor services. The amount of effort desired is that which, on the margin, adds to value of product as much as it adds to cost. Compensation for winning the CEO position should equal the value of the marginal products of the sum of efforts made by rivals seeking the post if preferences are risk-neutral and if the CEO post is merely symbolic of winning the prize compensation (rather than demanding of more effort and ability). With risk averseness, this prize should be set at a higher level; with risk preference, at a lower level. But these adjustments for risk also would be required by a marginal productivity system of compensation.

To set the prize and the junior-level management wages at their appropriate tournament levels requires one to possess knowledge of, or expectations about, productivity. To the extent that such knowledge is difficult to come by, the prize system suffers from the same problems as would a pay-for-productivity system. What is needed to justify the use of tournaments, *if* one adopts the information cost rationale, is a reason for believing that tournaments reduce the cost of acquiring information or reduce the error in setting wages. The reason set forth by Lazear and Rosen (1981) is not quite satisfying in this respect.

> The essential point follows from the theory of measurement . . . that a cardinal scale is based on an underlying ordering of objects or an ordinal scale. In that sense, an ordinal scale is "weaker" and has fewer requirements than a cardinal scale. If it is less costly to observe rank than an individual's level of output, then tournaments dominate piece rates and [output] standards. On the other hand, occupations for which output is easily observed save resources by using the piece rate or [output] standard, or some combination, and avoid the necessity of making direct comparisons with others as the tournament requires. (p. 848)

This is correct insofar as the question being answered is "Who should be promoted?" It is incorrect if the question is "What are the appropriate levels for CEO and junior management compensation?" Good productivity estimates, not rankings, are needed for the answer to the second type of inquiry, but these estimates presumably are difficult to secure if information is costly. Thus, the information cost rationale for relying on tournament compensation undermines one's ability to set the prize and junior compensation levels. It is therefore difficult to conclude on the basis of the information cost rationale that tournament theory is important to an explanation of managerial wages structure.

Suspicion about this rationale is reinforced by the natures of those situations in which we know tournament compensation to be important. The activity for which rank-order clearly is the dominant style of compensation is a tournament between rival athletes, but the cost of using measured productivity to determine compensation in sporting events is not much greater, if greater at all, than the cost required to establish rank. The cost-saving rationale fails precisely in the case in which rank-order compensation is clearly important. Determining who ranks first, who second, and who third requires a metric of performance that *is* closely linked to productivity – fewness of strokes in golf, number of sets in tennis, number of points in basketball, order of crossing the finish line, etc. If this metric were largely unrelated to productivity, it would not be deemed an acceptable metric for determining rank.[59]

This same metric just as easily can be used to compensate according to productivity. In a golf tournament, for example, it would be easy to compensate by absolute score, as in piece rate systems, with compensation proportional to fewness in number of strokes. No additional knowledge is required to substitute this absolute productivity compensation system for a winner-take-all tournament system. This is true for many competitive sports. Competing teams could be paid by number of points scored minus number of points the opponents score, rather than by who wins the game. That rank-order compensation is used for most competitive sports, even though absolute productivity would seem to be fairly easily measured, suggests that the reason for rank-order compensation is not always to be found in the supposed reduction in information cost.

Professional sports are viable because rules of play can be devised and enforced fairly easily to create contests in which outcomes are fairly independent of exogenous considerations. This makes for relative ease in measuring productivity as well as rank. Commonality of playing conditions across contestants, plus the ability to monitor and discipline infringements of playing rules, allow rank-order of finish to be a "fair" criterion by which to judge best, next best, and the remaining contestants.

Realization of "level playing field" conditions is much more costly to achieve in a contest between rival managers. This is an aspect of the difficulty in measuring management productivity, and, although it implies greater information cost, it also reduces the usefulness of tournament compensation as a method for rewarding business management. Whether the information problems inherent in the management situation favor greater reliance on tournament compensation is therefore not clear. The costly measurement of management productivity would seem to make it worthwhile to reduce this cost if one could do so by resorting to rank-order compensation, but the absence of a simple index by which to determine acceptable rank-order makes tournament compensation less effective in stimulating efficient effort levels.

When level playing field conditions can be achieved, an easily devised index of winners and losers can be chosen. The acceptability of the index, in turn, makes it easier to choose closely matched contestants. The ability to pit the best matched contestants against each other reduces the probability that there will

---

59. The professional sports contest also does not fit well the opportunism scenario set forth by Malcomson.

arise large differences in levels of performance. Avoidance of these large differences reduces the severity of one of the important problems engendered by rank-order compensation. This is the expected loss of effort from rival contestants if a gap between scores becomes so large that the chance of reversing the outcome is very small. Compensation by productivity rather than by rank encourages effort from both contestants even if there is a large gap in performance levels. It is worth noting that one important objective of sports leagues is to arrange matters so that, over time, a rough equality among the strengths of teams is achieved. Absent a rough equality among contestants, it is doubtful that rank-order compensation could long survive.

A level playing field and enforceable rules of play reduce the severity of another important problem of rank-order compensation, the encouragement this compensation system otherwise gives to sabotaging the efforts of one's rivals. Compensation according to productivity does not give rise to a similarly severe sabotage problem, since one person's compensation is more or less independent of another's. Rank-order promotion makes the performance of rivals crucial in determining one's own chances.

Rank-order compensation has advantages in the sports setting, but these are not linked to savings in information cost. Great effort by contestants seems the primary justification for relying on rank-order compensation in this setting. Productivity is measured by customer satisfaction, not by physical output, and in the realm of sports what customers want is "all-out" effort. The compensation system should be designed to bring forth this effort. If the previously specified preconditions (level playing field, enforceable rules, and well-matched contestants) can be met fairly easily, an activity can *become* a sporting event. A rank-order compensation system will bring forth high levels of effort under these conditions because even a well-performing second-place contestant loses out on the big prize. It is the enhanced compensation implication of small differences in performance that raises the joint productivity of the contestants as measured by consumer satisfaction in witnessing the sporting event. This is a different rationale for tournament compensation from that based on information cost. Compensation by productivity awards close seconds almost as much compensation as first placers, discouraging maximal effort when scores are close. The joint product of contestants determines the quality of the contest, and joint effort is very likely to be greater if rank-order, established by a plausible index of doing better rather than by absolute productivity, is used to award contestants.

The business setting, competitive as it is, simply does not have much in common with sports contests in these respects. In the competition between rival business executives (in the same firm), these preconditions are difficult to achieve. The tasks of executives are likely to differ in many respects, and the exogenous conditions that affect the performances of these tasks are difficult to take into account. Simple, acceptable indexes of rank that bear a plausible relationship to productivity are not obvious. These complications also make it difficult to assure evenly matched rival executives. Reliance on rank-order may discourage effort in this setting, since those who expect not to win receive no compensation for extra effort made to win; additionally, because rules that level the playing field are difficult to devise, rank-order compensation may encourage the sabotaging of the efforts of rivals. Hence, in a business setting a rank-order compensation system may yield smaller productivity for the team than a system relying on time on the job and other rough indices of general productivity. The balancing of these indices requires judgment, not the simple observation of score. Empirical work would seem to be needed to establish whether the tournament rationale is a powerful explainer of managerial compensation. Not much guidance is given by tournament theory for such a study. In the original formulation of tournament compensation theory, the main concern seems to have been to demonstrate that this compensation system is potentially efficient. Not much attention was given to developing testable consequences. Thus, Lazear and Rosen demonstrate that under certain conceptual conditions (i.e., competitive labor and product markets) and solution standards (i.e., Nash equilibrium) rank-order compensation can lead to an efficient allocation of productive inputs. It is shown that there exists a set of prizes, say $W(1)$ and $W(2)$, that, when offered on the basis of rank-order performance, result in efficient labor effort and/or investment in human capital. This conclusion reflects the desire of the authors to examine the efficiency potential of rank-order compensation. However, there is also a positive aspect.

If the Nash solution concept is accepted and if the error term that connects input effort to output is assumed to be normally distributed, the theory also shows that the optimal spread between $W(1)$ and $W(2)$ – that spread which yields the efficient solution – is increasing in the variance of the error term. This makes a claim for predicting the spread between prize rewards if tournament compensation is used. It does not, however, make a claim that tournament compensation becomes more effective as a substitute for productivity-based compensation as the variance of the error term increases.

An intuitive explanation may be given for the predicted spread between compensation levels. A larger spread between $W(1)$ and $W(2)$ encourages more effort and/or human capital investment on the part of workers, because the reward for outranking one's rival is greater. More worker effort and human capital investment are not always desirable from the viewpoint of employers. Competitive equilibrium requires firms to pay wages that compensate for the cost incurred to bring forth labor supply. The firm views such cost as worth incurring only if the marginal revenue product realized by the firm from additional worker output exceeds the marginal cost to workers of the additional effort and investment in human capital brought forth by the wages offered.

Prospective workers will be more reluctant to undertake labor effort and human capital investment if rank-order is determined mainly by forces different from those that reflect this effort and investment. The larger is the variance in the error term that connects their labor input to output, the greater is the chance that rank-order will be determined by just such forces. Hence, larger variance of error term discourages investment by workers. Since (in a two-employee contest) the employer pays both workers, one at high- and the other at low-reward levels, he or she is largely indifferent to the fact that rank-order is being determined in part by exogenous factors. The employer would have workers invest or exert effort as if exogenous factors were not at work. Since larger spreads between payment levels lead to more effort and investment by workers, the larger is the variance in the error term, the larger is the spread in prizes that serves the employer's interest. This makes payment to the winning worker greater than with a narrower spread, but it also makes the payment to the losing worker lower.

This conclusion is not suggested by productivity-based compensation theory. Let wages be based on estimates of productivity, but with these estimates subject to error. Now, if workers are risk-averse, the greater the variance in this error term, the less inclined workers are to exert effort and make human capital investments. This reduces average productivity and average compensation levels, but it carries no necessary implications for the spread in compensation for different ranks in the corporate hierarchy. The increased spread predicted by Lazear and Rosen for a tournament compensation system results from the incentive conveyed to lower-level workers by the presence of a larger prize, a prize that is independent of what their productivity will actually be if they win the promotion. If usable indexes of the importance of the error term in the institutionally established connection between compensation and effort can be found, tournament theory can be subjected to empirical examination.

There have been a few empirical studies (although not of this point), but they bear at best only tangentially on tournament theory. A positive relationship exists between the steepness of the compensation gradient for different levels of top management and time between promotions (Leonard, 1990). Golf performance improves with skewness in the reward schedule (Ehrenberg and Bognanno, 1990). The percentage compensation gap between adjacent rungs in the top management pay structure increases the higher up the pay structure are the adjacent rungs that are being compared (Main, O'Reilly, and Wade, 1993).[60] These findings do not reject tournament theory. They are consistent with the theory, but they are consistent with many other plausible theories. For example, disproportionality in the size of the pay gaps can be explained by

---

60. This finding is based on data similar to that used in the next section, where it finds confirmation.

disproportionality in responsibilities and in other measures of productivity. The need for further empirical work is clear.

An empirical study of management compensation

The statistical study undertaken here examines both the importance of tournament-style compensation and the factors that influence the amount CEOs are compensated. The analysis is cross-sectional, comparing across firms the averages of data calculated over the 1978–84 time period. Three data sources are used. The source that has been tapped specifically for the present study is proxy filings with the SEC. This is used to obtain compensation data for successive levels of management in the hierarchical management structure of 100 manufacturing corporations over the years 1978–84. The 1978–84 period has been chosen because it contains a number of years that fall into time periods covered by the second and third data sources. These other sources are the 1985 Demsetz-Lehn study of ownership structure and the 1991 Murdoch study of the variation across firms in the degree to which compensation changes in accordance with changes in the market performance of firms.

All firms in the SEC sample are also in the Demsetz-Lehn sample, allowing for a full 100-firm sample when data from only these two studies are used. Some firms in the SEC sample are not in the Murdoch sample, and when data from these two samples are combined, sample size is reduced; the reduction differs with the variables being examined, but its general magnitude is slightly more than 20 firms. Data definitions and sources of data are given in Table 6.1. Tables 6.2 and 6.3 give summary statistics for selected variables, with Table 6.3 devoted to compensation variables.[61]

Discussion of variables and of their roles in the analyses

The roles of these variables in the analyses of the two problems studied here will be discussed as the empirical work unfolds, but a few aspects of the variables require preliminary commentary. Two measures of CEO compensation, **s1** and **p1**, are available. **s1** is salary plus cash bonus, and it is obtained

---

61. The mean value of a5 in Table 6.2 is slightly higher than it is in the entire Demsetz and Lehn sample (27.2 for the 100 firm sample, 24.8 for the D-L 511 firms); this is due largely to the fact that the 100 firm sample used here contains no utility firms. One item in Table 6.2 merits comment: the maximum value of CEO tenure, Y. For a CEO to have 50 years as a director of a corporation is exceptional. The firm for which this value obtains is Northwestern Steel & Wire. The CEO's age was 70 at the time he is recorded to have been a director for 50 years. Northwestern Steel & Wire is a very closely held corporation that began its life 50 years prior to the recording of CEO age for this study, so the firm started when the CEO was 20 years old. If these numbers are reported correctly, and I have found no reason to doubt this, its 70-year-old CEO must have been involved in originating the firm.

Table 6.1. *Data definitions and sources*

For each firm:

s1, s2, s3, s4: Salary plus cash bonus (in thousands of dollars) averaged over 1978–84 for 100 firms, where number indicates ranking of salary with indexing CEO compensation. Data secured from SEC proxy forms for 100 firms

r12, r13, r14: Ratios, respectively equal to s1/s2, s1/s3, s1/s4.

esi, ... esj: Explained values of si, ... , sj, calculated from OLS regressions of each variable on log of firm size and five-year average stock market-measured rate of return.

dRij = si/sj − esi/esj = rij − esi/esj = unexplained deviations of actual values of **rij** from predicted values.

p1: CEO compensation (in thousands of dollars) as determined by firm's compensation plan. This broader measure of compensation includes **s1,** deferred compensation, savings on company loans, changes in discounted expected pension benefits, and income from stock options, restricted stock awards, and performance share units. (Data from Murdoch study.)

up1: Unexplained deviation of **p1** from predicted value where the predictions are derived from OLS regression estimates of the relationship between **p1** and the two variables, log of firm size and five-year average stock market measured rate of return.

sp1: Sensitivity of **p1** to firm performance as measured over time for each firm by the dollar change in **p1** per $1000 change in the market value of equity. (Data from Murdoch.)

fsize and lfs: Firm size (in thousands of dollars) and log of firm size, respectively, as measured by the value of equity plus book value of long-term debt. (Data from Demsetz-Lehn study.)

a5: Ownership concentration as measured by the percentage of shares owned by the five largest shareholders. (Data from Demsetz-Lehn study.)

ra5-da5/a5, where **da5** is the difference between actual **a5** and the predicted **a5** for the 100 firms in the present sample. Predicted **a5** is obtained from a regression relating **a5**, as dependent variable, to firm size and firm-specific risk, as independent variables, for the 406 firms contained in the nonregulated portion of the Demsetz-Lehn sample.

stdr: Standard deviation, calculated over time for each firm, of the market measure of the firm's monthly rate of return. (Data from Demsetz-Lehn study.)

stspl: = stdr x sp1: Variance in expected monthly CEO compensation as measured by **stdr x sp1.**

asr: 1978–80 average of annual returns as measured by stock price changes and dividends. (Calculated from Murdoch study.)

ydir: Number of years CEO in office. (Data from Murdoch.)

caps: Capital structure as defined by ratio of equity to **fsize.**

cr4: Four-firm concentration ratio for firm's four-digit SIC industry.

Table 6.2. *Summary statistics for selected variables*

Variable	Observations	Mean	Standard deviation	Minimum	Maximum
s1	100	492,785.3	187044.7	131978	987836
p1	79	734,889.3	561029.1	174154	3934127
fsize	100	1,741,607	2829134	37462	1.78e+07
a5	100	27.1776	17.8557	6.9	86.88
da5	100	−.3427169	.7064401	−2.482898	.728879
stsp1	100	.08286	.0211503	.04	.143
sp1	82	22.50281	26.42658	−15.09	96.48
asr	81	.1787531	.1114931	−.137	.470
ydir	78	14.24872	7.990103	4	50
caps	100	.7746241	.1652864	.1654019	1

from the SEC sample. Values of salary plus cash bonus are also available for lower levels of the management hierarchy; these are designated **s2**, **s3**, and **s4**, where the number indicates the number of steps down the compensation ladder. **p1** comes from Murdoch's data, and it is a broader measure of CEO compensation. It includes **s1** plus calculated values of stock options, restricted grants of shares, and firm loans to the CEO. This broader measure is not available for lower levels of the management hierarchy. The study of salary *structure* is possible here only when compensation is measured in the narrower fashion defined by **s**.

Normally, one would think that the more inclusive measure of compensation, **p1**, is the better tool by which to reveal forces operating on CEO compensation. Sometimes it is better, but not always. **p1** is affected by the vagaries of the stock market, and different values of **p1**, during some time intervals, may reflect the stock market more than company compensation intentions. Suppose we are interested in how firm size impacts CEO compensation. Assume that large firms rely *less* on performance-related compensation. Then, during a period when the stock market has risen, the correlation between **p1** and firm size will tend to be negative. The CEOs of small firms will experience high compensation because the stock market has risen and a larger fraction of their compensation, by assumption, derives from stock holdings and options. During a period when the market has fallen, the correlation between firm size and CEO compensation will tend to be positive. If, on the other hand, large firms rely less than do small firms on performance-related compensation, these correlations will tend to be of signs opposite to those just described. If we are to ascertain how firm size affects CEO compensation generally, and if we rely on **p1** to measure compensation, it is necessary to select periods of time that give appropriate representation to "bull" and "bear" stock market episodes. **s1** is

Table 6.3. *Summary statistics: Compensation structure*

Variable	Observations	Mean	Standard deviation	Minimum	Maximum
p1	79	734,889	561,029	174,154	3,934,127
s1	100	492,785	187,044	131,978	987,836
s2	100	357,202	136,220	92,551	700,280
s3	100	271,855	104,825	92,551	513,017
s4	100	239,004	94,680	82,486	476,065
s5	100	211,637	86,967	78,511	430,655
r12	100	1.405	.262	.884	2.341
r23	100	1.328	.213	1	2.172
r34	100	1.144	.107	1	1.609
r45	100	1.139	.095	1	1.455
		Summary statistics: Compensation structure if *s1 > s2*			
p1	77	744,745	564,930	174,154	3,934,127
s1	97	495,331	188,667	131,978	987,836
s2	97	354,858	136,718	92,551	700,280
s3	97	270,540	105,713	92,551	513,017
s4	97	238,829	95,751	82,486	476,065
s5	97	212,194	88,032	78,511	430,655
r12	97	1.419	.253	1.014	2.341
r23	97	1.327	.215	1	2.172
r34	97	1.139	.097	1	1.464
r45	97	1.135	.093	1	1.455

more likely to exhibit a consistent positive correlation to firm size, because its value is less dependent on stock market values. Because s1 is the less mercurial and speculative component of compensation it is sometimes better suited to revealing compensation principles.

Variables s1, s2, . . . are used to construct compensation ratios, designated by rij. These measure compensation relatives between hierarchical levels of management. For example, r12 = s1/s2, r13 = s1/s3. Approximate average differences between s1 and s2, between s2 and s3, and between s3 and s4 are, respectively, 40 percent, 30 percent, and 14 percent. Promotion from higher rank brings with it a larger increment to compensation.

Variables a5 and ra5 are two measures of the degree to which a firm's ownership structure is concentrated. a5 is the fraction of shares owned by the five largest shareholders of a corporation's stock. The Demsetz-Lehn study shows that a5 is dependent on firm size and firm-specific risk. ra5 has been constructed with this in mind. The construction is based on predictions of a5 generated from OLS regression of a5 on firm size and firm-specific risk, the regression being calculated from the much larger sample of *manufacturing* firms used in the Demsetz-Lehn study. For each of the 100 firms in the present sample, **ra5** is the ratio formed by dividing the difference between actual **a5** and predicted **a5** by actual **a5**. It is thus the forecasting error for **a5** scaled by **a5**, and it measures the degree to which ownership concentration is excessive relative to expectations based on firm size and firm-specific risk. **ra5** turns out to be somewhat more significant than **a5**, and consistently so, in its relationship to compensation. It is the ownership structure variable relied upon here to indicate the degree to which owners are able to protect themselves in their agency relationship with professional management.

An unpredictedly high value of **a5** (a high value of **ra5**) may be taken to indicate a situation in which concentrated ownership is especially productive as a mechanism for monitoring management; this is one reason shareholders are willing to take a more concentrated ownership position (for given values of other determinants of ownership concentration) even though this increases the firm-specific risk to which they are exposed. An atypically low **a5** may indicate situations in which concentrated ownership is a poor monitoring mechanism. With **ra5** interpreted as measuring the efficiency of ownership concentration in performing the monitoring function, there should be a negative relationship between **ra5** and CEO compensation if management entrenchment is an important source of high CEO compensation. More effective monitoring by owners should lead to better control over CEO compensation, and a significant negative coefficient on **ra5** may be taken to indicate the existence of a management entrenchment problem.[62]

For **ra5** to be a measure of the effectiveness of ownership concentration as a tool for monitoring and disciplining management, it follows that **ra5** should be correlated with the availability of information about management productivity. Tournament theory rationalizes a large spread between CEO compensation and junior management compensation as necessary to encourage effort because information about productivity is lacking. Hence, viewed from the perspective of the information-cost rationale for tournament compensation, **ra5** should correlate negatively with measures of the compensation gap between CEO and junior compensation levels. Thus, **ra5** provides a tool by which to assess the importance to compensation of both information-based tournament theory and management entrenchment.

Firm size, **fsize**, offers a reasonable index of management productivity. Merge two firms and ask whether the CEO of the new firm has a more difficult

---

62. This rationale implicitly assumes that the determination of ownership structure in the Demsetz-Lehn study is modeled incompletely, and that firm characteristics omitted from their model impinge on the degree of ownership concentration and possibly on the effectiveness of owner monitoring of management.

and important task than the CEOs of either of the two smaller premerger firms. Larger firms are more difficult to manage, and those selected to manage them are more likely to have established a proven record of superior management capability. The underlying relationship between CEO compensation and **fsize** is nonlinear, however, and the regression equations to be presented use the log of firm size, **lfs**. This substitution improves the explanatory power of the regression equations.

Profit is measured by **asr**, the five-year average of monthly market-measured returns to shareholders. This variable offers a second index of management productivity. Other compensation studies rely heavily on measures like **asr** to gauge CEO performance.

Ydir reports the number of years a CEO has been in office. Theory does not inform us as to the likely impact of CEO tenure on hierarchical compensation structure, and this variable is included mainly to discover this relationship empirically and to control for its impact. Since **ydir** may correlate with successful performance and/or management entrenchment, its inclusion is not simply for purposes of discovery.

sp1 is the sensitivity of broadly defined CEO compensation to changes in the firm's market rate of return. **stdr** is the standard deviation of a firm's market rate of return measured over time. The product of **sp1** and **stdr**, designated here as **stsp1**, tells us by how much the monthly value of CEO compensation may be expected to vary over time. **stsp1**, then, is a measure of the riskiness inherent in the CEO's compensation stream and, as such, allows us to assess the importance of risk to the level of CEO compensation. This variable also may be interpreted as proxying for the variance in the error term that links management effort to compensation, since the market price of a firm's shares may change from month to month for reasons that are quite independent of management effort; in this respect, it offers, as does ownership concentration, a method of assessing the importance of information-based tournament theory as an explanation of wage differences. It could be the case, however, that the expected monthly variability in the value of management compensation is not a good index of the longer term (and possibly more important) error-prone looseness in the connection between management effort and compensation. Yet, if long-term expected variability in management compensation is measured and used instead of **stsp1**, there is danger that errors in measuring effort will be confused with true differences in management productivity. For example, changes in market rates of return, measured from one decade to another, are much more likely to reflect changes in the basic business affairs of a firm than they are to reflect the error component in compensation. Changes measured over shorter time periods, such as from month to month, are less likely to reflect basic changes and are more likely to reflect the error component in compensation plans. Not knowing the best way to define the relevant length of the period by which to measure the error component makes **stsp1** somewhat more ambiguous than diffuseness of ownership as a measure of the degree to which error in measuring productivity may be present.

The capital structure variable, **caps**, is constructed to correlate positively with the importance of equity in the firm's financial structure. It is used to assess the relevance of free cash flow to CEO compensation levels. The free cash flow theory alleges that interest payments on debt constrain the behavior of management by reducing the degree to which management can pursue its own ends at the expense of shareholders. CEO compensation is an obvious "own end," and, to the extent that there is validity in the free cash flow theory, **caps** should correlate positively with CEO compensation (since **caps** is larger if the ratio of equity to total assets is larger).

subs is a dummy variable that takes the value 1 if the manager whose compensation is being measured is in charge of a firm's subsidiary. The CEO is assumed to be in charge of the firm, so **subs** runs from **subs2** to **subs4**, where the number tagged to the end of **subs** indicates the place of the manager in the firm's hierarchical compensation structure. Thus, if the fourth manager down the hierarchical ladder manages a subsidiary, the value of **subs4** is set equal to 1 (and 0 otherwise). **subs** is used to indicate the ease with which the productivity of lower-level management can be measured. If lower-level managers manage separately reporting subsidiaries, their productivity should be easier to measure than if their activities are buried in a hierarchical structure, whose productivity cannot so easily be partitioned. Tournament compensation should be less important if performance of the second level of management is easier to measure. However, because a manager who heads a subsidiary may possess greater capability than a manager who doesn't bear such an identifiable responsibility, an inverse relationship could also arise for reasons of relative productivities; the gap between CEO compensation and the compensation of a second-level manager who heads a subsidiary should be smaller, for either reason.

Tournament theory is deficient for present purposes in its lack of discussion of the attributes of firms that make them more likely to rely on tournament-style compensation. Had these attributes been specified, it would have been possible to see whether they correlate with structural differences in compensation levels. The absence of this discussion has made it necessary to adopt the compensation relatives between different levels of management as indexes of degree of reliance on tournament compensation. As between two firms that exhibit different pay relatives, that with the larger pay relative is deemed more likely to rely on tournament-style compensation. Pay relatives surely are very imperfect indexes. The larger pay relative may reflect a greater difference between the productivities of higher and lower levels of management rather than greater reliance on tournament compensation. Still, the central refrain in Lazear and

Rosen is that high CEO compensation is adopted by firms in order to create a larger compensation gap than would be dictated by the ability of the CEO. This provides incentives to motivate junior executives to compete more intensely for higher office than they would if CEO pay were set by CEO productivity. Since Lazear and Rosen assert that there is no significant difference between the abilities of the person chosen to be the CEO and the abilities of losing rivals, larger pay relatives cannot be attributed to greater differences in productivities. Given this assertion, pay differences would be trivially small if they were determined by ability differences. Acceptance of this assertion makes the size of compensation relative a good index of reliance on tournament-style compensation.

There are thus joint hypotheses at work in the Lazear and Rosen discussion of tournament theory. One is the presumption that ability differentials between levels of management are small. The other is that larger pay differentials than would be called for on the basis of ability differentials are needed to achieve desired effort levels at junior levels of management. The size of the compensation gap may be taken as an index of the importance of tournament compensation for a firm if the theory being tested is based on an acceptance of the belief that there are no large capability differences between the CEO and managers next in line. In this case, compensation ratios r_{ij} become a useful index of the importance of tournament compensation to the compensation plans of corporations. However, since r_{ij} has s_1 as one of its components, a measured correlation between r_{1j} and s_1 could simply reflect errors in measuring compensation.

Unwillingness to accept the claim that there are no significant differences in capabilities between winner and losers imposes a requirement to take productivity differences into account when explaining compensation relatives. An attempt is made to do this by estimating coefficients of **lfs** and **asr** in an OLS regression that examines the variation in executive compensation across firms. **lfs** and **asr** are taken as useful indexes of management productivity; so the estimated regression equation yields predictions of compensation based on productivity. The regression is run separately for the two top levels of compensation, s_1 and s_2. These coefficients are used to calculate compensation levels as predicted by these productivity indexes. For different levels of management, call these predicted values $es_1, es_2, \ldots$, and form the ratios es_1/es_2, $\ldots$, es_i/es_j; these are the compensation relatives to be expected on the basis of productivity differences. Subtract these from the actual compensation relatives to measure the portion of the actual compensation relative not explained by productivity differences, labeling the difference **dR$_{ij}$**. **dR$_{ij}$** is zero if the two compensation relatives are equal, positive if actual compensation relatives exceed the predicted relatives, and negative if actual compensation relatives are less than the predicted relatives. **dR$_{ij}$** is used as a "productivity-adjusted" substitute for **r_{ij}**. A by-product of substituting **dR$_{ij}$** for **r_{ij}** is a reduction in the seriousness of an errors-in-variables problem. Where a correlation between **rij** and **si** might be attributed to errors in measurement, it is unlikely that a correlation between **dRij** and **si** can be explained as easily in this way.

dRij may be interpreted as that part of the gap between hierarchical levels of compensation that is unexplained by productivity differences, so that tournament theory is supported if **dRij** is related appropriately to variables chosen as indicators of which firms are expected to rely in greater degree on tournament compensation. Three variables serve in this capacity: ownership concentration, junior management of a subsidiary, and a proxy for variance of the error component that links management effort to management compensation. These have already been discussed and identified as **ra5, subs**, and **stsp1**. Tournament theory is supported if **dRij** relates negatively to **ra5** and **subs** and positively to **stsp1**.

cr4 is the four-firm concentration ratio applicable to the four-digit SIC industry in which a firm is located. It is used to reflect the structure of the market that best defines substitutable employment opportunities for managerial personnel. Does the labor market offer managers fewer good substitute positions if the product market is dominated by a few large employers? This variable relates mainly to compensation levels rather than to the gap between CEO and junior-management compensation levels, since lack of easily substitutable opportunities should affect management compensation generally.[63]

Testing tournament theory

Tables 6.4A and 6.4B present evidence pertaining to the importance of tournament theory to compensation structure. Table 6.4A uses simple pay relatives, **rij**, as dependent variables, whereas Table 6.4B relies on productivity-adjusted substitutes, **dRij**. These measures of compensation relatives are presumed to correlate with the importance of tournament compensation across the firms studied.

The sets of explanatory variables in Table 6.4A vary in only three respects: different measures of ownership concentration are exhibited, **s1** and **p1** are used as alternative measures of CEO compensation, and three different levels of junior management are examined. The different levels of junior management give rise, respectively, to dependent variables **r12, r13**, and **r14**, and, respectively, to subsidiary dummy variables **subs2, subs3**, and **subs4**. Table 6.4A fails to give strong support for believing that tournament theory presents an important explanation of either wage structure or of the level of CEO compensation. If tournament theory is important, we would expect to observe a

---

63. In regression equations not exhibited here, in which **cr4** is an included variable, no relationship can be demonstrated to exist between salary differentials and **cr4**.

Table 6.4A. *Compensation relatives regressed across firms on CEO compensation, ownership concentration, riskiness of compensation, CEO tenure, and junior management of subsidiary*

	(1) r12	(2) r12	(3) r12	(4) r12	(5) r13	(6) r13	(7) r14
s1	8.5E-08 (0.43)	6.5E-08 (0.33)	1.4E-07 (0.74)		4.2E-07 (1.76)		
p1				5.9E-08 (0.83)		3.0E-08 (0.41)	5.7E-08 (0.68)
a5	.0011 (0.54)						
ra5		−.0260 (−0.54)	−.0365 (−0.77)	−.0128 (−0.26)	−.0776 (−1.33)	−.0762 (−1.25)	−.0498 (−0.72)
stsp1	−.0005 (−0.04)	.0002 (0.01)	−.0034 (−0.26)	.0007 (0.05)	.0210 (1.33)	.0142 (0.87)	.0256 (1.39)
ydir	−.0104 (−2.50)	−.0098 (−2.35)		−.0096 (−2.34)	−.0121 (−2.42)	−.0133 (−2.58)	−.0139 (−2.40)
subs2	−.0952 (−1.03)	−.0817 (−0.89)	−.0515 (−0.56)	−.0783 (−0.86)			
subs3					−.0268 (−0.72)	−.0451 (−0.49)	
subs4							.0183 (0.18)
cons	1.5260 (10.68)	1.5402 (11.21)	1.3576 (12.09)	1.5368 (17.23)	1.7949 (11.21)	1.9984 (18.35)	2.2048 (17.88)
adj. R^2	.04	.04	−.02	.04	.11	.06	.04
N	78	78	82	75	78	75	75

significant positive relationship between compensation relatives and the compensation received by the CEO, but only one regression equation in Table 6.4A, number (5), comes close to establishing such a relationship. This support is only apparent, however. A similar positive correlation is lacking when the broader measure of CEO compensation is used. Regression (6), which substitutes **p1** for **s1**, shows this. The plausible explanation for the different results obtained for the two measures of CEO compensation is that higher levels of more narrowly defined CEO compensation, **s1**, correlate with lower levels of profit-based components of CEO compensation. A CEO who obtains a large component of profit-based compensation also receives a smaller basic salary. This reduction in narrowly defined CEO salary will not apply to lower levels of management if the profit-based component is significantly less important at these lower levels; on average, this surely is the case. Because of this, the gap as measured by **r13** must decrease as the importance of profit-based components of CEO compensation increase, and this phenomenon is what accounts for the greater explanatory power exhibited by regression (5). In fact, **s1** and **sp1** (the latter measuring the sensitivity of broadly based CEO compensation to performance of the firm) exhibit a strong negative correlation of −.37. Allowing the profit-based component into our measure of CEO compensation avoids the implied measurement error, and we see that the substitution of **p1** for **s1**, eliminates the correlation between CEO compensation and salary differences.[64]

That this is not true with respect to **s2** suggests that profit-based compensation like that received by the CEO is more likely to extend to the second in command than to the third and fourth in command. Hence, when **r12** is the dependent variable, as it is in regression (1), no relationship to **s1** appears.[65]

The most believable interpretation of these coefficients is that they provide no support for the tournament theory. They exhibit only little explanatory power. This interpretation is supported in Table 6.4A by the absence of the predicted (1) positive relationship between compensation relatives and our index of the variance of error term in measuring productivity, **stsp1**, (2) negative relationships between compensation relatives, and (a) measures of ownership concentration and (b) **subs2**, **subs3**, and **subs4**.[66]

The remaining variable, CEO tenure (**ydir**), is uniformly more significant than other variables in its relationship to salary differentials. The negativeness of the coefficient of **ydir** suggests that junior-management compensation rises toward CEO compensation the longer the CEO has been in office. This could be because junior management functions in a more responsible way as the CEO moves closer to retirement. It could be that tenure in office of the CEO is

64. Had an equation regressing **r14** on **s1** been included in Table 6.4A, it would have shown a relationship to regression equation (7) similar to that shown between (5) and (6) for **r13**. In fact, the coefficient relating **r14** and **s1** is stronger than that which relates **r13** and **s1**, indicating that incentive-based compensation becomes weaker farther down the hierarchy. That the correlation between **r14** and **s1** fails to be confirmed in regression (7) of Table 6.4A, which uses more broadly based CEO compensation, **p1**, supports the interpretation given above for the difference between regression equations (5) and (6).

65. The simple correlations between **r12** and **s1** and **p1** for the firms reflected in these regressions are both equal to .12. Since higher values of **r12** definitionally must reflect higher values of CEO compensation and/or lower values of the second level of compensation, a .12 correlation is unimpressive.

66. Strangely, the gap between compensation of the CEO and the third highest-paid officer, as shown in the right half of Table 6.4A, is narrowed more significantly when the *second* officer heads a subsidiary than is the gap between compensation of the CEO and of the second highest-paid officer, as shown in the left half of Table 6.4A. The same phenomenon exists with respect to the gap between compensation of the CEO and of the fourth highest-paid officer; this gap is also narrowed more significantly when the *second* officer heads a subsidiary.

Table 6.4B. *Differences between actual and predicted values of compensa-tion ratios,* **dRij**, *regressed on compensation level,* **s1**, *ownership concentra-tion,* **a5** *and* **ra5**, *riskiness of compensation,* **stsp1**, *CEO tenure,* **ydir**, *junior management of subsidiary* **sub**

	dR12	dR12	dR12	dR12	r12
s1	1.17E-07 (.62)		1.39E-07 (.74)	1.14E-07 (.57)	6.49E-08 (.33)
es1		−7.30E-08 (−.29)			
a5			.0010 (.54)		
ra5	−.02611 (−.54)	−.0309 (−.65)		−.0261 (−.54)	−.0260 (−.54)
ydir	−.0096 (−2.33)	−.0103 (−2.59)	−.0103 (−2.48)	−.0096 (−2.28)	−.0098 (−2.35)
sub2	−.0779 (−.85)	−.0928 (−1.01)	−.0913 (−.98)	−.0780 (−.84)	−.0817 (−.89)
stsp1				−.0007 (−.85)	.0002 (.01)
cons	.1156 (.90)	.2181 (1.51)	.0995 (.73)	.1181 (.85)	1.5402 (11.21)
adj. R²	.06	.06	.06	.05	.04
N	77	77	77	77	78

correlated with tenure in office of his managers next in command, but that the time profile of the compensation of the latter increases more steeply than it does for the CEO. The negative coefficient is inconsistent with an important impact of CEO entrenchment on CEO compensation, since entrenchment of the CEO as measured by years served as director should widen the gap between CEO compensation and junior-management compensation unless junior manage-ment benefits disproportionately from entrenchment. More plausibly, the great-er the number of years CEOs retain office, the lower becomes their productivity relative to junior management.[67]

Table 6.4B substitutes **dRij** for **rij** and compares **s1** and predicted **s1, es1,**

---

67. The tables presenting the results of regression analyses do not include a variable for the age of the CEO, although I have calculated regressions using an age variable. The age variable coefficient is indistinguishable from zero, and including age alters no substantive result obtained without the age variable. The one change wrought by including CEO age is that the coefficient of **ydir** is somewhat more significant. The signs, significance, and general mag-nitude of other coefficients are not substantially altered.

as explanatory variables. Adjusting for that part of compensation relatives that may be attributed to management productivity differences across firms adds no confirming power in our search for evidence of the importance of tournament theory. Essentially, Tables 6.4A and 6.4B tell the same story. Perhaps sample size is too small to uncover evidence for the importance of tournament compensation. But, as we shall see, sample size is not too small to allow just two variables – firm size and market measured rate of return – to explain a large fraction of the variation in CEO compensation across firms.

Sources of variation in CEO compensation

In Table 6.5A, regression equations (1) and (2) use the narrowly defined CEO compensation, **s1**, as dependent variable; equations (3) and (4) use **p1**, the broader definition of CEO compensation. Equation (1) differs from equation (2), and equation (3) differs from equation (4), only by the choice of variable to represent the strength of management entrenchment. Equations (1) and (3) use **a5**; equations (2) and (4) use **ra5**. **a5** and **ra5** should correlate negatively with CEO compensation if management entrenchment explains a significant part of the variation in CEO compensation, but these regressions do not confirm a strong presence of management entrenchment. Support for the management entrenchment hypothesis is also lacking with respect to **caps**, the capital structure variable, whose coefficients also turn out to be insignificantly different from zero.

Since **cr4** may be taken to correlate inversely with the number of employment opportunities requiring tasks closely related to the CEO's present employment task, we might expect it to be associated with a negative coefficient; the fewer alternative employment opportunities, the smaller CEOs' compensation needs to be to obtain their services. However, it is also true that the greater is **cr4**, the fewer the number of substitute CEOs to which a firm can turn for experienced personnel to replace its present CEO; so the net effect on compensation from variations in **cr4** is unclear. Moreover, CEOs' capabilities may not be very specific to a firm or industry, in which case the market for CEOs' talents may extend well beyond the industry that currently employs them. Whatever the reason, the facts suggest that **cr4** does not correlate with monopsony power in the CEO labor market.

The tournament theory variables, **r12**, **r13**, and **r14**, as in Tables 6.4A and 6.4B, also show no statistical linkage to CEO compensation. That **r14** positively relates to CEO compensation in equations (1) and (2) but not in (3) and (4) is explained, as in Table 6.4A, by the negative correlation between **s1** and **sp1**.

The only regressors that significantly explain the variation in CEO compensation are **lfs** and **asr**, the variables that plausibly serve as indexes of CEO productivity. As between these two variables, the more important is the log of

Table 6.5A. *Management compensation regressed on ownership concentration, log of firm size, mean annual stock (market) rate of return, CEO tenure, market concentration, and ratios of CEO compensation to junior management compensation*

	(1) s1	(2) s1	(3) p1	(4) p1
a5	−191.88		−1039	
	(−0.25)		(−0.31)	
ra5		−15157		−78853
		(−0.82)		(−0.97)
lfs	115041	115021	298886	299157
	(10.33)	(10.44)	(6.00)	(6.08)
asr	232363	220284	1380773	1317321
	(2.04)	(1.95)	(2.77)	(2.68)
ydir	−2565	−2469	3382	3822
	(−1.54)	(−1.50)	(.047)	(0.53)
caps	4211	−107	−155585	−180246
	(0.05)	(−0.00)	(−0.42)	(−0.49)
cr4	−854	−857	−1592	−1575
	(−1.37)	(−1.38)	(−0.58)	(−0.58)
r12	−49673	−51608	330830	321354
	(−0.84)	(−0.88)	(1.27)	(1.25)
r13	25670	22053	−262078	−275766
	(0.32)	(0.28)	(−0.73)	(−0.80)
r14	135963	136898	224384	226983
	(2.04)	(2.09)	(0.75)	(0.78)
cons	−1312931	−1311498	−3851097	−3853806
	(−7.14)	(−7.32)	(−4.77)	(−4.91)
adj. R^2	.65	.65	.37	.38
N	76	76	73	73

firm size. The much greater explanatory power of equations (1) and (2), as compared to equations (3) and (4), is attributable to the fact that smaller firms rely much more heavily than larger firms on performance-based compensation. The correlation between **lfs** and **sp1** is −.43. Since performance is much less stable or predictable than is size, the correlation (which is .58) between **p1** and **lfs** will be weaker because of its larger performance-related component than is the correlation (which is .73) between **s1** and **lfs**.

Table 6.5B uses this information to focus attention on **lfs** and **asr**. This allows the full 100-firm sample to be used when the dependent variable is narrowly based management compensation (**s1**, **s2**, **s3**, and **s4**), because none

Table 6.5B. *Management compensation across firms regressed on log of firm size and average of five years of stock return*

	(1) s1	(2) s2	(3) p3	(4) p4	(5) p1
lfs	107225	78226	66584	60899	282620
	(9.61)	(9.22)	(11.61)	(11.90)	(6.85)
asr	291983	231242	101363	96078	1269670
	(2.46)	(2.57)	(1.67)	(1.77)	(2.94)
cons	-1026429	-758156	-661633	-613299	-3323822
	(-6.71)	(-6.53)	(-8.42)	(-8.75)	(-5.90)
adj. R^2	.55	.53	.63	.64	.42
N	100	100	100	100	78

of these variables come from the Murdoch study. Considerable explanatory power is derived from just these two variables. [Regression equation (5), which uses **p1** to measure CEO compensation, is presented so that comparisons can be made with the regression equations that use **s1**.]

Table 6.5B reveals that firm size contributes more to explanations of the variation in compensation, and average stock return contributes less, the more junior is the level of management being considered, but that the forces at work to explain compensation of the second level of management are much like those that explain CEO compensation. Regression (5), which uses broadly based compensation as the dependent variable, exhibits a much lower R^2 than does equation (1), which uses narrowly based compensation. This is not surprising, since performance-based elements of compensation are less surely linked to firm size than is narrowly based salary plus cash bonus.

In broad generalization, the statistical work already reported supports the following conclusions: (1) The greater is the reliance placed on performance in the CEO's compensation package, the lower the straight salary component tends to be (i.e., **s1** is inversely related to **sp1**); (2) the **relative** influence of performance (measured by **asr**) as compared to firm size is stronger for higher levels of management than it is for lower levels. While silent about specific cases, the preceding analysis, considered in broad terms, gives no reason to claim productivity theory is irrelevant to management compensation, although firm size, the most significant explainer of variations in management compensation, might reflect a more or less "mechanical" rule of thumb (i.e., a rule with no apparent rationale) as well as it reflects the importance of management productivity. No support is found for tournament theory as a specific alternative to CEO productivity in explaining variations in CEO compensation.

The intensity and dimensionality of competition

Economists are so familiar with the perfect competition model that they tend to confuse this with competition more broadly conceived, but our understanding of competition is seriously deficient once we leave the safe harbors of the perfect competition, monopoly, and Cournot oligopoly models. The main task of this commentary is to convince the reader of this. A subsidiary task is to give a summary evaluation of the antitrust experiment in the United States.

The problem of competitive intensity

Intuition clings to a notion of competing that is something like "effort expended to best the performance of others." *Performance* might refer to prices, qualities, technical progress, or any of an infinitely long list of activities in which persons engage. As we shall see in the next section, this variety of competitive activities is a source of much difficulty both for the theory of competition and for public policy toward competition, but we may begin our discussion by focusing more narrowly on price competition.

Is there price competition? Are prices set competitively? These are the questions most frequently asked in regard to the competitiveness of markets. This emphasis on price competition clearly owes its origin to our interest in the price system as an allocator of resources and to the formalization of this system through the perfect competition model. However, perfect competition, the central model of neoclassical economics, does not really involve competitive pricing activity. The equilibrium market clearing price that emerges from the perfect competition model may be termed a competitive price, but it results from mysterious market clearing forces and not the competitive pricing activities of firms. Each firm takes the price given to it by the market, and no firm competes with others by offering a lower price. Instead, firms compete by offering *output*, especially by offering output through entry. The firm competes by entering a market and adding its output to that of incumbents, but all firms in a given market produce the same good and sell it at the same unit price. Equilibrium obtains if neither insiders nor outsiders have an interest in changing the quantity they supply to the market. Competition in the perfect competition model is nothing more or less than the undertaking of profitable imitative output responses to given market prices, and it is best described just so – as *imitative output competition*. Competitive pricing, on the other hand, requires firms that have some control over the price of their goods; this implies, of all things, firm demand functions that are negatively sloped or firm output capacities so large that one firm can increase output enough to have a significant effect on market price. The quasimonopolist, the producer of a differentiated product, the oligopolist might entertain the notion of lowering price relative to rivals, but not the perfectly competitive firm.

The criterion by which to judge the intensity of imitative output competition is clear from neoclassical theory. Competitive intensity is at a maximum if firms produce identical outputs within a market structure so decentralized that no single firm can influence market supply. This criterion, which permeates the discussion of competition, has given rise to the market concentration doctrine. Increase the number of competitors doing the same thing and you increase the intensity of competition. The notion that this is the appropriate criterion by which to judge competitive intensity finds support from the standard model of monopoly, the logic of which is dependent on there being only one firm in the market.

There are other important competitive activities of relevance to economics, such as quality competition and competitive innovation, but, unlike imitative output competition, theories about these lack obvious criteria by which to judge competitive intensity. There is nothing equivalent to extreme decentralization by which to determine, even when one relies on "blackboard analysis," that competitive innovation or quality competition are at their theoretical maximum intensities. This is because their objective is not to replicate or imitate but to innovate and differentiate. Thus, innovative competition, or, as Schumpeter described it, creative destruction, works through changes in technology, organization, and product, and it works even if a market is monopolistic in the standard sense; it shows no respect for the existing condition of the market and works even if the innovator is a monopolist. Whereas the intensity of imitative output competition, as is well known, is related to the degree to which the individual is stripped of significance by extreme decentralization, the intensity of innovative competition is bound by no such relationship. A lone individual, or a small group of individuals (usually housed within one firm), creates a new market or revolutionizes an old one. People act as if they can influence outcomes, and they can. If competition is of the imitative output variety, no single farmer holds the price of wheat close to marginal cost. The aggregate of supplies from all individual farmers does this. But if competition is innovative, a Cyrus McCormick can reduce the entire cost function of grain production and a Marchese Marconi can create a radio industry.

This contrast, one element of which is the innovative individual, is important to a theory of competition, for it makes apparent that competitive intensity depends in part on effort expended by the individuals involved in the productive process. Imitative output competition *assumes* maximal competitive effort on the part of individual producers. Each firm produces at the lowest possible cost and produces at a rate that maximizes return. This follows from the perfect competition assumptions of profit maximization on the basis of full and free knowledge of technology and prices. In this case, an increase in the number of firms succeeds in reducing the control each firm has over market supply without, at the same time, reducing the effort made by the individual firm to realize the lowest cost output. The individual is freely endowed with the knowledge necessary to implement the best technology in an errorless way; therefore, competitive effort is always maximal even if no resources are devoted to it. The notion of *working to compete* by improving product, technology, pricing, and organization is foreign to the model.

Things are different in the case of innovative competition. Increase the number of firms engaged in innovating in a given line of business, and it is conceivable that there will be a consequent reduction in the expected reward faced by each provider of innovation. This might reduce the competitive effort made by any one firm. This is because the innovator is perceived to work at innovating, unlike perfect competitors, who do not work at imitative competition because they are possessed of complete knowledge of prices and technique and execute this knowledge errorlessly. The innovative competitor must commit resources to compete effectively. The significance of all this is that the intensity of competition is no longer solely a function of number of competitors. It is also a function of the effort made by each competitor. The point is akin to Leibenstein's X-efficiency, discussed earlier in these commentaries. The general level of competitive intensity might be reduced by adding more competitors if this results in sufficiently large reductions in the competitive effort exerted by each competitor. It is noteworthy that sporting events, such as golf tournaments, often establish criteria of play that limit the field of contestants to those few possessing comparably good skill at the game. This makes the tournament more attractive to fans. This is partly because they can view "the best" at play, partly because the tournament is more manageable, and partly because, when the best play against each other, they play harder. This last consideration implies that the competitive intensity of a contest is not always increased by adding more contestants.

Moreover, for a given prize the addition of more players reduces the expected prize for each player, and this reduces the effort made by each player in preparing for and in playing the tournament. If the number of players of comparable skill is doubled (an impossible feat) the expected prize to each is halved, so that each player should reduce by 50 percent the effort he or she would have exerted if the additional players had not been admitted. Summed over all players, effort remains unchanged. This suggests that the performance achieved from the contest also remains unchanged. This need not be so.

Competitors might be risk-averse, and risk is more likely to rise than to decrease with an increase in the number of competitors. It certainly is not so if lesser-quality contestants are permitted to compete. Take ten very high-capability performers and race them against each other. Take the same ten, but intersperse between them enough lower-quality contestants to make it difficult for each of the ten to monitor the other nine top contestants, and their effort is likely to diminish. Being well in front of all rivals one can see encourages a contestant to ease off a bit.

The measure of competitive intensity that seems implied in the preceding discussion is the effort expended by individuals or by an aggregate of individual efforts. Measuring competitive intensity by effort expended may be distortive. Suppose performance is measured by speed attained by the winner of the contest. The reduction in effort occasioned by an increase in number of players results in each player running more slowly. For a given prize, assume that a doubling of numbers of competitors reduces the effort given by each in half, so that total competitive effort remains unchanged. A likely outcome of the race is a slower winner (or a longer time to transit the course). The quickness with which a race course is traversed may the more appropriate index of competitive intensity. If it is, an increase in the number of even equally matched runners may reduce competitive intensity. Significant reductions in the expected prize, wrought by increasing the number of competitors, makes "turtles" of each competitor. Reduce the number of competitors and turtles are converted to rabbits. However, reduce the number of competitors very much, and they may find it better to collude to reduce effort and thereby to lengthen the best time taken to complete the course. The relationship between competitive intensity and the number of rivals may not be monotonic once the effort exacted from individuals is taken into account. The result may be compared to perfect competition. The perfectly competitive market uses market output as an index of competitive intensity, with output reaching its competitive maximum as the number of rivals increases to the point where all sense of rivalry is lost; a monotonic relationship is implied. Once perfect knowledge of technology and price is abandoned, market quantity may increase, decrease, or remain unchanged as the number of firms in the market is increased, depending on the force of considerations like those just discussed.[68]

68. Numbers affect performance through more than one channel. So the effect of number of contestants on performance is not always obvious. If the number of players is very few, as compared to very large, the person who actually has the potential for being fastest is more likely to have been excluded from the race. The consequence for performance of increasing the number of contestants is thus complex and not straightforward at all. The performance-numbers relationship is also affected by the evenhandedness of treatment of the contestants, their qualitative parity, the amount and distribution of rewards, and, of course, the probability of their colluding.

The analogies just drawn may distort the situation when it comes to economic performance. Typically there is no preset prize. The value the market puts on an innovation determines the prize, not some tournament administrator or government official. And there is no great stock of knowledge about which potential contestants offer the most promise of excelling; innovations often find their sources in very unlikely places. With open entry, the number of contestants that remain viable is determined by the market and will vary from market to market. However, it is presumptuous to conclude from the perfect competition and monopoly models that markets populated by fewer firms perform less well or offer competition that is less intense. Mergers can increase the intensity of competition, and so can communication between independent firms. This is because different organizations can learn from each other as well as collude with each other. Learning has benign consequences for performance, but this is ruled out by neoclassical models that assume that full knowledge of technology and prices is had by all.

When fully thought-out, these considerations may suggest that some restrictions on entry in some circumstances are socially desirable, but not in other circumstances. Indeed, the property right system – replete with patent, copyright, trademark, and secrecy protections – presumably can be an instrument for benign restrictions on imitative entry. Open entry, whatever this may mean, does not necessarily imply that larger numbers of competitors increase the probability that the market will deliver the performance sought by buyers or society. Telser (1994), in discussing the usefulness of core theory, offers the following example:

> ... regular limo service to O'Hare Airport ... makes scheduled stops at certain times and locations in the neighborhood where it picks up passengers. Demand is heavy at spring and Christmas breaks. Once we were waiting with several students for the 7 a.m. limo. ... Just before 7, a Yellow taxi pulled up, flag down, meter off and offered to take up to five customers to O'Hare for $8 each, non-stop, which is below the limo price. The taxi got a full load and left for O'Hare. No one remained for the regular limo service. Although the taxi driver and those who accepted his offer were made better-off, the incentive for providing the regular limo service was impaired ... thereby harming the interest of any residents of Hyde Park desiring regular limo service to the airport.

"Open entry" presumably denies to the market the more desirable option of maintaining regular limo service. Telser discusses the solution in terms of imposing an upper bound on the quantities that may be sold by certain sellers. In this example, the taxi presumably would be barred by regulation or collusive agreement from competing for passengers in this market.

This may be the solution in some cases, but in others the problem is simply in the definition of property rights. The curb side in this example is not owned but is treated by the city as a collective or communal good. Private owners of the curb side (or properly motivated government owners), with the right to bar vehicles from pulling up and taking on passengers, would bar taxies from pulling up a half-hour before the limo is scheduled to arrive. They would maximize profit (if Telser's example is correct) by being able to charge the limo a higher fee than would be possible without such a bar. Thus, by properly defining property rights, it is possible to reduce the number of competitors when this works to the advantage of buyers or society at large. All this is speculative, but it can become less so only after we realize that the theory of competition now part of the economic tool kit does not really address important aspects of competition.

The problem of multiplicity of competitive activities

Four dimensions along which competition may take place have already been touched on: output, price, quality (including reputation), and innovation. There is no sense in attempting to list yet other competitive activities. The list would never be complete. No matter. Even a few competitive activities make it impossible to set forth a measure of competitive intensity to which all will agree. One competitive mix, as compared to a second, contains more intensive innovation and quality competition and less intensive imitation and price competition. Which is the more intensively competitive mix as judged by the general level of competition? Even if one could measure competitive intensity along each and every single dimension of competition, our inability to convert units of competitive intensity from one dimension of competition to another makes the general intensity of competition ambiguous and even meaningless. There is a widely held but unarticulated belief that competitive intensity can be measured well enough so that scholars, lawyers, judges, and politicians can agree that a policy has increased (or decreased) the general level of competitive intensity. Although in one case or another this belief may be valid, as a general proposition it is just plain wrong. We have been encouraged in this belief by our heavy reliance on perfect competition, monopoly, and oligopoly models, all of which focus only on imitative output competition.

Our simplistic notion of competitive intensity ignores the heterogeneity of competitive actions and treats competition as a single-dimensioned parameter of behavior. This allows us to speak, write, and legislate as if the general level of competition can be more or less intense, measured as such, and predictably influenced by policy. From the policy perspective, however, the relevant policy question is not which of two mixtures of competitive activities is the more intensively competitive; it is which of the two mixtures of competitive activities is preferred. Some persons will especially value imitative competition. Others will attach a greater weight to innovative competition. Quite reasonable people can differ in their preferences across mixtures of competitive activities. To young parents just starting their families, competitive innovation is important. Their children will benefit. To an old person without children, today's price competition, and therefore imitative output competition, are important. Three sorts of considerations – the form of competition, its intensity, and its objective – help to form preferences. Competing by offering higher-quality goods is generally thought beneficial, competing by advertising is of questionable benefit, and competing by resort to violence is a cost, not a benefit. As to intensity of competition, competing via price is generally approved but, if carried to excess, it earns the "cut throat" label, and, if its objective is to put rivals out of business, it earns the "predation" label. As to "objective," the unrestrained sale of weaponry, and in particular of technical nuclear know-how, easily can make the world worse off even as it benefits some buyers of weaponry.

To make matters more difficult still, the degree of competition associated with one activity is often correlated with the degree associated with another. Often this correlation is negative, so that, even if we restrict our discussion to beneficial objectives, it is impossible to increase the intensity of competition in the pursuit of one desirable objective without thereby reducing the intensity of competition in the pursuit of other desirable objectives. Many subtle tradeoffs between forms of competition are involved even in a narrowly defined business activity, such as the tradeoff between competitiveness of the partnership and competitiveness of the individuals who make up the partnership. Innovative competition is encouraged by limiting output and price competition on already invented goods, so that up-front costs of innovation have a higher probability of being covered by revenues secured from the sale of these innovations. The fact that the intensities of many forms of competition are negatively correlated makes the measurement and judgment of competitive intensity all the more difficult. It is senseless to claim that a policy that increases the intensity of one form of competition also raises the general level of competition if, as a consequence, the intensity of another form of competition is reduced. When this happens, policy cannot be directed toward increasing the intensity of competition simultaneously along all the possible dimensions of competition, and this denies policy even the remote possibility of being able to unambiguously increase or decrease the general level of competition. One can speak of a particular mixture of competitive activities as more preferred to another, but not as more intensively competitive.

The inverse correlation between the intensities of many different forms of competition not only undermines the competitive intensity criterion, it also suggests that we exaggerate the differences between markets in competitive intensity when we judge competitive intensity by the standard derived from the perfect competition model. Modes of competition other than imitative output competition are likely to be inversely related in intensity to that of imitative output competition. A judgment that imitative output is weak is more likely to be made for a market in which innovative and quality competition is strong, and vice versa. Successful innovative competition, because it tends to gather market share and pricing power to the successful innovator, brings forth lower values of indexes of imitative competition, and quality competition, if successful, results in positive price-cost margins. When price-cost margins and market structure yield low indexes of imitative competitive intensity, the intensities of quality and innovation competition are more likely to be high. The consequence of giving great weight to indexes of imitative competition is to overstate differences across markets in the general levels of competitive intensities.[69]

If we agree that many relevant forms of competition relate inversely to each other and that no plausible method exists for converting intensities of different forms of competition into a common unit of intensity, then, it would seem, we also must agree that the Sherman Antitrust Act is logically impossible to carry out if its goal is interpreted as increasing the overall intensity of competition (or to reducing the overall intensity of monopoly). This should be the nub of the argument made by the UCLA/Chicago proponents of letting efficiency considerations guide antitrust policy.[70] Instead, although they have based their arguments on efficiency, they have not shown the fallacy in the belief that policy can use competitive intensity as its criterion. Thus, Bork (1978) championed efficiency on the claim that this is what legislators who passed the Sherman Act had in mind, and economists, including the author, championed efficiency because they perceived policy to have developed in some respects in an anticompetitive way (e.g., the attacks of antitrust authorities on vertical integration, marketing policies, and concentration). The stronger argument I believe is the one made here. Increasing the intensity of competition (or reducing the intensity of monopoly) is not a feasible goal of antitrust. Efficiency is at least a conceptually feasible goal. It is not an easy goal to pursue, however. Preferences, not just costs, matter. Misguided as the courts have at times been, perhaps it is in the service of this goal that they have sought to attenuate the Sherman Act's blanket prohibition of restrictive agreements with a "rule of reason."

Cost conditions, the outcomes of competition, and monopoly

The important varieties of competition found in the economy are not ad hoc; they are not exogenously given, and they are not solely the result of policy. If

---

69. Other reasons for bias can be stated. For example, Schumpeter tends to consider monopoly profit a "lightning rod" for attracting thunderbolts of innovative competition. On this view, high monopoly profit, as compared to low monopoly profit, is accompanied by more serious threats of being undermined by innovative competition.

70. As a small act of institutional immodesty, I note that the profession has allowed the Univerity of Chicago to appropriate to itself the efficiency doctrine of antitrust. The offering of this doctrine in a substantive, analytical way originated at least as much from work done at UCLA as from that done at Chicago.

competition is to be taken seriously as a scientific problem, economics has the task of explaining the mixtures of the competitive forms we observe. This task differs from that presumed by our current practice, which is to focus attention almost exclusively on deductions from superimposed models of the competitive process, such as models of perfect competition, monopoly, monopolistic competition, and oligopoly. This practice begins its work by presuming the applicability of a particular model of competition. It does not take as its task the problem of explaining the forms of competition we actually observe.

We have expectations as to what methods of competing are feasible. The existence of significant scale economies is likely to reduce the significance of imitative output competition, simply because increases in output coming from an existing large firm are likely to be cheaper than if they came from new, smaller firms. The competition that does take place is likely to occur periodically or episodically rather than continuously, and it is likely to be marked by rivalry to service the entire market or a large part of it rather than to add a unit of sales here and a unit there. The outcome of competition under this condition cannot be identical to the outcome of competition under cost conditions that tolerate atomistic market structure. Competition will yield concentrated market structures and multipart pricing, so absence of competition cannot be inferred from either of these.

Whether it is wise to use detailed regulation in substitution for periodic competition is an issue that cannot be resolved simply from a knowledge of the product markets. A comparison of the efficacies of regulation and of competition "for the field" is crucial to this judgment, but to use the standards of a single price for all, equal to marginal cost, and an unconcentrated market structure as tests for the intensity of competition is nonetheless clearly foolish if scale economies are so important. Competition for the field can be as intense as it is possible for it to be under these conditions and yet not satisfy criteria of competitive intensity that are appropriate for cost conditions approximating those assumed by the perfect competition model.

Problems arise for the measurement of competitive intensity even if scale economies are not so significant as to make one firm the lowest-cost supplier of the entire market's supply. If the typical firm in a multifirm market has production costs that are U-shaped over a nontrivial range of output, intense competition is unlikely to yield a price equal to the lowest average cost of incumbent firms. A quantity of product that is just sufficient to allow all incumbent firms to produce at rates of output that yield the lowest possible unit cost for all of them is not likely to be the same quantity that satisfies market demand at a price equal to unit cost. It will be a quantity that falls short of that needed to satisfy demand at such a price, and the price will be higher than would obtain in a perfectly competitive market in which no firm's output is subject to scale economies. The gap between price and average cost will be positive but not so large as to allow an additional firm to enter the market profitably. The residual demand that would reveal itself at a price equal to minimum average cost, but which remains unsatisfied at the higher price, is simply too small to allow the new entrant to produce at this average cost. This results not from too little competitive intensity, but from significantly U-shaped average cost functions. It is inappropriate to apply the criterion "observed price equal to observed average cost" to judge competitive intensity in such a setting. A price that does not exceed average cost by more than is made necessary given the U-shaped cost curve condition, would seem a more appropriate criterion.

Competitive activity in a market is not fully revealed in the experiences of those firms now in the market, it is also revealed in the experiences of firms who have sought to *become* incumbents but who have failed to do so. The tests we use to gage competitive intensity – market concentration, profit rate level, and price-marginal cost inequality – all rely on the existing firms for data, but reliance on data from incumbent firms is likely to bias our judgments about competitive intensity. As we shall see, cost conditions exert a strong influence on the degree to which this bias is likely to be present.

The general problem is well-known and easy to grasp. If one were to guage competitive intensity by the rate of return on investment made by winners in lottery games, the rate of return would be quite high, but a negative return is obtained if the calculation includes wagers made by losers. Now, although casual discussions of lottery winnings neglect the experience of those who have gambled and lost, there is no reason in principle that this should be so. The losses of each year's losers can be totaled with the winnings of each year's winners, and the algebraic sum can be divided by the total investment in lottery tickets in that year. The rate of return so calculated need not be biased, and, because of the nature of the game, it generally will not be biased. The nature of the game is that it is played entirely within one data collecting period. Each year's play is independent of other years.

This may be contrasted with an industry such as the biotechnology industry. In order to produce product during one data collecting period, a firm needs to invest in research for many periods; after these investments have been made, and if the Federal Drug Agency permits the product to be marketed, then and only then is it possible for profitable production to take place. The typical firm goes through several periods of losses to be able to bring a drug to the FDA and possibly to the market. Now, if the importance of firms that fail to reach the successful product stage is in steady state equilibrium, no serious data problem arises. Each year, on a proper reckoning of industry experience, the losses associated with failure will be tossed in with the profits. What is more likely to be the case is that present failures underrepresent the history of failure for past years. *More* failed attempts to enter the industry and become a viable producing firm have taken place in the early stages of the industry's development. The few firms that are alive and well have survived several years of lottery playing, and by virtue of having done so and won, they have earned the right to market a product. The losses of the many failing firms in the industry's earlier years play no role in the calculation of contemporary industry rate of return. These losses have been recorded during the year they occurred. To make the point clear, assume that entry attempts no longer are made at all and that only the winners of several past years of "lotteries" are the producing firms of the present. Let all these producing firms make large profits. Still, reckoned over the entire play, these profits might be more than cancelled out by the larger early losses of all who attempted to become players. These early losses were incurred not in the expectation of making a profit during the year they occurred, but in anticipation of making a profit several years later. Each of these early year experiences are therefore interdependent with later years. The game is not one of annual independent lotteries. The correct rate of return for the industry must trace the entire play; this extends to many more accounting periods than the current year's play.

These considerations play a role in those market situations characterized by indivisibilities of the sort discussed in the preceding section (and which frequently are described by theorists as possessing an empty core). Incumbent firms receive a profit that outsiders would like to enjoy, but if outsiders enter on the scale needed to survive at the current price, their entry lowers price below the cost of all active participants. However, competition (and equilibrium) in markets of this type cannot be judged until one recognizes the attractiveness of "being" an incumbent. An earlier competition to become an incumbent is implied, and, given the stream of profit expected by winners in this competition, potential incumbents as a class should suffer losses sufficient to make winning just a break-even a priori gamble. From this perspective, viewed across both segments of the game, the rate of return is competitive.

The "entire game perspective" creates a different view of the monopoly problem. Pushed far enough back, there is competition to secure monopoly, well-known in the literature as competition between rent seekers. This competition should balance the expected winning of monopoly profit with the bearing of losses in the attempts of many to become the monopolist. Summed over winners and losers, the rate of return is competitive. The entire process is competitive even if it has an end point, such as a valuable patent, that is depicted well enough by the monopoly model; there may be only one surviving firm, and this firm may price in excess of marginal cost, but in doing so it may receive only a competitive return summed over both segments of the process.[71] Policy toward competition cannot be framed on the basis of profit rate alone,

---

71. This view of the game ignores the possibility that monopoly may arise fortuitously, in which case no loss is borne in the process of the monopoly's acquisition.

and it cannot be guided only by the end point situation. Rather, it requires a determination of whether the entire process is a plausible way to achieve appropriate objectives. An end point patented medication yielding high profit and priced above marginal cost is insufficient grounds for intervention; this may be the best way to spur the development of desirable medications. On the other hand, an end point in which profit is competitive and price is equal to marginal cost may be undesirable if the product is nuclear weapons.

Cost conditions and false product differentiation

Competition along the quality dimension is almost always considered in the context of monopolistic competition, but there is a different and much neglected source of quality competition that has nothing at all to do with product differentiation or even with information cost. Its source is hidden by neoclassical production theory.

Consider a farming firm that grows "wheat" by combining fertilizer and several other inputs. Let the price of fertilizer decrease. Appropriately, the farmer substitutes fertilizer for other inputs. Production theory assumes that the nature of wheat remains unchanged during this adjustment. However, a change in the quantity of fertilizer relative to quantities of other inputs cannot be presumed to leave the quality of wheat untouched. Just as a change in the relative quantity of copper used to produce electric wire will change the wire's weight, conductivity, and strength; so a change in fertilizer can change the qualities of wheat that affect its market value. The degree to which product quality changes depends on how responsive quality is to changing the mix of inputs. For some goods, such as wheat, a quality change may be slight, but for other goods it will be significant.

Production theory is not designed to answer questions about changes in the nature of the goods being produced. Goods of a given quality are presumed, and input mixes requisite to their production are the concern of production theory. However, constant quality of output requires the special assumption, not explicit in production theory, that adjustments in input mix are constrained to those that yield the same quality output. This assumption yields a definiteness in the concepts of cost and demand that otherwise is lacking. If the price of fertilizer falls, farmers can be viewed as changing all inputs so as to minimize the cost of producing a constant *quality of wheat*. This is the view implicit in production theory. Alternatively, they can grow bushels of different quality "wheat" if they are willing to let the quality of wheat respond optimally to the fall in the price of fertilizer. If the second reaction is chosen, their new cost function differs from what it would be with the first reaction. Should they choose to allow the quality of "wheat" to vary, they also face a different market price (or, for imperfect competition, a different demand curve). The well-defined cost and demand framework established by standard production theory, which holds product quality constant, avoids such complications, but it does so at a cost. Profit-enhancing courses of action that would be chosen by real firms are ignored.

Methodology is somewhat different at the levels of analysis involving market supply and demand. Alterations in product quality that might accompany a change in input prices are recognized, but as intermarket shifts in resources. A reduction in the price of land shifts some agricultural resources from corn production to wheat production. The changed quality of output is labeled a change in product and is represented by an increase in the supply of wheat relative to the supply of corn. Standard production theory ignores the general problem of product quality change. The shift from corn to wheat is in principle the same as the more modest and less obvious shift (which is ignored by production theory) in the quality of corn that should accompany changes in input prices.

The underlying cause of product quality change is not only input price change, but any profit-maximizing motive for changing input mix. Operating a firm at different scale levels involves different input mixes if, as is generally the case, not all inputs are easily changed proportionately. The traditional U-shaped average cost curve derives from input indivisibilities that guarantee that changes in output are accompanied by changes in input mix. More generally, marginal products of various inputs fall at different rates as the scale of operations is increased. Production theory recognizes this by allowing the firm to use different input mixes to produce different output rates, but the theory does this in the context of a given, unchanging good. In principle, a complete adjustment will involve a change in the quality of the good also. If the marginal product of labor falls more quickly than that of other inputs as scale is increased, then the firm that produces television circuitry will substitute printed circuitry for hand-made. This alters performance attributes (such as frequency of breakdown, cost of repair per breakdown, and so on) and generally leads to a different market price. The firm does not move along a horizontal demand curve defined for a given quality product as its scale of operations increases, although this is what it could do if profit was served by maintaining a given quality of good. Instead, it moves from one price to another, from one demand function to another, or from one market to another, because it alters the quality of its product. These quality changes can take place even though the physical characteristics of the product remain unchanged. Slight differences in the quality of services and in the reputational capital of the firm shift its product into a different quality class. Just as profit-motivated changes in output may be viewed as competitive activity of the imitative output variety, so we can view these changes along the quality dimension.

Statistical estimates of the firm's demand elasticity are unlikely to correct for these quality changes. Smaller output rates make larger quantities of the fixed inputs available to the firm, creating "excess" capacity by which to serve buyers more quickly or more thoroughly. The quality of output is likely to be higher when there is less quantity produced than when there is more. It is a common observation that, when an economy moves into a recession, the quality of services received by buyers increases. A firm with fixed inputs that produces a small output rate, perhaps because product prices have decreased, should receive a higher price per unit than if the quality of service had not increased. After adjusting for changes in the general level of prices due to inflation and deflation, a negative relationship between price and output arises because the quality of the good has not been carefully controlled. These different prices do not belong on the same firm demand function since they reflect varying quality of product, with higher quality more likely to be associated with smaller output rates. To take these prices as associated with a single quality of product when statistically estimating the firm's demand function is to exaggerate both the degree of negativeness in the slope of demand and the prevalence of monopolistically competitive markets.

Cost conditions and real product differentiation

Significantly positive costs of information are a serious source of difficulty. Pure price-taker behavior is ruled out by such costs because consumers cannot know for certain the qualities of goods offered by rival sellers. Competition is then directed, at least partly, toward efforts to do a better job than rivals of assuring buyers about quality. Reputations must be established, sellers must be time- and transaction-tested, and branding becomes important. Goods for which information problems abound are those for which we expect buyers to develop attachments to brands, reputation, and past performance. These attachments serve as imperfect but usable "guarantors" of reliability, and they imply the emergence of negatively sloped demands for the outputs of individual suppliers of these goods. The information problem cannot be done in. It is simply a reflection of resource scarcity, and it cannot be decoupled from negatively sloped demand. Adoption of a price-cost margin standard of competitive intensity seems foolish in this situation. It is competitive activity itself that yields negatively sloped firm demand as firms strive to find novel means by which to overcome consumer lack of confidence that is borne of information cost. The existence of a positive margin is part of the competitive way of coping with information cost. Each firm will have a noticeable ability to raise price without losing all its sales and an equally noticeable inability to win all the sales of rival firms by setting a lower price. Costly information weakens the reliability of the guidance that can be given by price alone, unlike the guidance that can be given by price in the full knowledge world of perfect competition. The competitive activities of sellers allow buyers to derive confidence built upon reputation and brand name capital.

Buyer welfare is likely to be increased by business investments in reputation and brand name capital, especially if there is no obstacle to the entry of firms that rely very little on such capital. The availability of products from firms with different offerings of price and reputation allows buyers to choose between products of "less differentiated" price-based rivals and products of "more differentiated" brand name rivals. That reputations and brand names attract enough buyers to remain viable is a strong signal that many buyers benefit from these investments and, by implication, that the higher price-marginal cost margins they face from the negatively sloped firm demand functions that these investments necessarily create are but a different perspective of this benefit. It is inappropriate to use the criterion of equality between price and marginal cost to measure the competitive intensities of such markets because this criterion signifies a certain loss of welfare only if goods are known by all to be perfect substitutes.

The works of Chamberlin (1933) and Robinson (1933) are preeminent in the history of the product differentiation literature (but both have surprisingly little to say about information cost). I focus on Chamberlin's work. His theory invokes a Bertrand expectations psychology by assuming that each firm makes its pricing decisions on the expectation that all other firms occupying the same product *group* hold their prices unchanged.[72] The group, unlike the market of neoclassical theory, is an ambiguous concept. Chamberlin does not tell us how to determine whether a firm is or is not in a group, since no specified degree of substitutability divides members of the group from nonmembers. Alteration in the membership of the group, since it changes the number of product varieties it includes, also changes the group's "aggregate" demand, but with any given number of firms the group's aggregate demand still escapes definition because the many different firms within the group each faces its own price and its own units of output. The lack of a clear notion of market demand was recognized by Stigler some time ago.[73] This is a weakness of the model, but it purchases a realism not found in models that assume homogeneous goods markets; by taking product substitutability to its upper limit, homogeneous goods models allow unambiguous equilibria to be deduced but they generally falsify and exaggerate the substitutability between the outputs of different firms. Monopolistic competition's acceptance of vague, imperfect product substitutability attains greater realism in terms of product substitutability, but it sacrifices the well-defined equilibrium (although Chamberlin incorrectly wrote as if his model does offer a determinate equilibrium).

---

72. The logic of this expectation carries within it implications about the outputs of rivals.
73. See Stigler (1950) and Demsetz (1993).

Chamberlin's model assumes open entry. This and his large numbers assumption for group membership constitute the competitive part of monopolistic competition theory. But open entry into the group does not imply the imitative entry assumed by neoclassical theory for perfect competition. Sellers within a Chamberlin group maintain differentiated products. This assumption, necessary to the definition of monopolistic competition, bars producers of perfect substitutes from entering into or belonging to a group. With this constraint, the model claims to, but cannot really, deduce a zero-profit equilibrium for incumbent firms. If products are differentiated, there is no assurance that the entry of additional differentiated products is profitable simply because existing product varieties enjoy profit. The degree of substitutability between product varieties may be too small and the range of output over which any one variety's average cost falls may be too large to allow entry to have the fineness of effect necessary to guarantee that incumbents operate at a zero profit equilibrium. Thus, the central assumption of monopolistic competition, that firms produce imperfectly substitute product varieties, undermines the usefulness of the price-marginal cost equality standard and the zero profit standard for measuring the intensity of competition. Firms can compete as intensely as is possible under the restraint that they cannot produce identical products, yet they can fail to satisfy these standards of maximum competitive intensity.[74]

The zero profit equilibrium has been used by Dixit and Stiglitz (1977) to define the extent of the Chamberlin group. They do this by letting the entry of new product varieties reduce the profit to the group. That product variety whose entry brings the profit of the group to zero is the boundary that sets this group apart from other Chamberlin groups. This purely mechanical definition of a group will not do. The substitutability between the last product variety to enter, whose entry reduces the group's profit to zero, and the next in line to enter may be no less than between product varieties already in the group. Surely, it is substitutability that counts. If the firms in a group as defined by Dixit and Stiglitz were to collude, the higher price would quickly bring yet new product varieties into the group. One must conclude that the Chamberlin group still defies definition.

Empirical studies reveal a correlation between profit rate and the degree to which firms in a group use advertising, but it is not clear just what this finding signifies. Costly information, we have seen, creates a demand for investments in reputation, brand name capital, and research. The consequence of these investments is to produce a mixture of physical good and consumer confidence. Investments in these inputs is largely cast in the form of intangible capital, and

---

74. Absent the zero profit equilibrium, there also is no necessary conclusion that equilibrium is marked by excess capacity.

this capital is very firm-specific. These investments are of a sort that they lose their value should an attempt to enter and remain in a product group fail. If entry is to serve its equilibrating role, the expected rate of return on these firm-specific investments should be competitive, but this means that the losses of those who fail to "make the grade" and who never enter or fall from the data base that defines the group must be counterbalanced by supracompetitive profit for those who succeed in being in the data base of viable firms. Rational expectations in a competitive setting, given firm-specific investments and a positive probability of failure, requires this showing of supracompetitive profit. Since the specificity of these investments is very likely to correlate positively with advertising intensity, rational expectation theory leads us to expect a correlation between profit rate and advertising intensity even in a setting of high-intensity competition. This problem is no different from the contrast previously discussed between entering the farming industry and remaining a viable farmer, as compared to entering and remaining a viable firm in the biotech industry.

The correlation between profit rate and advertising intensity may reflect not only this, but also the accounting artifact discussed in the commentary on the use and misuse of accounting data. Accounting practices fail to treat investments in firm-specific brand name and reputational capital in the same way that they treat tangible capital. This can result in an upward distortion of profit rates for advertising-intense firms.

Competition that takes place along the reputation and branding dimensions of firm activity thus presents a set of theory and measurement problems that are too often ignored in attempts to assess competitive intensity. These relate to the rational expectations and accounting bias discussions just completed, but they run even deeper than these. Costly information and product heterogeneity make all group (or market) definitions arbitrary, and it is not implausible that the more intensively is the use of inputs like advertising, the greater is the degree of ambiguity that surrounds the definition of the market. The profit rate that tends to be statistically correlated with advertising intensity may not reflect greater barriers to entering the group or market, as it often is interpreted to reflect. Rather, it may result from weaker substitutability between the product varieties within the group. The lower level of substitutability, in turn, reflects the higher cost of knowledge acquisition and/or greater differences in consumer tastes across potential product varieties in settings in which trademarks are legally protected. Economies of scale can be more important than would seem to be the case for the larger "market" that contains these "less substitutable" product varieties. This can give rise to profit and price-cost margins of the sort we associate with the protections afforded by patent, trademark, and copyright, *or* they can derive from the increased relevance of input indivisibilities.

Information cost and problems of coercion, fraud, and interbrand rivalry

The introduction of significant information cost fundamentally changes the analysis of firms and competition. Because products, suppliers, and purchasers can have varying qualities that cannot be known with certainty, the exchange economy requires the production and dissemination of information. Even a monopoly must inform prospective buyers of the availability and nature of the good it produces. Information conveyance is not the task of firms only. It is a joint product of sellers and buyers. At a minimum, buyers bear the cost of having their time and attention diverted from other uses. This component of the cost of receiving information necessarily involves an element of coercion. Anyone who wishes to communicate must catch the attention of the party targeted to receive the communication. This attention getting cannot be an entirely voluntary affair. The communicator cannot arrange to convey this attention on a completely voluntary basis; the act of soliciting permission to deliver a message is itself a message that requires an initiating coercive element of attention getting. Even should the communicator wish this attention to be voluntarily, an attention-getting process must begin by acquiring the voluntary permission of the other party, and this must involve an element of intrusion or attention-getting coercion. This element of coercion is unnecessary if competition is perfect, but simply because the perfect competition model presumes that all knowledge necessary for exchange is possessed. Thus, one consequence of costly knowledge is to introduce the "serpent" of coercion into the Libertarian Garden of Eden. We bear some attention-getting cost involuntarily every time we see a billboard, hear a commercial, and view the computer E-mail menu of arrived messages. Even the attempt to avoid these initiations of communications implies an involuntarily borne cost. However, much of the information-receiving cost borne by buyers is voluntarily borne, such as the cost of newspapers, radios, telephones, televisions, and other information-receiving devices. But whether voluntarily or involuntarily borne, these costs simply reflect the fact that information is not free.

Is a mixture of competitive activities that includes sizable amounts of information-conveying costs less desirable than one that includes less such cost? It might be helpful to this judgment if communication of "objective fact" could be separated from persuasive communication, so that the former might be allowed and the latter discouraged. There is no way to make this separation in convincing fashion, since to inform people of the availability of a good is to persuade persons to purchase the good, and it often is the case that an increase in the amount of one type of information provided brings an increase in the amount of the other. I am not sure we would want to make this distinction anyway. Persuasion is not without its value. It can be productive. Anyone who has raised children, "educated" students, and remained married must know this. And it is a common occurrence to be persuaded to purchase products on one day and to find on the next day that they nicely fulfill wants not otherwise easily satisfied. Of course, there is fraud and misrepresentation, and labeling requirements and assorted similar regulations may improve communication, but in the final analysis the most reliable protection comes from a system that tolerates the competitive selling of quality and reputation.

Some information conveyance is directed toward shifting sales from rivals to one's own firm; this almost necessarily results in the protection of one's own sales from the competitive efforts of others. Advertising for the purpose of reallocating a given market between sellers in the same Chamberlinian group is often thought wasteful because it merely shifts sales between firms. However, one never knows when a plug for one seller's brand will convey information of real value to buyers, but, more to the point, there is a way to reduce this type of communication. Organize the Chamberlinian group into a monopoly, so that interfirm rivalry ceases. This reduces the intensity of interfirm advertising competition, presumed here to be undesirable, but it also reduces the intensity of price competition. Policy is again fraught with difficult tradeoffs.

Summary evaluations of U.S. competition policy

By now in this commentary, it should be clear that economics has much work before it is to lay claim to a rich understanding of the problem of competition. The world does not wait for economists, however. It establishes and enforces public policy toward competition, both through an explicit competition policy, such as the Sherman Antitrust Act, and through property, contract, and tort law also. Where the emphasis between these two sources of competition policy should rest is an issue about which opinion is divided. However, the explicit, specialized antitrust policy that we do have, and shall continue to have, highlights the problems caused by the tradeoffs previously discussed. Because of these tradeoffs, no single evaluation, by me or anyone else, is convincing in all its details to those who seriously consider the issues involved. That convincing recommendations are difficult to come by is attested to by their absence from the legislation that has created the antitrust policy of the United States.

It is in the process of enforcement of competition policy that we learn which dimensions of competition are to be tolerated and encouraged and which penalized. Policy enforcement, like economic theory, is far from perfect in its pronouncements; so I conclude this commentary with a summary evaluation of U.S. antitrust enforcement. There can be no doubt at this point in the present commentary that the opinions I shall express are speculative and reflective of my own perceptions of economic behavior. The large weight I give to efficiency, as compared to competition, is consistent with earlier parts of this commentary.

Horizontal price agreements

The first substantive issue that faced U.S. courts in enforcing the Sherman Act is the legality of price agreements. Their chosen resolution of this issue has won long-standing acceptance in subsequent cases (excepting the 1933 *Appalachian Coals* case) and widely based support from a large plurality of antitrust economists. The precedent not only holds price agreements to be illegal; it admits no defense whose purpose is to convince the court that the price agreed to is reasonable. Justice Peckham, in two early cases (*Trans-Missouri*, 1897; and *Joint Traffic*, 1898), held that the only reasonable price is the price set by competition.

A blanket prohibition of price agreements gives a clear signal to businesspersons. It also removes from the court the burdens of judging the reasonableness and significance of a price set by agreement between sellers. These are important practical advantages, and they make a strong case for blanket prohibition when buttressed by neoclassical theories of competitive and cartel prices. Neoclassical theory hardly admits the possibility of reasonableness of prices set by agreement. The assumptions of its central model, perfect competition, are controlling. Market participants are presumed to possess complete information about technology. This leaves little else for businesspersons to talk about other than raising price. In truth, as the present commentaries have emphasized, infomation is imperfect and costly to obtain. Since other businesspersons are sources of technical and organizational information, it would be surprising if some meetings between businesspersons fail to serve the socially useful function of transmitting this knowledge. Price manipulation may not be the end point of all such meetings, although it is easy to see the temptation to include some discussion of price. Beyond its informational assumptions, perfect competition also insists on firm size so small as not to confound establishment of a stable theoretical equilibrium based on the independent actions of sellers. Recent writings based on the theory of the core suggest the possibility that production indivisibilities may bring forth firm size requirements that undermine this theoretical equilibrium, and that this might make cooperative agreements on price desirable. On all counts, perfect competition rejects the possibilities that meetings between businesspersons might serve socially useful purposes, and the per se prohibition of price agreements is consistent with the biases set in place by this model.

However, it is no mistake for the court to guide its decisions in regard to price agreements by the presumption that businesspersons have important interests of their own in setting price, and these interests very often conflict with broader social interests. A general, broadly based rejection of price agreements is in order. What may not be in order is to extend this rejection to the status of a *per se* prohibition. It is difficult to find reason to object to price agreements that set price for only a small share of the output in a market (*Appalachian Coals,* 1933).[75] When only a small share of the market is involved, one might suppose that the agreement is but a stepping stone to a broader agreement, but that supposition is itself founded on a view of markets that sees no purpose in price agreements other than to reduce output. If other purposes can be supplied, the case for attacking all agreements as if they were designed to achieve the same objective is diminished. It is also difficult to find objection to a price agreement among sellers that sets a *maximum* price. In *Arizona v. Maricopa County* (1982), doctors agreed to set maximum prices for certain medical procedures they performed, and not all doctors joined in this agreement. Cartel theory offers no good explanation of this, and I find no sensible purpose for the agreement other than one that defendants claimed for it – that of reducing the risk to health insurance providers in not knowing the limits to the liabilities they might face when policy holders used these procedures. This agreement presumably enabled the insurance companies to provide their service for a lower level of insurance premiums than they otherwise would have charged and hardly constitutes cause for the court's guilty verdict. Because the corpus of price theory includes no serious attempt to explain such anomalies, it does not offer reliable guidance in such cases. Price agreements also can be used to maintain the quality of a product or service, as in resale price agreements and uniform pricing by franchises. A franchise operation can be viewed simply as a guise by which rivals reach an agreement on identical price, but it also can be viewed as a consequence of a desire by a franchise to ease the problems it faces in monitoring and controlling quasi-independent franchise outlets so as to be assured that a standardized quality of product and service is provided. If one outlet can charge a lower price than a neighboring outlet, it can divert business from nearby outlets, since customers have been given reason to believe that quality is standardized across all outlets. The loss of business by neighboring outlets might undermine their attempts to invest in quality-enhancing assets and service, even while the price-cutting outlet is also cutting the quality of its good. Hence, maintenance of a standard of quality can be facilitated by the establishment of uniform prices.

These theoretical arguments see social value in price agreements, and an antitrust policy that allows some defense in terms of the reasonableness of price might be preferred to one that offers only a blanket prohibition. However, if our

---

75. The court's decision in *Appalachian Coals* strayed from precedence by exonerating the defendants, but antitrust scholars view the decision as an aberration from the rather steady blanket prohibition of price agreements.

choice is between no prohibition of price agreements and a blanket prohibition, the blanket prohibition seems preferable to me. Smith's famous dictum seems appropriate here:

> People of the same trade seldom meet together, even for merriment and diversion, but the conversation ends in a conspiracy against the public, or in some contrivance to raise prices.[76]

A test of reasonableness, however, might be even better. Whether or not it is depends on how adept the courts are in separating reasonable from unreasonable price agreements. Justice Peckham judged the court a poor vehicle for doing this, and perhaps it is, but I believe that some conditions make it easier for the court to make correct decisions about reasonableness. If sellers are setting maximum rather than minimum prices, it is more likely that the agreement is ameliorating underlying externality or informational problems than that it is harming buyers Similarly, price agreements are more likely to serve socially useful purposes if the combined market share of those entering the agreement is too small to convey power over price. When conditions like these appear, I believe a test of reasonableness is appropriate. Price agreements claimed to be reasonable because of their role in making market conditions more stable, as might be claimed by the theory of the core as applied to a market in which firms need to be very large to realize low costs, are more suspect and less easy to designate as socially reasonable.

Market structure

With the court's position on horizontal price agreements behind it, the next issues to rise to prominence were firm size and market structure. U.S. antitrust policy has developed in a manner that distinguishes between control over price exerted through collusive agreement and control exerted by the apparent dominance of a market by one or a few firms. Control of the former type is barred per se, whereas the latter type becomes illegal only if judged *unreasonable*. Two aspects of this distinction call for explanation. Should there be a distinction? If yes, on what basis should it be made?

If the same market share is controlled through a price agreement as is controlled by a single firm, it is entirely reasonable to believe that greater control over price can be exercised by the single firm. This firm does not need cooperation from other firms. Hence, *if judged solely by the likely degree of*

---

76. It should also be noted that Smith's very next sentence proclaims that, "It is impossible indeed to prevent such meetings, by any law which either could be executed, or would be consistent with liberty and justice . . . [but] law . . . ought to do nothing to facilitate such assemblies; much less to render them necessary." (Adam Smith, *The Wealth of Nations* [New York: Modern Library, 1937, p. 128].)

control over price, antitrust legislation ought to treat a very dominant firm more severely than it would a price agreement linking several sellers who together possess the same market share. A problem with such a policy is immediately encountered. Let there be 20 equal-sized firms in a market. Should two of them attempt to set price through an agreement, the per se doctrine makes their agreement illegal. These two, operating cooperatively on pricing, between them control but 10 percent of the market. An attempt to create parity of treatment for an equivalent market structure would hold a firm that sells 10 percent of the market in violation of antitrust. Surely, such parity is foolish, for no firm size is so small that its market share could not be the equivalent of that which could be put together through a price agreement. The per se prohibition of price agreements can be, and has been, deployed to strike agreements down even if the combined shares of the agreeing firms is too small to affect market price significantly. Extending this doctrine to market structure would leave no firm size protected against prosecution.

To address the problem before us, it is therefore necessary to back away from the per se doctrine and substitute one that requires a showing that market price can be significantly affected by a price agreement before this agreement can be declared in violation of antitrust. Parity of treatment then requires the break-up of a single firm that controls a market share equal to or in excess of the share that is large enough to make a price agreement between smaller firms illegal. And what if this single firm were to be replaced by a small number of oligopolists? Control over price by this oligopoly is likely to be weaker than it would be with a working price agreement covering smaller firms that in combination possess the same share; so it does not follow from the illegality of a price agreement covering a given market share that the same share possessed by noncolluding oligopolists should also be illegal. However, suppose, for the sake of argument, that a price agreement involving control of a given market share by several firms delivers the same degree of control over price as if the same market share were possessed by fewer, larger firms not linked through such an agreement. That is, higher concentration substitutes for collusive agreement. The theory of the firm has not been concerned with determining the point at which a tight market structure becomes the equivalent of price agreement. We are not sure exactly how high the concentration must become before we reach the control over price delivered by a working collusive agreement, but we know there must be a degree of concentration that is the equivalent because we believe that a single very dominant firm obtains more control over price than is secured by several firms cooperating through a price agreement. Suppose we could agree on the degree of market concentration that is the equivalent of an illegal price agreement. We still might not want these two situations – price agreement and market structure – to be treated the same by antitrust; control over price is not the sole consideration.

It is relatively cheap to enter into a price agreement that encompasses enough share to be considered illegal, and no great cost is borne by participants if the agreement should break down. Therefore, many price agreements will be made solely for the purpose of raising price and reducing output. It is cheap to play the price agreement game because the agreement does not usually call for serious modifications in the inner organizations, sizes, and efficiencies of the firms involved. In contrast, efficiency can be affected seriously if firms become larger in order to establish an oligopolistic structure that delivers the same degree of control over price, even if this is accomplished through merger. If this were done solely to gain greater control over price, it would come at the risk of creating less efficient firms that could not compete successfully with smaller rivals. Hence, oligopoly formed simply to control price, a control that could last only a short time, is less likely than the formation of a price agreement for the same purpose.

The second reason for distinguishing between price agreements and concentration is that social benefits derived from price agreements are less plausible than if derived from concentrated market structures. The *usual* price agreement results from an attempt by sellers to benefit at the expense of buyers, not from the need for resolving some dynamic entry-exit or informational problem. A concentrated market structure, however, often arises for reasons fundamentally different from the desire to control price, although the strict prohibition of all price agreements might on occasion lead to market restructuring whose main purpose is to substitute for a price agreement. An examination of the histories of industries whose structures have become concentrated reveals that product innovation and technological change have played important roles. To penalize firms for having competed successfully in these socially beneficial ways is to undermine social reliance on profit guidance, creating the necessity for substituting nationalization or detailed regulation for the give and take of market rivalry. This important cost is not the usual outcome of penalizing price agreements.

The histories of U.S. industries experiencing increasing market concentration supports the notion that society derived some benefit as these structures became more concentrated. Meatpacking became concentrated because some firms adopted refrigerated storage and shipping technology, and this allowed them real advantages and won them large market shares. The introduction of refrigeration also accounts for the abilities of a few beer brewers to displace highly localized breweries. Henry Ford's notion of mass producing identical copies of lower-priced automobiles at lower cost through assembly line techniques significantly increased concentration in the U.S. automobile industry. Duke's willingness to produce and market machine-rolled cigarettes when other tobacco firms refused to do so won for his American Tobacco Company the lion's share of the cigarette business. Proctor & Gamble's innovation of detergent into the cleansing products market accounts for a large part of its post-WWII success. That there were economies of scale to be won in steel production is attested to by the fact that the U.S. Steel Corporation, created out of a merger of mergers, has continued to grow in size even while it has lost market share to faster growing rivals. Although IBM did not make the first computer, it was a leader in mass producing computers and it outpaced Univac in introducing new models. The fundamental industrial structural change that took place in the U.S. between 1880 and 1920 also reflected the dramatic reduction in transport cost accomplished through the completion of the railroad network. This allowed locally successful firms to enter distant markets from which high transport cost had hitherto barred them.

Some of these changes reflected the emergence of scale economies, but others reflected superior products and technology not necessarily related to scale economies. Even if production cost exhibits constant returns to scale, the development of superior products or superior technologies by some firms can lead to market concentration simply by reducing the level of unit cost for these firms. Ultimately, such increases in market concentration are limited by rising marginal cost or diminishing marginal preference for a particular good, but this may not occur until large market share has accrued to superior firms.

For some time during and after such episodes, the profit rates recorded by firms of different sizes in these industries should differ to reflect the superiority of the innovating firms. These firms should record higher profit rates than their less successful rivals. This difference in profit rates need not persist, for other firms will successfully imitate or innovate around the successes of the earlier innovators, but there might be a considerable period over which there is a pattern of profit rate differences. Studies of *intra*industry profit rate patterns reveal that large firms in more concentrated industries record higher profit rates than small firms, and that this tendency is strongest in the most concentrated industries (Demsetz, 1973, 1974, and 1989).

It is difficult to imagine an explanation of this that is based solely on the exercise of monopoly power, for if there were no differences in the efficiencies of firms within an industry, a market price raised through market concentration should benefit firms of all sizes equally. A difference in product quality or production cost across firms within an industry is needed for systematic differences in profit rates to exist. In highly concentrated industries, the firms with the more significant innovative history record the higher profit rates, at least until the onslaught of competitive innovation catches up with them. Nothing guarantees continuing superiority, and, I am convinced, large size generally breeds inefficiencies sufficiently great to result in eventual reductions in market concentration. This takes time, however, and noticeable intervals of time will pass before the impact of product and cost breakthroughs on market structure and intraindustry differences in profit rates disappear.

U.S. antitrust policy has created a policy that treats market concentration more preferentially than it treats price agreements. However, a more strict treatment of market concentration occurred midway in the history of antitrust. From 1890 to 1911, concentrated market structure confronted little opposition. In 1911, in two famous cases, *Standard Oil* and *American Tobacco,* high market concentration was treated as part of the reason for finding defendant firms guilty and for calling for their dissolution, but high concentration became relevant only when accompanied by a record of behavior by defendant firms that the court thought predatory. Absent such behavior, market concentration was not construed to be a violation (U.S. Steel, 1920). Then, in deciding the *Alcoa* case (1945), Judge Learned Hand came perilously close to making high market concentration a per se violation of the Sherman Act, one that required structural remedy. Hand's position has not persisted in U.S. antitrust courts. Over the last quarter-century, courts have returned to a position that is better described by the precedent set in *Standard Oil* and *American Tobacco.* The post-1970 documentation of divergent profit rates between firms in the same market and the suggestion of a superior firm explanation of market concentration played a role in this shift.

Two different views of the sources of high market concentration are contained in the preceding discussion:

- Market concentration arises solely to gain control over price.
- Market concentration arises because of product and technological breakthroughs that spur the growth of one or a few firms, or that make the optimal firm size larger.

Of course, even if market concentration arises because of product and technological breakthroughs, it can augment price-setting power. Still, higher profit rates for larger firms in concentrated industries may have the size of the firm as their source rather than the exercise of control. If firms need to be large to compete effectively, there may not be room in the market for another firm even if the market clearing price is above the unit cost of incumbent firms; the entry of another firm might force price below the unit cost for all sellers. Price remains above unit cost not because control over price is exerted by incumbent firms, but because it is uneconomic to fine-tune supply to eliminate a positive margin between price and unit cost.

One interesting but largely unexplained finding in market concentration studies is consistent with this. The correlation between concentration and profit rate tends to exist only for high market concentration industries. The correlation is weak or nonexistent for eight-firm concentration ratios less than about 60 percent. This discontinuity, it turns out, can be explained by appeal to large firm economies. In industries whose concentration ratios lie between 0 and 60 percent, the variation in concentration ratio is not fundamentally due to variations in firm size. It is due to variations in market size combined with approximately constant firm size across markets. Within this range of market concentration, smaller markets exhibit higher concentration ratios. In industries whose concentration ratios lie between 60 and 100 percent, the variation in concentration ratio is fundamentally due to variation in firm size, not market size. The more concentrated is the market the larger is the size of the leading firms. Mismatching between the aggregate output of incumbents and output that would yield "competitive" returns should be more likely and more severe in this latter group of markets because entry by an optimally sized firm is more difficult. Within this range of concentration ratios, price becomes more likely to exceed unit cost as the market becomes more concentrated simply because of this indivisibility problem. For these industries, we expect, and we find, a stronger correlation between profit rates and concentration (Demsetz, 1989).

Mergers

A few words may be said about the merger route to market concentration. Mergers sit somewhere between internal firm growth and price agreements in terms of the probability that they are likely to be undertaken solely for the purpose of controlling price. To the extent that the merger involves basic reorganization of the firm, it is more like internal growth than like a price agreement, and to this degree merger is unlikely to be attempted solely for the purpose of getting better control over price. Of course, the larger the market share brought about through merger, the greater is the degree of control of price that is likely to obtain. This implies that antitrust should be suspicious of mergers that result in very high market concentration when no substantial reorganization of the firm is involved. But even such mergers may yield lower cost or other types of efficiencies, and result in social benefits that exceed the social losses that may be associated with a greater ability to control price (Williamson, 1968).

A defense based on a showing of such efficiencies should be allowed but might be difficult to sustain since

- the claimed efficiencies are unlikely to reveal themselves empirically until several years have passed, and
- the merging firms may have erred in joining and may not realize these efficiencies even if obtaining them was the sole reason for the merger.

Although the Department of Justice in the United States considers the pros and cons of a merger in which it has an interest, it has proclaimed merger standards that, if breached, are likely to trigger official opposition. These involve two dimensions of market structure, the increase in market concentration wrought by the merger and the level of market concentration. However, the record of enforcement of antitrust reveals that these standards do not offer a good guide as to which mergers are actually opposed and which are not.

Mergers are a studied phenomenon. They seem to be somewhat profitable as measured by a comparison of premerger and postmerger stock prices summed over both firms, but especially profitable for owners of the acquired firm. They seem to be neither very profitable nor very unprofitable, on average, as measured by premerger and postmerger accounting rates of return. The very large gain usually experienced by shareholders of the acquired firm reflects the expectation by the acquiring firm of profits to be made out of the acquisition. This expectation is sometimes realized and sometimes not, and this explains the failure of accounting profit rates, on average, to show much gain or loss from a merger. It is a mistake to argue that lack of large gains in accounting profit, summed over both firms, is evidence that merger activity lacks social justification. Merging is a competitive activity like other methods of competing. There is no reason to expect it to yield high returns even when it yields social benefits. An analogy is useful. Most start-up firms fail, but it would be specious reasoning to bar the formation of new firms on this basis. A few firms succeed, and these may yield great social benefits even if they themselves experience rather modest profits because of the quick entry of imitators. Similarly, some mergers may yield great social benefit even while they record rather modest profit gains.

Since mergers, as compared to internal growth of firms, are plausibly a less risky substitute for price agreements when price agreements are barred by the antitrust authorities, it may be reasonable to face them with somewhat tougher standards when markets are highly concentrated. But efficiency defenses should be permitted.

Predatory Practices

Although the preferential treatment accorded market concentration as compared to price agreements is justified, the particular criterion used by the courts is a dangerous one. High market concentration is excused if it has arisen in the absence of *predatory* behavior. Predation has become the touchstone upon which to judge acquisition of influence over market price. The correct criterion, which differs from predation, avoids penalizing the control over price that might arise with a merger or with internal growth if concentration has arisen because of differential firm superiority. Superiority may be judged by quality of product and service as well as by cost.

When is a price predatory and when is it simply competitive? We do not have a correct answer to this question. The most common answer put forth is that a price that is set below marginal cost is predatory, but this begs the issue of how price and marginal cost are to be measured. It is frequently the case that firms in promoting their products will give samples away. Is price below marginal cost? Not if price is calculated as the present value of the revenue stream per unit of product that is expected to be sold as a result of the "give-away." Surely, the firm engaged in promotional activity expects this measure of price to exceed the cost of the unit given away, or it would not be profitable for it to engage in the promotion. Correctly viewed in this expectational sense, price exceeds marginal cost even if nothing is charged for the units of good being given away. From this perspective, no firm, even one bent on securing a dominant position, ever sells at a price below marginal cost. A firm seeking a dominant position in this way expects the present value of revenues from future sales to exceed its losses on current sales.

The logic and calculation in these two cases are precisely the same; there is no way to distinguish them through price/cost comparisons. Hence, to attack as predation a pricing policy that delivers goods to buyers at a low price may be to attack an honestly competitive price of a promotional sort. A policy that deprives buyers of the opportunity to purchase at lower prices today in the belief that protecting firms from the low prices of rivals today keeps more firms around "tomorrow," and that this assures buyers of lower prices tomorrow, is wrongheaded. It is highly speculative and implicitly based on the notion that interest rates are negative. A "bird in the hand" should be worth more than a "bird in the bush," not less. Such a policy is likely to reduce incentives to price competitively to win share from rivals and amounts to a legalization of a minimum price agreement. The court, in second-guessing market price, presumes that it possesses knowledge of the future that it cannot possibly possess, and this is true even if one firm is able to purchase another at a lower price because of the low price it has set for the good it sells.

Not only is the theorizing in regard to predatory behavior speculative, but it fails to recognize the great difficulty in profiting from strategic predation by a practitioner firm that is no more efficient than its alleged prey. Pricing below cost to deter entry imposes greater losses on the incumbent firm than on the would-be entrant, since the former loses much on its large market share while the latter loses practically nothing. Unless the incumbent firm enjoys lower cost than the would-be entrant, such a policy is very likely to fail. Similarly, any attempt to bid up the prices of inputs in order to penalize a rival or deter entry cannot work if the alleged predator does not have lower cost; with equal cost, he loses just as much by paying higher input prices as an equally sized rival, and he loses more if he is larger. I have yet to uncover a rationale for predatory behavior that escapes from this dilemma if one thinks deeply about the practice. This means that reliance on an antitrust doctrine seeking to penalize predation runs a high probability of penalizing efficient firms for competing aggressively.

This is an especially dangerous policy because we have no reliable logic that reveals when a price is predatory and when it is merely competitive. I have already argued that the distinction cannot be drawn in terms of a price-less-than-marginal-cost standard, but this cost-based standard is foolish anyway. Why is a firm punished less severely by a rival that cuts price but keeps price above marginal cost than it is by a rival whose price cut brings price below marginal cost? If price is cut by the same amount, the same loss in revenue is incurred. And, whether or not the rival's new low price covers its cost, it may fail to cover the suffering firm's cost. I can see no way to distinguish price cuts according to whether they are predatory or simply competitive. If we are to trust in market competition, predation must be abandoned as a standard to apply by antitrust authorities. This is because trust in market competition implies that if there are predatory price cuts, they are too unlikely to succeed, too infrequent, and too difficult to separate from beneficial price cuts to make a policy opposing them wise. Some methods of competing are more obviously against social interest and are more easily detected and separable from beneficial methods of competing. Rivals should be penalized for competing by burning down each other's factories or by engaging in fraudulent advertising. These competitive techniques should be penalized because we believe firmly that they yield no significant benefits to society. This cannot be said of price competition.

Vertical Business Practices

The domain of topics here includes the full-blown vertical integration of firms that normally buy from or sell to each other and more limited control exercised by one firm over another when these firms buy from or sell to each other. Mergers of firms or agreements between them at any given level of production are not directly involved. If they were, the problem they might create for policy would be subsumed in policy toward agreements between competitors or market concentration. I believe no issue of real concern to antitrust policy is raised by vertical business practices. What one firm legally can do for itself if it were completely vertically integrated should not be barred if accomplished through vertical mergers or vertical control over the business practices of other firms.

Consider first the issue of vertical control over the business practices of other firms. Let a firm be organized in vertically integrated fashion from product manufacturing to retailing. It enters into no price agreements with other firms when it retails its product and does not hold a dominant position in the retail market. Therefore, it cannot exercise significant control over retail price. What it does to organize production within itself is a management problem of no concern to antitrust. The firm should have no fear of antitrust authorities.

Take the same manufacturing and retailing activities and divide them up into separately owned firms, with one manufacturer and several independent owners of subsets of the original retail outlets. The independent manufacturing firm offers to sell its product to owners of the independent retailing firms, but it does so only on condition that each retailer refrain from reselling the product into the territories of other retailers. The agreement is voluntarily entered into by retailers who could have refused and chosen instead to deal with a rival manufacturer.

Now, if the fully integrated firm would have violated no antitrust law by instructing its own managers of retail outlets to refrain from selling to customers located beyond a given distance from their retail outlet, then why should the manufacturer selling to independent retailers be penalized for territorial limitations on retailer sales? No good reason comes to mind.

We might be interested in understanding the purpose served by territorial limitations, just as we might be interested in understanding the purpose served by restricting freedom of action of retail managers in a fully vertically integrated firm, but it is difficult to see how the answer should lead to antitrust penalties. To the question of legality under antitrust laws, it is sufficient to say that vertically separated firms should be able to do anything they would have been permitted to do had they been vertically integrated into a single firm.

The same conclusion holds for the act of vertically integrating firms. If the firms about to be vertically integrated are not guilty of violating antitrust's concern about price control in any relevant market, then putting them together in a single vertically integrated firm should not be objected to on antitrust grounds. The darkest days in U.S. antitrust policy dawned during the twenty-year period following the end of World War II. During that period not only did high market concentration come close to being a per se violation of the Sherman Act, but there was also considerable interference with vertical mergers. Fortunately, the intensity of concern about vertical integration has waned during the last quarter-century.

Powerful arguments now exist in economic theory that describe efficiency advantages to strengthening vertical controls of one firm over another in the vertical chain of production, even to the extent of full vertical integration. These include especially the ability of quasi or full vertical integration to reduce the severity of opportunism and free-rider behavior (Klein, Crawford, and Alchian, 1978; and Williamson, 1983). For example, in cases in which economies in advertising lie with retailers, it is important to manufacturers that such advertising takes place. Disincentives to advertise will arise if retailers can invade each other's market areas, for then it becomes possible that one retailer's advertising campaign will redound to the benefit of a rival if this second retailer is allowed to sell the same good in the geographic area in which the first retailer advertises; to bring about an amount of advertising that is closer to the optimal, the manufacturer may find it desirable to restrain independent retailers from selling into neighboring market areas. In this case, voluntary territorial restrictions promote the efficient provision of information to buyers.

It is true that some economists have expressed concerns about the impact of vertical controls, and especially of full vertical integration, on the conditions of entry into a market. The necessity for would-be entrants to operate at more than one level in the vertical chain of production does, in a sense, impose greater capital requirements than would exist if they could enter at only one level. But for the greater capital requirement to exist, it is necessary for vertical integration to be efficiency enhancing. If vertical integration were detrimental to efficiency, two firms, each entering at one of two adjacent vertical levels, could raise capital more cheaply than the one firm that chooses to operate at both levels. Thus, the alleged barrier created is no different from the barrier set before a would-be entrant who refuses to use efficient technology. It would be less capital-demanding if a firm could enter into automobile production by investing in only half an assembly line, but if a full assembly line is more efficient, the fact that successful entry requires the full investment hardly constitutes a barrier to entry that is of social concern.

It is sometimes the case that vertical restraints practiced by business derive from the legitimate control of output and/or price, as when a firm has won patent or copyright protection for the product it produces. Presumably, society finds protection of market power an acceptable cost to bear in order to encourage creative activities.[77]

There are issues bearing on the efficiency implications of various dimensions of patent and copyright policies, but these relate only tangentially to antitrust issues. In the absence of antitrust prohibition, inventors might profit from marketing their inventions or the services from it in a way that relies on tie-in sales. Tie-in sales, possibly because they invoke discriminatory pricing (but for other reasons also) can increase the profit patent holders derive from their inventions. Antitrust might be, and in the United States is, used to bar price discrimination, but it should be clear that this does not reduce market power interpreted as freedom from rivals so much as it simply reduces the profit to be secured from the market power that exists. The use of antitrust in this way may be thought of as the equivalent of a tax on the profit from invention and, as such, as an adjunct to patent and copyright policy. Whether or not it is wise to

---

77. The economic issues involved in patent and copyright are well-known. Two key issues are thought to prompt legal protection of creative activity. The investment that goes into invention is, to a large extent, front-loaded in the sense of being made before any product comes to market. Absent legal protection, imitation might be easy. When it is, inventors will find it difficult to recoup their investment because price will settle at the lower unit cost of imitators. To allow easy imitation is to undermine the incentive to invest in invention. The way in which inventors can protect their investment in the absence of patent and copyright is, when possible, to keep their inventions secret. Patents and copyright encourage inventors not to rely on secrecy, and by doing so they bring into the open the knowledge upon which others can build. Thus, this protective policy not only encourages invention. It also encourages the spread of information.

use antitrust in this way depends on how one judges the consequences of doing so. Limiting the profit secured by inventors reduces incentives to invent. Reducing the degree to which they can formulate price policy, as in the adoption of price discrimination, usually, but not necessarily always, reduces the extent to which the invention will be used. Limiting the wealth to be secured from a patent may be thought desirable even if unwanted consequences accompany this policy. But open tax policy would seem preferable to using antitrust for this purpose.

References

Alchian, A. A. "Uncertainty, Evolution, and Economic Theory," *Journal of Political Economy* (1950), 211-21.

———— and Demsetz, H. "Production, Information Cost, and Economic Organization," *American Economic Review*, 62 (1972), 777–95.

Auerbach, P. *Competition: The Economics of Change.* Oxford, Basil Blackwell. 1988.

Bain, J. S. "Relation of Profit-Rate to Industry Concentration: American Manufacturing, 1936-1904," *Quarterly Journal of Economic* (August 1951), 293.

Ball, R. and Brown, P. "An Empirical Evaluation of Accounting Income Numbers," *Journal of Accounting Research*, 6(2) (1968) 159–78.

Barnard, C. *The Functions of the Executive.* Cambridge, Mass., Harvard University Press, 1938.

Beaver, W., Clarke, R., and Wright, W. "The Association Between Unsystematic Security Returns and the Magnitude of Earnings Forecast Errors," *Journal of Accounting Research*, 17(3) (1979) 316–40.

Becker, G. S. "Irrational Behavior and Economic Theory," *J. of Political Economy*, (1962), 1–13.

Bergstrom, C. and Rydqvist, K. "The Determinants of Corporate Ownership – An Empirical Study on Swedish Data," *J. of Banking and Finance* (1990) 14, 255–69.

Berle, A.A. and Means, G.C. *The Modern Corporation and Private Property.* New York, Macmillan, 1933.

Bork, R. *The Antitrust Paradox: A Policy at War with Itself.* New York, Basic Books, 1978.

Bowles, S. and Gintis, H. "The Revenge of Homo Economicus: Contested Exchange and the Revival of Political Economy," *J. of Economic Perspectives* (Winter 1993), 83–102.

Bradley, M. "Interfirm Tender Offers and the Market for Corporate Control," *J. of Business* (1980), 345–76.

Chamberlin, E.H. *The Theory of Monopolistic Competition.* Cambridge, Mass., Harvard University Press, 1933.

Chandler, A. *Stategy and Structure: Chapters in the History of the American Industrial Enterprise.* Cambridge, M.I.T. Press, 1962.

————. *The Visible Hand: The Managerial Revolution in American Business.* Cambridge, The Belknap Press of Harvard University Press, 1977.

Clark, J. M. "Toward a Concept of Workable Competition," *American Economic Review* (1940), 241–56.

————. "Competition: Static Models and Dynamic Aspects," *American Economic Review* (1955), 450–62.

Clyde, P. S. *The Institutional Investor as an Effective Monitor of Management.* UCLA unpublished doctoral dissertation, 1990.

Coase, R. H. "R. H. Coase's Lectures," *J. of Law, Economics, and Organization* (Spring) 1988.

Conlisk, J. "Costly, Optimizers Versus Cheap Imitators," *Journal of Economic Behavior and Organization* (September 1980), 275–93.

Cornell, B. and Landsman, W. R. "Security Price Response to Quarterly Earnings Announcements and Analysts' Forecast Revisions," 18 (1989), 680–92.

Demsetz, H. "The Cost of Transacting," *Quarterly Journal of Economics*, 82(1) (February 1968a), 33–53.

―――. "Why Regulate Utilities?" *Journal of Law and Economics* (April 1968b), 55–66.

―――. "Inconsistencies of Monpolistic Competition," *J. of Political Economy*, 80 (1972), 592–7.

―――. "Industry Structure, Market Rivalry, and Public Policy," *J. of Law and Economics* (April 1973), 1.

―――. "Two Systems of Belief About Monopoly," in *Industrial Concentration, the New Learning*, edited by Goldschmid, Mann, and Weston. Little Brown, 1974.

―――. "Accounting for Advertising as a Barrier to Entry," *J. of Business*, 52(3) (1979), 345–60.

―――. "The Structure of Ownership and the Theory of the Firm," *J. of Law and Economics*, 26(1) (1983).

―――― and Lehn, K. "The Structure of Corporate Ownership: Causes and Consequences," *J. of Political Economy* (December 1985), 1155–77.

―――. "Corporate Control, Insider Trading, and Rates of Return," *American Economic Association: Papers and Proceedings*, 76(2) (May 1986), 313–16.

―――. "Theory of the Firm Revisited," *J. of Law, Economics, and Organization*, 4 (1988a), 141–63.

―――. *Ownership, Control, and the Firm. Vol. 1 of The Organization of Economic Activity.* Oxford, Basil Blackwell, 1988b, 236–48.

―――. *Efficiency, Competition, and Policy. Vol. 2 of The Organization of Economic Activity.* Oxford, Basil Blackwell, 1989, 112.

―――. "George J. Stigler: Midcentury Neoclassicalist with a Passion to Quantify," *J. of Political Economy*, 5 (1993), 793–808.

Dixit, A. K. and Stiglitz, J. E. "Monopolistic Competition and Optimum Product Diversity," *American Economic Review*, 67 (1977), 297–308.

Dodd, P. R. and Ruback, R. "Tender Offers and Stockholder Returns: An Empirical Analysis," *Journal of Financial Economics* (December 1977), 351–74.

Ehrenberg, R. G. and Bognanno, M. L. "The Incentive Effects of Tournaments Revisited: Evidence from the European PGA Tour," *Industrial and Labor Relations Review*, 43 (Special issue, February 1990), S74–88.

Ellsberg, D. "Risk, Ambiguity, and the Savage Axioms," *Quarterly Journal of Economics* (1961), 643–69.

Fama, E. and Jensen, M. "Agency Problems and Residual Claims," *J. of Law and Economics* (1983), 327–49.

Fisher, F. M. and McGowan, J. J. "On the Misuse of Accounting Rates of Return to Infer Monopoly Profits," *American Econ. Review*, 73(1) (1983), 82–96.

Galbraith, J. K. *The New Industrial State,* Boston, Houghton Mifflin, 1967.

Gerson, J. *The Determinants of Corporate Ownership and Control in South Africa.* University of California, Los Angeles, unpublished Ph.D. dissertation, 1992.

Gibrat, R. *Les Inequalities Economiques.* Paris: Recueil Sirey, 1931.

Grossman S. and Stiglitz, J. "Information and Competitive Price Systems," *American Economic Review* (1976), 246–55.

Haltiwanger J. and Waldman, M. "Responders Versus Non-Responders: A New Perspective On Heterogeneity," *The Economic Journal*, 101 (1991), 1085–1182.

Hart, O. "An Economist's Perspective on the Theory of the Firm," *Columbia Law Review*, 89 (November 1989), 1757–74.

Hayek, F. A. "The Use of Knowledge in Society," *American Economic Review*, 35 (1945).

Hirshleifer, J. "Economics from a Biological Viewpoint," *J. of Law and Economics* (1977), 1–52.

Hoffman, E. and Spitzer, M. "Experimental Tests of the Coase Theorem with Large Bargaining

Groups" (1986) in *Readings in Public Sector Economics* by S. Baker and C. Elliot. Lexington, Mass.: Heath, 1990.

Ijiri, Y. and Simon, H. A. *Skew Distributions and the Sizes of Business Firms.* Amsterdam, North-Holland, 1977.

Jarrell, G., Brickley, J., and Netter, J. "The Market for Corporate Control: The Empirical Evidence Since 1980," *J. of Economic Perspectives* (1988), 49–86.

Jensen, M. C. and Meckling, W. H. "Theory of the Firm: Managerial Behavior, Agency Costs and Ownership Structure," *Journal of Financial Economy* (1976), 305–60.

Jensen, M. C. and Murphy, K. J. "Performance Pay and Top-Management Incentives," *J. of Political Economy* (1990), 225–64.

Joskow. "Contract Duration and Relationship-Specific Investments," *American Economic Review* (1987), 168–85.

Kim, Y. *Reputation, Managerial Labor Market and Chief Executive Turnover in Large Corporations.* University of California, Los Angeles, unpublished Ph.D. dissertation (1993).

Klein, B., Crawford, R.G., and Alchian, A.A., "Vertical Integration, Appropriable Rents, and the Competitive Contracting Process," *J. of Law and Economics,* 21(2) (1978), 297–326.

Knetsch, J. and Sinden, J. A. "The Persistence of Evaluation Disparities," *Quarterly J. of Economics* (1987), 691–6.

Knight, F. H. *Risk, Uncertainty, and Profit.* New York, Harper & Row, 1965; first published in 1921.

Kormendi, R. and Lipe, R. "Earnings Innovations, Earnings Persistence, and Stock Returns," *J. of Business,* 60(3) (1987), 323–45.

Lazear, E. P. and Rosen, S. "Rank-Order Tournaments as Optimum Labor Contracts," *J. of Political Economy* (1981), 841–64.

Leibenstein, H. "Allocative Efficiency vs. X-Efficiency," *American Economic Review* (1966), 56, 392–415.

Leijonhufvud, A. "Capitalism and the Factory System," in *Economics as a Process; Essays in the New Institutional Economics,* edited by Langlois, R.N. Cambridge University Press, Cambridge, 1985.

Leonard, J. S. "Executive Pay and Firm Performance," *Industrial and Labor Relations Review,* 43 (Special issue, February 1990), S13–29.

Lewellen, W. G. *The Ownership Income of Management.* New York, Columbia Press for NBER, 1971.

———— and Huntsman, B. "Managerial Pay and Corporate Performance," *American Economic Review* (1970), 710–20.

Machlup, F. "Theories of the Firm: Marginalist, Behavioural, Managerial," *American Economic Review,* 57, No. 1 (March 1967), 9.

Main, B. G. M., O'Reilly III, C. A., and Wade, J. "Top Executive Pay: Tournament or Teamwork?" *J. of Labor Economics* (1993), 606–29.

Malcomson, J. M. "Work Incentives, Hierarchy, and Internal Labor Market Markets," *J. of Political Economy* (1984), 486–507.

Mandelker, G. "Risk and Return: The Case of Merging Firms," *Journal of Financial Economy* (1974), 303–35.

Manne H. G. "Mergers and the Market for Corporate Control," *Journal of Political Economy* (1965), 73, 110–20.

Markham, J. W. "An Alternative Approach to the Concept of Workable Competition," *American Economic Review* (1950), 349–61.

Marris, R. *The Economic Theory of Managerial Capitalism.* London, Macmillan, 1974.

Marshall, A. *Principles of Economics,* 8th ed. New York, The Macmillan Co., 1920; first published in 1890.

References 173

Masten, S. "The Organization of Production: Evidence from the Aerospace Industry," *J. of Law and Economics,* 27 (1984), 403–18.

Mitchell, M. and Lehn, K. "Do Bad Bidders Become Good Targets?" *J. of Political Economy* (April 1990), 372–98.

Murdoch, J. *Executive Compensation: The Use of Incentive Contracts to Attenuate an Agency Problem.* University of California, Los Angeles, unpublished Ph.D. dissertation (1991).

Nelson, R. and Winter, G. *An Evolutionary Theory of Economic Change.* Cambridge, The Belknap Press of Harvard University Press, 1982.

Penrose, E. *The Theory of the Growth of the Firm.* Oxford, England, Basil Blackwell, 1959.

Prowse, S. D. "Institutional Investment Patterns and Corporate Financial Behavior in the United States and Japan," *Journal of Financial Economics* (1991), 1–24.

———. "The Structure of Corporate Ownership in Japan" (1991), unpublished manuscript.

Robinson, J. *The Economics of Imperfect Competition.* London, Macmillan & Co., 1933.

Roe, Mark J. "A Political Theory of American Corporate Finance," *Columbia Law Review* (1991), 31–53.

Roll, R. "The Hubris Hypothesis of Corporate Takeovers," *J. of Business,* 59 (April 1986), 197–216.

Rosen, S. "Authority, Control, and the Distribution of Earnings," *Bell Journal of Economics* (1982), 311–23.

Schumpeter, Joseph A. *Business Cycles.* New York, McGraw-Hill, 1939.

Scitovsky, T. "A Note on Profit Maximisation and Its Implications," *The Review of Economic Studies* (1943), 57–60.

Shleifer, A. and Vishny, R. "Large Shareholders and Corporate Control," *J. of Political Economy,* 94 (1986), 461–88.

Simon, H. *Administrative Behavior.* New York, Macmillan, 1947.

Smith, A. *The Wealth of Nations* (1776). Glasgow Edition, edited by R. H. Campbell and A. S. Skinner Cannan, 1979, 741.

———. *The Wealth of Nations.* New York, Modern Library, 1937, 713–14.

Smith, V. "Rational Choice: The Contrast Between Economics and Psychology," *J. of Political Economy,* 99(4) (1991), 877–97.

Sraffa, P. *Production of Commodities by Means of Commodities.* Cambridge, Cambridge University Press, 1960.

Stigler, G. J. *Five Lectures on Economic Problems.* London, Macmillan, 1950.

———. "Extent and Bases of Monopoly," *American Economic Review* (1942), 2–3.

———. "Economics of Information," *J. of Political Economy,* 69 (June 1961), 213–51.

———. "The Xistence of X-Efficiency," *American Economic Review* (1976), 66, 213–16.

Sundqvist, S. *Owners and Power in Sweden's Listed Companies.* Stockholm, Dagens Nyheters Forlag, 1986.

Telser, L. G. *Economic Theory and the Core.* Chicago, Ill., University of Chicago Press, 1978.

———. "The Usefulness of Core Theory in Economics," *J. of Economic Perspectives* (Spring 1994), 151–64.

Thaler, R. "Mental Accounting and Consumer Choice," *Marketing Science,* (Summer 1985).

Tversky, A. and Kahneman, D. "The Framing of Decisions and the Psychology of Choice," *Science* (January 1981), 353–58.

Veblen, T. *The Engineers and the Price System,* New York, Viking Press, 1921.

Williamson, O. E. "Hierarchical Control and Optimum Firm Size," *J. of Political Economy,* 75 (April 1967), 123–38.

———. "Economies as an Antitrust Defense: The Welfare Tradeoffs," *American Economic Review* (March 1968), 18.

———. *Corporate Control and Business Behavior,* Englewood Cliffs, N.J., Prentice-Hall, 1970.

References

———. "Managerial Discretion, Organization Form, and the Multi-Division Hypothesis," in *The Corporate Economy*, edited by R. Marris, and A. Wood, London, Harvard University Press, 1971.

———. "Markets and Hierarchies: Some Elementary Considerations," *American Economic Review*, 63 (May), 316–25.

———. *Markets and Hierarchies: Analysis and Antitrust Implications*. New York, The Free Press, 1975.

———. "Credible Commitments: Using Hostages to Support Exchange," *American Economic Review* (1983), 83.

———. *The Economic Institutions of Capitalism: Firms, Markets, and Relational Contracting*. New York, The Free Press, 1985.

———. "Comparative Economic Organization: The Analysis of Discrete Structural Alternatives," *Administrative Science Quarterly* (1991), 269–96.

Case citations

Appalachian Coals, Inc. et al. v. United States, 288 U.S. 344 (1933)
Arizona v. Maricopa County Medical Society et al., 495 U.S. 328 (1982)
Atlantic Richfield Co. v. U.S.A. Petroleum 495 U.S. 328 (1990)
Standard Oil Company of New Jersey et al., v. U.S., 221 U.S. 1 (1911)
U.S. v. Joint Traffic Ass'n., 171 U.S. 505 (1898)
U.S. v. Trans-Missouri Freight Ass'n., 166 U.S. 290 (1897)
U.S. v. Aluminum Co. (Alcoa), 148 F.2d 416 (2d Cir. 1945)
U.S. v. American Tobacco Co., 221 U.S. 106 (1911)

Index